GREAT AUSTRALIAN WORLD WAR II STORIES

GREAT AUSTRALIAN WORLD WAR II STORIES

FROM THE ANNALS OF THE RSL
EDITED BY JOHN GATFIELD

ABC Books

> **Warning:** The stories contained in this compilation are first-person accounts of World War II and are true reflections of the writers' experiences. In order to preserve the authenticity of these accounts the language used and the views expressed are faithful to the original story-telling. The publisher acknowledges that some of the language used and the views expressed may be harmful or cause offence to some readers.
>
> The stories include descriptions of war, violence, torture and death that some readers may find distressing.
>
> **Publisher's note:** The publisher does not necessarily endorse the views expressed or the language used in any of the stories.

The ABC 'Wave' device is a trademark of the Australian Broadcasting Corporation and is used under licence by HarperCollins*Publishers* Australia.

First published in Australia in 2018
by HarperCollins*Publishers* Australia Pty Limited
ABN 36 009 913 517
harpercollins.com.au

The right of John Gatfield to be identified as the author of this work has been asserted by him in accordance with the *Copyright Amendment (Moral Rights) Act 2000*.

This work is copyright. Apart from any use as permitted under the *Copyright Act 1968*, no part may be reproduced, copied, scanned, stored in a retrieval system, recorded, or transmitted, in any form or by any means, without the prior written permission of the publisher.

The authors gratefully acknowledge the permission granted to reproduce the copyright material in this book. Every effort has been made to trace and acknowledge copyright. Where the attempt has been unsuccessful, we would be pleased to hear from the copyright holder to rectify any omission or error.

HarperCollins*Publishers*
Level 13, 201 Elizabeth Street, Sydney NSW 2000, Australia
Unit D1, 63 Apollo Drive, Rosedale, Auckland 0632, New Zealand
A 53, Sector 57, Noida, UP, India
77–85 Fulham Palace Road, London W6 8JB, United Kingdom
2 Bloor Street East, 20th floor, Toronto, Ontario M4W 1A8, Canada
195 Broadway, New York NY 10007, USA

A catalogue record for this book is available from the National Library of Australia.

978 0 7333 3915 8 (paperback)
978 1 4607 0359 5 (ebook)

Cover design by Hazel Lam, HarperCollins Design Studio.
Cover image: El Kantara — this group of happy soldiers are some of the wounded at 2nd Australian General Hospital after the Battle of Bardia. Courtesy Australian War Memorial (005218)
Typeset in 10/15pt ITC Bookman by Kelli Lonergan
Printed and bound in Australia by McPhersons Printing Group
The papers used by HarperCollins in the manufacture of this book are a natural, recyclable product made from wood grown in sustainable plantation forests. The fibre source and manufacturing processes meet recognised international environmental standards, and carry certification.

Contents

Introduction	1

Singapore Falls

My Unit in the Fall of Singapore By E. (Jimmy) James, ex-WO1, 2 Echelon, AIF	5
Dinner at Brigade: A Singapore Story By Lieutenant Colonel J.W. Wright	9

Prisoners of the Japanese

Sister Berenice Twohill: A Prisoner at Rabaul Interview with John Gatfield	19
Remarkable Courage as a Prisoner of War By Chris Neilson	26
Eighteen Months on the Burma Railway By Sergeant Roy K. Smith	32
Christmas in Captivity: Three Memorable Days on the Railroad of Death Author unknown	37
An Elephant Tale By E.C. Yates	42
Bicycle Camp, Hell Ship and Death Railway By Dallas Cressey	44
Hail to the Brave Byoki By 'Banjo' Binstead	50
The Specialists By Hugh V. Clarke	53
Salvation By Len Ikin	58
A Day to Remember By NX59783	62
The Day the Nips Came In By 'Krani'	67

Caring for Prisoners of War   69
   By June Kerr

New Guinea and the Kokoda Track

Correspondent's War Diary   73
   By George H. Johnston

Sanananda Epic: Heroic End of Captain Cobb   78
   By Trooper Bob Ebner

Epic Crossing of the Buso River   81
   By Brigadier H.B. Norman, DSO, MC

Ambush Knoll   88
   By 'Commando' (Colonel R.S. Garland, MC & Bar)

The Bulldog Road   97
   By George Macris

That Big 2/33rd Battalion Tragedy   100
   Author unknown

River of Death   102
   Author unknown

Attack on Hill 710: Wewak 14 to 24 May 1945   108
   By Lieutenant Colonel B.S. O'Dowd MBE (RL)

Midnight Marauder   114
   By Leading Aircraftman A.D. Darby

Butchers of Milne Bay   116
   By G.F. Donohoe

The Bridge   119
   By NX145805

Underage but Signed Up   122
   By John Montgomery

Nursing in New Guinea   125
   By Hazel Dalton

Tarakan and Sandakan

Tarakan Island: The Death of Lieutenant T.C. Derrick, VC   131
   By Emmett O'Keefe

Brothers Inseparable Until Death   134
   By Mark Wells

Mopping Up at Sandakan   139
   By Tom Turner

The Sandakan Underground   142
   By Paddy Funk

Repatriating POWs to Australia   148
   By Joan Dowson, Red Cross Field Force Officer

The First Japanese POW on Australian Soil   153
   By Sergeant Leslie Powell

The War in the Middle East

First Stop, Bardia!   159
   By NX2621

The Battle of Mahomed Aly Square   166
   By H.J. Moore

Diary of a Digger of Tobruk   168
   By A. Hertzberg, Sgt, AIF, Abroad

Incident in Cairo: 1942   171
   By F.C. Turner (Maletti), ex-RAANS

Ajax Won at Cairo Race Meeting   173
   By Rex C. Testro

They Dived in with Messerschmitt-Like Accuracy   176
   By 'Dan R', AIF

With the 7th Div Cavalry Regiment   178
   By Norman Grinyer

Rats with Guts   185
   XBy 'Poopdeck', ex-2/13 Battalion

El Alamein: Gate of the Road to Victory   187
   By A.E. Bannear

Mussolini's Way   190
   By John W. McWilliam, MM

The War at Sea

HMAS Yarra: A Survivor's Story   193
   By Alfred George Orton

Out of School and Under Kamikaze Attack   198
   By Gilburd 'Gibb' Woods

The Luck of the Draw   203
    By Frank Glover

The Sinking of HMAS Perth   206
    By Fred Taylor

The Tobruk Run   210
    By Lieutenant Fred Gill, RAN

Collision in the North Atlantic   216
    By Frederick (Frank) Finch

Poker Game Went to the Bottom the Day
They Sank the Brave Limerick   220
    By Harold 'Snow' Mackrell

Greece and Crete

Scrap Iron   227
    By Petty Officer A.W.C.

Strewth! The Evacuation of Nurses   233
    By Una Keast

Escape After the Battle of Crete   237
    By Signaller S.L. Carroll MM

Dasher   244
    By SX1543

Prisoners of the Nazis

Escape from a Prison Train in Greece   251
    By Norton Foster

A 'Lousy' Trick   259
    By U.G. Ryan

Stalag 383's £5000 Spitfire   260
    By Keith H. Hooper

Escape from Marburg   263
    By an ex-member of the 2/1 Battalion

The Long March: Dombrova, Poland
to Regensburg, Bavaria   268
    By WX827 Pte G.C. Anderson, HQ Company, 2/11th AIF

The War in the Air

The Spy   275
    By Slim Johnson

Raid on Berlin: I Learned from This By Flight Lieutenant Bob Nielsen, DFM	277
Bombers, Fighters — and the Occasional Church Spire By Squadron Leader Keith Thiele, DSO, DFC & 2 Bars	280
Old Pilots Never Die By Ted Kirk	288
Rendezvous Over Essen By Pilot Officer, Bomber Command	293
Air Raid on Revigny: A Long Hard Day at the Office By John Clulow	298
On the Russian Front, 1942 By Wing Commander Robert Holmes	302
Darwin: February 1942 By Tom Griffith, 25570 ex Sgt RAAF	305
Darwin 1942: A Pilot's Close Call By Harold Stuart McDouall	308
The Fourth Mine By Leo M. Kenny, RAAF	313
An Amazing Rescue After Air and Sea Attack By Pilot Officer Keith Shilling	315

On Stage and Back Stage

Among the First Army Servicewomen to See Operational Service Overseas By Ailsa Jean Livingstone	321
On Stage with Peter Finch By Pat McKenzie	324
Service Totally in the Dark By Joy Granger	328
A Story of Mateship By Connie Noble	331
I Was Sixth Divvy's Telephonist By Marien Dreyer	333
Abbreviations	337
Acknowledgements	339
About the editor	341
Index	343

Introduction

My father never talked about his service or his experiences in World War II. He never attended reunions or marched on Anzac Day. He had served as a gunner in the Middle East with the New Zealand Army Field Artillery, and was repatriated after being wounded and losing much of an upper arm and shoulder. His only brother was killed in action and buried in Libya.

While I can understand why my father wanted to forget the war years, I regret that he never sat down and talked about them. This was part of our family's history yet we never learned about it. We never understood fully what impact the war had on his life, his beliefs, or his emotional well-being.

For more than twenty years I have worked closely with the Returned and Services League of Australia in NSW and with the wider veteran community. During this time I have listened to many men and women talk about events and incidents that occurred during their time in uniform. Some stories I have written for the RSL magazine *Reveille*; others I have read in sister publications interstate.

The stories these veterans tell are not necessarily heroic although frequently they are poignant. Always they are personal. These individual narratives fill in the gaps that are left by the histories of battles and campaigns and the broad sweep of wartime histories. These are the memories of the men and women who volunteered. As our WWII generation dwindles in number, their stories deserve to be read again and must be preserved.

This collection of WWII stories begins with the fall of Singapore, overrun by the Japanese army early in 1942. I chose this as a starting point because the loss of Singapore had an enormous impact on Australian lives. There were 15,000 Australians taken prisoner; in the years to come the horrors of the Thai–Burma Death Railway and the Sandakan camp would be exposed. From Singapore, the Japanese advanced south, attacking Australian cities by air and by sea, capturing Rabaul and progressing over the Kokoda Track in New Guinea to pose a threat to invade Australia.

All this occurred while thousands of Australians were serving in the Middle East, at sea on the oceans of the world, and in the air, with the RAF Bomber Command in particular.

When I compiled the collection of stories from the Great War for *The RSL Book of World War I*, very few were available written by women, and those were recorded by nurses. That is the major difference with this collection from WWII. Throughout this book the reader will find numerous reminiscences by women who took a far more active role in serving both at home and overseas, and in many different ways, sometimes in secret, as will be seen from the final section which I titled 'On Stage and Backstage.'

I have learned that every man and every woman who has served the nation in a time of conflict, including in recent years in our peacekeeping missions, has a story to tell. The earlier volume of WWI articles provided a remarkable insight into the lives of those who volunteered 'for King and Country.' I hope this collection provides the same understanding of how Australians fought against Nazi Germany and Japanese imperialism.

John Gatfield

Singapore Falls

'I think it is just patrol activity we are hearing.'

— Brigadier to Lieutenant Colonel John Wright

My Unit in the Fall of Singapore
By E. (Jimmy) James, ex-WO1, 2 Echelon, AIF

During the night of Sunday, 8 February 1942, one and a half divisions of Jap troops, with artillery, crossed the Johor Strait and landed on the north-west side of Singapore Island, beginning immediately an onslaught on our 'West' Force.[1]

The next morning the whole of the Allied Air Force evacuated Singapore and became based on Sumatra, and the way was open for a Jap onrush. My unit was working on records at Holland Road, about eight miles south of the Jap landing, but air raids and artillery fire became so frequent that we evacuated to Balmoral House, Stephen Road, another eight miles farther south, which we did on 10 February.

The next day, at about 1100 hours, we were blitzed from the air with anti-personnel bombs. The Japs had no opposition in the air and could do what they liked with us. Our casualties were three killed and 10 wounded.

At 1300 hours six-inch shells began to fall around us, so we moved farther south again.

All this time the 'West' Force, with the 3rd Indian Corps as 'Centre' force,[2] was putting up a mighty effort, but without avail. Unfortunately the giant 15-inch guns at Changi, which could have been very helpful, were not mounted so that they could be turned far enough to send their shells into the oncoming Japs.[3]

Sensing a quick victory, the Japs became berserk. They went wild, shooting up everything — everywhere. Some had seeped through our lines, and as they were dressed as peasants it was difficult to detect them. They procured arms and ammunition from pro-Jap natives in Singapore City, and established themselves in trees in the streets, from which they kept a continuous sniping. I saw, myself, three of these men tumble out of trees when fired on.

At this stage all troops, whether frontline or otherwise, were in it up to their necks. The Australian field ambulances had set up in St Andrew's Cathedral, where they were treating the wounded as best they could under an incessant bombardment.

At the Alexandra Military Hospital in Singapore, the critical day was 13 February. During the morning, routine work was continued, but in the afternoon, at 1340 hours, the Japs hove in sight, attacking towards the sisters' quarters, from where the sisters had been previously evacuated.

As a number of Japs reached the rear door of the hospital, Lieutenant Watson went from the reception room with a white flag to indicate the surrender of the hospital. The Japs took no notice at all of the white flag, and made for Lieutenant Watson, whom they bayonetted savagely to death. The Japs then ran amok on the ground floor.

One party entered the operating theatre block, and at this time operations were being performed in the corridor between the sisters' bunk and the main theatre — as the best-lighted and most sheltered area in the hospital. The Japs climbed into the corridor, motioned the staff to move along, and then, for apparently no reason at all, set upon the unarmed staff with their bayonets. Lieutenant Roberts was bayonetted twice through the thorax and died immediately; Captain Parkinson was bayonetted to death, as were Corporal McEwan and Private Lewis.

The patient on the operating table was also bayonetted. Captain Smiley got it too but struck away the blade, which hit his cigarette case in his left-hand pocket. The Jap lunged at him again and wounded him in the left of his groin. Captain Smiley pretended to be killed, and fortunately, in falling over, he fell on top of Private Sutton, who was unharmed. The Japs left them both for dead.

My Unit in the Fall of Singapore

In the meantime another party of Japs had gone into the wards and had ordered all the patients and orderlies who could do so to go outside of the hospital. About 200 patients and orderlies assembled outside, and these had their hands tied behind their backs with cord, in packs of five. Some could only hobble and others had their limbs in plaster. One or two collapsed and had to be revived.

The 200 were then marched away to the native servants' quarters, where they were herded into three rooms, each about 10 feet by 10 feet with over 60 in a room. So crowded were the men in these small rooms that it took minutes to raise one's hands above the head. Sitting down was impossible, and the men were forced to urinate against one another.

During the night several men died and others suffered badly from thirst. Water was promised but never given.

In the afternoon the Japs were seen leading off small groups out of sight, and the ensuing screams, with the Japs wiping their bayonets as they returned, left no doubt as to what had happened to each party. Very few of the men in the groups were ever seen alive again.

Later the Imperial Japanese Army GOC called at the hospital and expressed his regret at the incidents, and said that the staff would have nothing more to fear; his visit was to be regarded as that of a direct representative of the Emperor, which, he said, was a high honour to the hospital.

But we still had memories of the senseless shooting; of the 70 in a 10 foot by 10 foot room; and of the groups being led away around the corner, never to return.

Mufti, June 1954

Warrant Officer Class 1 Enoch James, *was born on 14 June 1897, enlisted at Randwick in July 1941. He maintained careful*

7

records of the 8th Division prisoners of war in Changi, often burying these records to conceal them from the Japanese guards. James was discharged from the army in March 1948 having served with 2 Echelon in Malaya.

Notes:
[1] The overall commander at Singapore, Lieutenant-General Arthur Percival, had allocated the western part of the island to the two brigades from the Australian 8th Division, commanded by Major-General Gordon Bennett.
[2] General Percival assigned the 3rd Indian Corps under Lieutenant-General Sir Lewis Heath to the north-eastern sector, known as 'Centre' force.
[3] Five of these large guns were installed on Singapore to defend approaches to the naval base from the sea. Three were based at Changi, site of today's international airport. This article repeats the commonly accepted myth that the guns could not be turned to fire at the Japanese troops crossing the Johor Strait from Malaya. In fact four of the five could be swung around but were ineffective against troops because they were supplied with armour piercing rather than high explosive shells.

Dinner at Brigade: A Singapore Story
By Lieutenant Colonel J.W. Wright

On the night of 10/11 February 1942 the Japs were consolidating their landings in the north-west and northern shores of the island, and had commenced strong thrusts towards the city and port of Singapore. My regiment of 25-pounder Australian field artillery had been driven out of our original positions on the north-west sector, where it had been in support of the AIF brigade responsible for the defence of that sector.

Overwhelming numbers of crack Japanese assault troops had swarmed ashore from boats and rafts at night on a 10-mile frontage of virgin foreshores, unprotected by any form of fixed defences or barbed wire, and opposite the narrowest portion of the Straits of Johor. The order to withdraw the guns came about 0500 hours.

After being in action all night on 8/9 February and most of the day following, we had just settled into the new positions the AIF brigade had ordered outside the north-west fringes of the city. Returning to my HQ, which had been set up in a deserted bungalow, shortly after 1700 hours, after a tour of the new gun positions, a signal from division was passed to me. It ordered the regiment to make an immediate move across the island to support a counterattack which the North Indian Brigade had been ordered to launch.

The signal stated that the attack was to commence at 1800 hours, preceded by an artillery bombardment. I spread out my map, measured the distance to the position stated as the HQ of the North Indian Brigade, and identified it as an Indian mosque about a couple of hundred yards east of the Bukit Timah Road and about a mile south of the village of Bukit Panjang.

It was every yard of 10 miles from our present position. We had to get there, find out the plan of attack and arrange the artillery support, select gun positions, occupy them, provide communications and be ready to support the attack at 1800 hours.

The time factor plus the distance to be travelled made it an utterly unrealistic order to give supporting field artillery. It was obviously compiled by a staff officer with little or no technical knowledge of field artillery procedure. But it was an order from division and the attempt had to be made.

After telling my second-in-command to join me at the Indian mosque as speedily as possible with the battery reconnaissance parties and the gun groups to follow and await further orders, I set out in my car with my driver and adjutant, accompanied by my despatch rider on his motorcycle.

The mosque was at the end of a gravel-surfaced lane, lined each side with large trees in full leaf, up a fairly steep hill about 20 yards in on the east side of the main road.

Fighting Starts

By my watch it was just 1800 hours, the time the attack was ordered to commence. As I walked the few yards to the mosque entrance I became aware of the sounds of fighting not so far away to the north: small arms fire and machine-gun bursts, and an occasional grenade. Entering the mosque, I identified myself to an English officer I found sitting at a desk and asked for the commander of the North Indian Brigade.

He got up and went into a screened-off inner part and returned with a stoutish elderly brigadier, who came towards me with outstretched hand, saying, 'Glad to meet you again, Colonel.'

I saluted and shook hands. 'Reporting to you with my regiment, sir. Under your command for a counterattack, I understand.'

Dinner at Brigade: A Singapore Story

The brigadier looked at his watch. 'Glad to have you with us, Colonel. You did well getting here in the time. However, I won't need your recce people and guns tonight. You can send them word to stand by in readiness for a move early tomorrow.'

The brigadier continued, 'Now, about the counterattack. It has been impossible to mount it within the time ordered. In any case, I haven't got the troops to do it with. I suggest you go inside with your officers and make yourselves comfortable while I go and see division. When I return, which should be in about 45 minutes, I'd like you and your staff to join us at mess.'

He turned and called out to the officer we had first met. 'This is our intelligence officer,' the brigadier told me. 'He is also our mess secretary. Here,' he said to the officer, 'take the colonel and his staff inside and look after them. They'll be stopping for mess.'

He went outside and entered his car, which had driven up while we had been talking, and drove away down the lane.

New Use for a Mosque
The mess secretary informed us that the brigade mess was functioning in all departments and that the bar was well stocked. On his invitation we named our choice of liquid refreshment and, while we were waiting, he called one of the stewards and instructed him to take my car driver and despatch rider to the brigade mess for other ranks. Our drinks now appeared on a polished silver tray carried by a mess steward formally garbed in a trim, well-starched white jacket with dark blue red-striped trousers and clean black shoes.

All this time my ear had been well cocked to the sounds of fighting, which I felt certain were now a good deal closer to us than when we had driven in about 20 minutes earlier. I noticed that my own adjutant seemed more conscious of the distant sounds of warfare than the sparkling glass of Tiger Beer he held in his hand, but the host seemed quite oblivious to everything outside the mosque.

We sipped our drinks and made casual conversation, trying to seem unconcerned at the steadily nearing sounds of conflict. Bursts of machine-gun and small arms fire were clearly distinguishable, also grenades and an occasional louder explosion, unmistakably a mortar bomb.

I remarked to the others, 'From the sounds and direction from which they are coming, that fighting we hear is a good deal closer to us than the village of Bukit Panjang, which is supposed to be in our hands. Don't you agree?'

They did agree. The IO for the first time seemed to become aware of what was happening outside the mosque, for an expression of grim concern suddenly replaced the appearance of cordial affability which his countenance had previously displayed to us.

This new awareness on his part did not prevent him from remembering his duties as our host, for he ordered another round of drinks.

I looked at my watch and began to wonder if the brigadier would be coming back; it was now over half an hour since he left. It was pitch-black outside. I went to the door to have a look — and to listen!

Returning to my seat, I was trying to make up my mind what to do if he did not return soon, and with these thoughts in my mind, the main door of the mosque opened and the brigadier walked in, accompanied by the COs of the two infantry battalions which comprised the North Indian Brigade. He seemed quite calm and unperturbed, made the necessary introductions and suggested we go in immediately and commence dinner.

Plans Made at Dinner
When we were all seated the brigadier said, 'I saw the GOC and he agreed that we postpone our counterattack until 0900 hours tomorrow. We can discuss it while we dine. I'm hungry and I expect you gentlemen are all the same.'

Dinner at Brigade: A Singapore Story

We sat down at one long table and two waiters in starched white jackets, etc., commenced to serve dinner. Spotless white damask cloths covered the table, with napkins to match, rolled neatly and inserted in the glasses in the best hotel tradition. The cutlery and silver were of the best quality and sparkled with brightness; the varied glassware was highly polished.

I thought to myself, *Are we at war or am I dreaming?* I felt like pinching myself to see if I was asleep or awake. As I swallowed a delicious soup, hot and tasty, the explosions of grenades and mortar bombs sounded much closer, as did the bursts of automatic fire. Too close for me to feel comfortable! I began to lose my appetite!

I looked around the table. The brigadier and the two battalion COs seemed completely unconcerned and only interested in their dinners. *What business is it of mine*, I thought. *I'm only a guest in another mess. But I am concerned! Very much! Those are my guns and that is my regiment not very far away.*

I said to the brigadier, catching his eye for a moment, 'The sound of that fighting up the road seems much closer and seems to have intensified in the past 10 minutes.'

He replied soothingly, with a smile, probably sensing my apprehension. 'I think it is just patrol activity we are hearing. They're holding the line there. I don't think their CO is worried about the situation.'

He looked across the table to the CO in question, who merely nodded and looked grim, not deigning to reply, and went on with his dinner.

I looked at my own officers, the second-in-command and the adjutant. They returned my look somewhat worriedly, but went on with their dinners. Could I blame them? It was possibly the best meal they had been near for a couple of months.

I finished my soup. A fish course came next, served from silver entrée dishes.

13

There was some conversation between the brigadier and the other two COs regarding possible numbers for the counterattack in the morning. The dinner went on; the main course was now being served. If my memory serves me right it was roast chicken with vegetables. I could now hear confused shouting between explosions and bursts of MG fire.

The brigadier said something to his IO, who seemed to have been keeping an anxious ear cocked to the sounds outside. He went out and came back a few minutes later looking very concerned and, bending over, whispered something to the brigadier.

Just then two mortar bombs burst not more than 50 yards from the mosque, and fragments splattered on the roof and walls. A long burst of MG bullets rattled through the roof, several falling on the table, breaking a couple of glasses, and more fell on the floor. Another mortar bomb exploded, this time shattering most of the windows, the glass falling inside the building.

Grenade explosions now seemed to be just outside the building and loud, furious shouting interspersed with bursts of automatic fire indicated that hand-to-hand fighting was occurring only a few yards away.

A waiter, white jacket and all, rushed into the room from the side door, shouting, 'The Japs are just outside, sir.'

The brigadier rose unhurriedly from his unfinished dinner, wiping his mouth carefully with his damask napkin, and without any sign of concern or agitation spoke to us calmly and clearly. 'Gentlemen, I apologise for interrupting your dinner. Conditions in our immediate neighbourhood seem to be somewhat disturbed. I suggest we postpone further discussions. You should leave now and return to your respective commands for the night. By morning the position may have become clarified. I suggest we meet again at 0700 hours tomorrow to continue this discussion. Good evening, gentlemen.'

I never saw a building empty so quickly. The lights in the mosque went out immediately as we scrambled in the darkness to get to the door. I did not even have an opportunity to thank the brigadier for his hospitality.

Jap Fighting
Outside there was frenzied shouting and shooting as the brigade defence platoon fought Japanese in the darkness, lit up now and then momentarily with brief flashes from grenade explosions. The combat appeared to be all on the Causeway side of the mosque, which enabled us to reach my car on the Singapore side, where the driver was already in his seat with the engine running, and the despatch rider alongside on his motorcycle.

Our second-in-command could not find his utility truck or driver where he had left them. I called to him to ride back with us, and he jumped on the car running board. We crawled down the lane slowly in the darkness, not daring to switch on the car lights, while bullets from friend and foe whistled through the trees over our heads.

Turning carefully onto the main road in the direction of Singapore, my driver paused to accustom his eyes to the darkness and to pick up the edges of the main bitumen road. The darkness was absolute, but as our eyes grew more accustomed to it we found we were only a few feet away and alongside a dark mass of some large vehicle. A few yards ahead we could just make out another similar dark mass. The second-in-command stepped off the running board for a closer look. Re-entering the car hurriedly, he said quietly, 'Those are tanks! We have not got any in Malaya, so they must be Japs!'

I leaned over the back of the front seat and spoke softly into the driver's ear. 'Drive slowly past them without lights, and when you get about 200 yards beyond the second one, switch on your lights and drive like hell! We must get back quickly to warn the regiment.'

The remainder of that night was a nightmare in my recollection. It will be sufficient to say that by making two rearward moves during the hours of darkness and being warned by the sounds of fighting on each flank, the whole regiment avoided being surrounded and cut off by the Japanese thrust along each side of the Bukit Timah Road.

On the western side, sometime about the middle of the night, both AIF and RAA headquarters were overrun, the occupants getting out with only the clothes they were wearing, losing all equipment and records, etc.

The invitation to mess at brigade ceased to exist that night; I never saw the brigadier again.

Reveille, February 1971

John William Wright, DFC *was born at Quirindi, NSW, on 4 January 1893. He served in WWI initially with the 12th Light Horse, then transferred to the Australian Flying Corps as a pilot where he was awarded the Distinguished Flying Cross, was wounded and later became flight commander of 4 Squadron. He enlisted for WWII at Paddington, Sydney, in March 1940, was taken prisoner of war, and was discharged in January 1946 with the rank of lieutenant colonel, and died 3 November 1986.*

Prisoners of the Japanese

'War either makes or destroys a man. He either becomes a man or he's an animal.'

— Sister Berenice Twohill

Sister Berenice Twohill: A Prisoner at Rabaul
Interview with John Gatfield

In January 1942 a Japanese fleet landed thousands of troops at Rabaul, on the north-eastern tip of the island of New Britain. A force of approximately 1400 Australians was stationed there — most were to die: in the immediate battle, in captivity, or in attempting to escape across the Solomon Sea to New Guinea. Among the civilians to remain in Rabaul was Sister Berenice Twohill of Our Lady of the Sacred Heart Convent. Born near Murwillumbah, she was in her early twenties when she was posted to Rabaul in October 1939 to teach at the St Joseph's school for children of mixed race. For three years and nine months she was a prisoner of the Japanese. As she told John Gatfield, the war started for her within hours of Japan attacking Pearl Harbor on 7 December 1941.

I remember it so well. At 11 o'clock the children used to go out to play. Two policemen came along. They said, 'Pearl Harbor was bombed this morning and we're at war with the Japanese and we've come to collect the two little Japanese boys. They'll be all right — their father's already on his way to Australia, and they'll have to go with their mother out to the mission. The school will have to be closed.'

The bishop came to us individually and said, 'You're supposed to go to Australia.' We all said we'd rather stay and carry on, and Canberra said, all right, on one condition: that you do Red Cross work. So we made our red crosses and put them on our white dresses. And we went out to the mission at Vunapope. There were about 35 sisters there.

19

JG: When the Japanese arrived in Rabaul there was no hope of holding them back, was there?

No hope whatever, and the army knew that. And they pleaded and pleaded, but were told, 'No danger, there's no danger.' They said, 'Either send help or evacuate us', but the army did neither.

Father Barrow, who was parish priest at Rabaul, was with the soldiers who were told to stay to face the Japanese and was taken prisoner with those who survived. He became very sick with dysentery and was dying, and was sent to the mission. He told me first-hand information about the battle. I want that emphasised. There was a battle, even though nothing much has been written about it. Those Australians fought to the death. They were abandoned, sacrificed. When the [Australian] government found out they'd refused to send any help until it was too late, they said, 'We'll forget them — they never existed.' That's why it's all been hidden.

Other soldiers had been told to go to the bush. Some had been there only a little while and knew nothing at all about the bush. A lot of them died unnecessarily because you should never starve in the tropics with so many vegetables and things around — they'd be surrounded by food and wouldn't even know it — they got sick and died of starvation.

> *The Japanese confined the sisters to the mission and held other civilians, including priests and missionaries, under house arrest. Rabaul became a central assembly point for prisoners brought in from other islands.*

The day the Japanese landed, by 11 o'clock they were out at the mission and we were all imprisoned. From that day on we couldn't speak to a native or anybody else.

The majority of Japanese guards were just little boys. They

had no idea of where they were or what they were doing. All they had was their army outfit, a spade hanging here, and a bayonet. They always had bayonets and they'd come around to us and say, 'Blood of Australian soldier', and throw it up in our faces, but we'd just laugh at them and say, 'It's only tomato sauce', but we didn't know, it could have been true.

Bishop Scharmach was Polish and had been conscripted into the German Army and was a stretcher-bearer in World War I. We were interned in our building and had no contact with anyone else until the bishop got the upper hand and demanded that he come and visit each of us every day. He was the only person we had contact with for about nine months, apart from the Japanese guarding us all the time.

For the first two weeks or more we were terrified, absolutely terrified. We didn't know what would happen to us. Until the bishop got on top. He got a guarantee that no sister would ever be touched — we were safe. But before that, one of our sisters had a little place where she looked after about eight little babies whose mothers had died. Now they tried their best to get into that place over and over again. It was barred, thank goodness, but the bishop went straight to the top and complained about it. Then we felt relatively safe.

JG: Is it going too far to say that the bishop may have saved your lives, that he put his life on the line to argue on your behalf?

He definitely did save our lives. Over and over again he did that. He came and told the six Australian army nurses and the other civilian nurses, 'I've got bad news, all the women have to go to Japan.' He said to the nurses, 'I can't stop you [from being taken] because you really don't belong to the mission, but the sisters, over my dead body will they take you.' They didn't dare. They became really afraid of the bishop — he stood up to them. He was a remarkable man, so none of us left, and he really saved our lives. He was fearless. His trust was all in God, and he'd say, 'We'll get through.'

We were searched every day because they thought we had radios and were sending news to Australia about how many planes went out. If we had only had the means to do it! Because we counted every plane that went out and every plane that came back. And they'd come and say, 'Oh, we brought down 10 Australian planes today', and we knew that was the number they'd lost. They always told us exactly the opposite, but they didn't know we were counting them all. We watched everything from our convent, overlooking the harbour. We had the most beautiful view.

After the nurses went, we were moved into the bigger compound, together with all the fathers and brothers. So it was better for us, although we didn't see anything, because we had contact with them.

> *The Japanese provided nothing for their captives. For the first several months the prisoners lived on food supplies which had been hidden in the days before the Japanese invasion.*

They hid it everywhere. Where I was cooking there was a little native hut with an attic upstairs. We'd packed that with stuff. We would quickly put up a ladder and then pull it down because we had this soldier going around and around. That went on for 10 days, perhaps, until one day somebody didn't get the ladder down quickly enough and he saw it. The Japanese were strange. It never seemed to enter their minds, *Where are they getting the food from?* It was never questioned. But this day he saw the ladder and up he went. Then we were banished. We'd learned by this time that they were frightened of two things: malaria and TB [tuberculosis]. We had a Dutch sister superior, and any time they'd come close to where we'd hidden food in the convent, she'd say, 'Malaria — no! no! no! — malaria.' And they never went in.

JG: Did you witness any atrocities yourself?

Oh yes. Captain Gray. [Captain John Robert Gray, AIF NX191431, is buried at Rabaul.] After we were moved into the compound with native huts and barbed wire, we saw him tied up to a coconut tree. They tormented him and did all sorts of things. They were trying to get information out of him, and he'd only been there a week and knew nothing. They tormented him for days and days, and there was not a thing we could do — we just had to watch it.

We had some seminarians who were allowed to stay, and they were down behind us, and they saw this doctor, who was a nasty doctor, bringing a man down with two other soldiers just behind their place, and they saw him cut his heart out while he was alive. They witnessed that.

We also saw them belting the natives. They'd bring them out in front of us, put them over a beam, turn them upside down and belt them. And that's what was going to happen to us if anything upset them. Others we saw taken down to the cemetery, and we'd hear the shots. When they'd lose planes they'd take it out on us. They gave us nothing to eat — they just guarded us. We didn't run away because it was always if one ran away, 10 would be beheaded. If two ran away, 20 would be beheaded. All this was always written up.

JG: As the war went on, did the Japanese come under attack themselves in Rabaul?

Oh yes. We watched that begin. And it was the most marvellous sight, to see hundreds and hundreds of them, all in formation, just like silver birds coming in, and drop their bombs. And we'd watch them day after day. At night we were down in the trenches. By degrees the bishop and the men would build these big trenches, or tunnels, under the mountains. We could stand up in those.

One morning the planes came from a different direction, over the hills behind us, so we didn't hear them coming. They dropped their bombs on Vunapope. We knew that would happen because the Japanese had brought out their ammunition and put it just beside us with a red cross on top of it. From then on we knew we were doomed. So they'd come over every day and every night and they'd bomb us and bomb us. And we'd be crouched, hundreds of us, in these tunnels under the mountain, and we'd just wait for it to collapse. But it didn't. Whether they knew we were there or not, I don't know.

After we'd been there for a while they brought out their little Japanese nurses and put them on one side of us. And they put a hospital for their shell-shocked soldiers next to that. They had no protection like we did. When we came back from the tunnels one day all these bombs had exploded and there were bits of Japanese bodies everywhere. We had all these arms and legs and heads all over our place. We had to pick them up and pass them over.

> *The sisters were given no more than a litre of water to share between 10 for washing every morning. Everyone suffered from prickly heat and they could spend up to eight hours a day in the stifling tunnels while Allied bombers attacked Rabaul.*

The fathers decided they'd get an air shaft right through to the top of the mountain. And they worked day and night. And the day it came through, this gust of wind went through the tunnel and we thought it was just wonderful. And what happened? The Japanese came along and said, 'We want you to go to a safe place now.' They'd only been waiting till we got that shaft through and tricked us.

Then they took us down to this valley at Ramale. We got to the top and you couldn't see the bottom through virgin forest. Eventually we got to the bottom and you couldn't see the sky.

Not the slightest bit of sunshine got through for weeks. There were a couple of huts for us. You were sopping wet all day but it was heaven compared to living in the trenches. We just lived on weeds for months. You had to boil everything. I got malaria; there was so much malaria. Others got beri-beri and dysentery. We had our own little cemetery down in the Ramale Valley and all those bodies were taken back after the war to Vunapope.

I don't bear them [the Japanese] any grudge at all. I look at it this way: every soldier fights for his country. War either makes or destroys a man. He either becomes a man or he's an animal.

Reveille, March–April 2002

Sister Berenice Twohill *of Our Lady of the Sacred Heart Convent was born at Tumbulgum near Murwillumbah, NSW, on 9 November 1916, the eighth of 11 children. She was one of about 350 missionary Fathers, Brothers and Sisters who were interned on New Britain by the Japanese for the duration of the war. She was liberated by Australian troops in 1945. In later life Sister Berenice Twohill lived in the Sacred Heart Convent in Kensington, Sydney, working in particular among the homeless. In 2016 she celebrated 80 years as a daughter of Our Lady of the Sacred Heart and also her 100th birthday. The 2010 telemovie* Sisters of War *was based on the wartime captivity experiences of Sister Berenice and army nurse Lorna Whyte (Johnston). Their friendship lasted until Mrs Johnston's death in September 2013. Sister Berenice Twohill died on 3 November 2017, just a week short of her 101st birthday.*

Remarkable Courage as a Prisoner of War
By Chris Neilson

Chris Neilson experienced the absolute brutality of torture, starvation and degradation by his Japanese captors, yet not only did he survive, he laughed in their faces. The son of a former Danish naval captain who settled at Cooktown, North Queensland, he spent his youth prospecting for gold and tin, and as a professional fisherman, a bare-knuckle boxer and a canecutter. When war was declared, Chris joined the 2/9 Infantry Battalion and transferred to a signals unit in E Section 8th Division. His first taste of action came at Muar on the west coast of Malaya.

They were already in action and when we went there, there was dead all round. The Japs had already made a bayonet charge and they'd repelled them. The major said, 'Get over there and make sure they're dead.' There was Jap dead and Australian dead, so I thought I'd be safe there. I got a signal through and just then a Jap nearly got him [the major]. I said, 'Sir, have you got a good rifle? I can see him. Just show your head and bend back again.' I was a trained sniper, and I hit him right here [through the head]. Incidentally I think I'm the only signals wireless operator who ever went into action with a bayonet.

After five days and five nights there were 120 of us left out of the battalion. The commandant took on a machine-gun nest and didn't realise there was another one on the other side, and they got him. So there was only the doctor, an artillery bloke and myself, and my offsider [Max Robinson]. So I said, 'Doctor, pick out a walking wounded.' He picked him out and said, 'Do

Remarkable Courage as a Prisoner of War

you know where we're going?' I said, 'I'm a bloody bushman from North Queensland. I know the jungle and the mudflats and everything.'

So I took the wounded man across the hill and we joined up after walking all night and the next day with the 2/19th Battalion. I'll never forget — every hour we got a message from Malayan command, the British. I'd say, 'When is this help going to come? We've been cut off, encircled.' 'Help's on the way,' they said. 'Nearly there.' Later on we found out there wasn't a Brit left in Malaya, not one Brit. Only our two battalions, a thousand of us. Then we found, when Yamashita[1] was charged with murder, he said, 'The only excuse I can make for my men killing all the wounded in the trucks was when they found out a mere battalion had held up the Emperor's two divisions for five days and nights, they slaughtered everyone.' We found out the only people who came to help us came as far as Johor, just north of Singapore, and it was a Scottish battalion and they covered us while we retired back to Singapore.

And the silly bastards. Bennett [Australian commander Major-General Gordon Bennett], he tried his hardest to stop the British from cutting the water off — the water came from Johor. Singapore had no water, and as soon as they cut the water off, we were buggered. That was the bloody Brits for you. It wasn't the soldiers' fault — they were champions and they said they tried to get up to help, but the command said no. It was a hell of a balls-up.

The first working party — we were building a shrine — and two of the Japs got a young Chinese woman. They stripped her down, both raped her on the spot, then put a bayonet into her, ripped up her guts and killed her. So I said, 'This is no place for me.'

The night that Singapore fell, Chris and a companion had tried to escape — his mate was killed by a Japanese patrol and Chris made it back to the Australian lines. Chris then went scrounging for wireless parts and was asked by a young Chinese to join a guerrilla group operating in the jungle near Malacca. Chris and a radio technician, Bob Green, agreed, but the day before they were to be smuggled across to Johor Bahru, Green went down with dysentery. Chris nursed him for five days, then carried him 16 kilometres back to the camp, where he reported to the senior Australian officer, obtained quinine and other drugs for Green, and went to sleep.

We just went to sleep. And the bloody commandant, our own Colonel Oakes, rung up the Kempeitai [the Japanese military police] and told them we'd tried to escape and to come and get us. This bloke had read out to every one of the troops that anyone caught escaping would be executed on the spot. And he still rung up the Kempeitai and put us in. I wasn't allowed to name him when I came home — I'd have got in a lot of trouble for naming him. They had to cover it up, they said — they didn't want the Australian people to know this bastard had turned us in for execution.

You should have heard the bloody Japs — they swarmed around us — hopples and handcuffs, and they chucked us into a truck and into the YMCA building — that was the Gestapo headquarters. I'll never forget it. Ten hours a day. The first five hours they'd interrogate us. The bloke behind would be pushing his sword into you, just enough to bleed you. All the bashings, you couldn't name the hidings you'd get, the slap in your face, bleeding from your bloody ears. We went back that night after 10 hours — I was buggered. And there were 17 people in the billiard table room in the YMCA building. A Chinese woman was there — her son had escaped through the slats — must have been a skinny little bugger — and they held her and said if the son gave himself up they'd let her go. There was one 20-gallon bucket in the corner for the lot of us. I asked her in Malay if she wanted to have a leak and she said, 'Yes.' I said, 'Fellers, would you turn your back? She wants to get on the john.' Just then this officer came in. He'd only be about 25 — he was the commandant's son. He could kill with his hands. He was the most brutal capable bastard I ever saw in my life. He said, 'Who ordered?' I said, 'No one ordered, sir. You being a gentleman yourself, I asked them to turn their backs.' And he hit me here and he hit me there — I don't know how he did the throw but I landed on a billiard table, and he came over and hit me with the sword. Talk about a bloody mess. From then it was five days, 10 hours a day, then they sent us to Outram Road Jail to be executed.

I don't know why, but on the 29th day, the day before we were due to be executed, 17 May 1942, we were taken back to court. Evidently one of the judges believed us when we said we were city boys who'd been lost looking for food. He battled for us, and the prosecuting attorney said, 'You sons of English criminal swine. You'll wish you'd been executed. Three years' solitary confinement.' And in the cells we went. God almighty. Half the blokes went mad straight away.

Bob Green came to see me in Cairns, years after. He said, 'What happened? I remember going out and getting sick. I don't remember coming back and the Japs taking us to jail.' I said, 'You emptied a shit bucket over your head and you were running around mad, and they sent you out to Changi.' He said, 'It's only a few years ago that it's got home to me that I was a prisoner of war.'

I was 14 months in solitary confinement and then I went back again for five months.

John McGregor and I only had a ball of rice twice a day for 14 months. Nothing else. The first Christmas there, they said, 'Are you Christians?' 'Oh yes, we're all Christians all right.' So we thought we'd be getting a good dinner today, for sure. And the bloody bastards. The Japs eat a lot of those little fish. They'd heaped up all the bloody bones and mixed it with our rice for Christmas dinner. So I chucked it in the shit bucket, and it was the worst thing I could have done — it fermented and outflowed on the step and they put the bloody aluminium dish with rice in it in the shit.

> *After his first spell in solitary confinement, Chris was down to six stone two pounds [40 kilograms]. He had a depressed fracture of the skull, which gave him a headache every day for the rest of his life, and both hands were broken. He had more than 200 infected scabs on his body from wounds caused by the Japanese jabbing him with bayonets and swords.*

My skin was like shark skin. What they did, they had a sheet and soaked it in red palm oil. They wrapped me in it, and after about three weeks I shed my skin. All the skin came off in great sheets.

> *One of the ploys Chris used to maintain his sanity while in solitary confinement was to tap Morse code messages to other inmates. He and others also used a piece of bamboo or fishbone to keep a record of executions on the whitewashed walls.*
>
> *He had also been reported as having been executed, and both his family and his unit had been told he was dead.*

My poor old mother — she said, 'No, I'll never have it.' Everyone else said, 'Mrs Neilson, the Red Cross doesn't make mistakes — they've sent word that he's been executed.' 'I don't care,' she said. 'He's my firstborn. I feel he's still there,' she said.

I always thought I'd get back home. McGregor and I used to put a tiny bit of cloth behind the lock on the cell door so we could jerk it open. We reckoned that when the executioner came for us, we'd yank it open, throw our latrine buckets over them, brain the bastards with our wooden pillows, and grab their swords off them and fight our way out.

The escape plan wasn't necessary. Chris survived to return home, and described his experiences as 'just a bad memory'.

Reveille, March–April 2004, interview with author

Christian Henry Ernst Neilson, *was born at Cairns on 2 March 1913, enlisted in April 1940. With the rank of signalman, 8th Division Corps of Signals, he was discharged in January 1946 and died 1 November 2005.*

Note:
[1] Tomoyuki Yamashita (8 November 1885 — 23 February 1946) was the Japanese general who directed the invasion of Malaya and Singapore. He later commanded the Japanese defence of the Philippines from advancing US forces. After the war, Yamashita was tried for war crimes committed in the Philippines by troops under his command and found guilty. Yamashita was sentenced to death, and executed by hanging.

Eighteen Months on the Burma Railway
By Sergeant Roy K. Smith

Everyone thought that the Japs would not come down the west coast [of Malaya] where the jungle was thought to be impenetrable. But of course they did. When that was known some of our chaps were sent over but they were cut to ribbons. We were drawn back to Singapore. Then the air raids started. Jap planes in groups of nine dropped daisy cutter bombs. We were taught to drop flat but the civilians ran, and they were cut down in droves. General Percival soon found that he had almost no supplies and Yamashita had taken most of the island. So we surrendered.

The Japanese then found they had some 60,000 slaves for labour and within a few months our three battalions, about 3000 men, were moved out and into two ships. Our ship took 1000 and the other, which was a bit larger, 2000. We were packed into the holds where there wasn't room to lie down. Singapore is practically on the equator and anyone who has been there will know that the heat catches the breath. In the holds the heat was a solid block.

Latrines consisted of a sort of scaffolding hanging on the side of the ship. As a concession to cleanliness there was a hand pump. A mate would pump salt water over me after using the latrine. The problem was that the salt which dried on the body was then mixed with sweat in the holds, and the resulting dermatitis and the itch were an additional turn of the screw.

We were offloaded onto barges at Victoria Point, the southernmost part of Burma, where there was an airfield. This had been dynamited by the British as they pulled out, and our job was to repair it by filling in the holes and packing them to airfield standard with our feet. Some of the charges hadn't gone off but because of the typically British neat spacing of the charges we were able to tell where explosive was buried and no one was lost digging it up.

There was a concrete pillbox which would be in the road so it had to go. A Japanese engineer measured a hole which we dug and then pushed the pillbox into it. Would you believe he then wanted us to dig another hole to take the excess soil? After a lot of Japanese discussion we finished by stretchering the soil off the 'drome on bamboo poles threaded through sacks.

After a couple of months we were shipped to Rangoon where we worked round the rail and marshalling yards.

And then to the big one. The Japs wanted to build a railroad some 400 kilometres from Bangkok to Thanbyuzayat near Rangoon. Thousands of men at the Bangkok end started to build towards us, and we worked as battalions at our end. The battalions leapfrogged one another. One would build forward and another would work back from up ahead until we met, and then the same procedure for the next distance. Camps were known by their distance from Thanbyuzayat. By the time we had got to 75 Camp our three battalions, 3000 men, had to be merged into one battalion, as by then the treatment we got resulted in half the men being unfit for duty or dead.

For some reason the dreadful treatment meted out to the men at Bangkok was not repeated at our end, although there were instances I do not like to look back on.

I was in charge of a platoon of about 100 men. One of them had a very badly ulcerated leg. We had to carry rock from the quarry so I told him to drop out. As we were coming back from the quarry I heard him scream — a guard was kicking him in the leg. Before I stopped to think I hit the Jap. The penalty for hitting a guard is death, but because I was No. 1 of the platoon I was taken instead to the guardhouse where there was a sort of bamboo rail. I had to lean over that and was beaten with bamboo rods till I passed out. When I woke up my mates were bathing my back with salt water but next morning I could not move. I had intended to lie there but the guard raised a storm, demanding No. 1. So I was finally carried out and stood on parade.

That guard gave me a bad time for two days but fortunately the guards were rotated to another camp. Much later, in another camp, a guard clubbed my toes with the butt of his rifle till I lost my toenails — which are still not right.

A young chap tried to escape from one camp but was brought back. The penalty for escape was death. One of our officers tried to save him by saying that this young man was weak in the head and did not know what he was doing. Unfortunately the Japs saw through the ruse and he was convicted. Normally escapers were shot but for some reason on this occasion the Jap officer was required to execute him with a sword. As the boy knelt, the officer swung the sword as hard as he could, but mis-hit across the boy's shoulders. The officer then had to try again and this time killed him. I saw the officer go back to his hut and I felt that the whole thing had got to him. Anyway he did not come out of his hut again and days later disappeared.

I had got to 110 kilometres, where there was a camp, when I got a very bad foot. It was twice the size of the other one and red hot and purple. The men who were sick, such as those with beri-beri, dysentery, malaria, cholera and so on, had to work, as the camp commandants merely said that they had nothing wrong with them. But the men with something to show, such as bad wounds, went back to 55 Camp where there was a crude hospital and some doctors. Depending on the condition of the ulcers and wounds and the extent of the gangrene, a man might have to have a leg amputated. All the surgery I saw was to remove part of a leg. This was due to the sharp little chips which flew up, as picks were used on rock in the quarries. Little puncture wounds so easily got infected. In my case I must have scratched the side of the foot and it wasn't possible to keep out the mud. My boots had rotted away to nothing a long time before. We were all barefooted.

At 55 Camp in my time there were 64 amputations but only 27 men survived. A Dutch doctor had got his hands on some cocaine and he used to inject this into the spines of the men until their legs were numb. Then Colonel Coates and Major Hobbes would amputate with the sort of saw that butchers use in their shops. Those of us who could get about were given camp duties, as well as helping with the operations. There was no way of knowing how long the numbness would last so several of us had to stand by to hold the man down in case the cocaine wore off.

While you were working you got three cups of boiled rice a day. A bad consequence of being hospitalised meant that the Japs said that if you couldn't work you didn't need full rations, so you only got three half-cups of rice each day.

My foot was so hot and I was so afraid that I would lose it that I tried to cool it in a stream that ran through the camp. As I sat there I felt an odd sensation in the foot and, looking down, I could see a school of tiny fish busy chewing at the rotting flesh of my ulcer. I watched until the wound was as clean as a whistle. To this day I believe that those fish saved my foot and indeed my life. I was able to keep it clean until it healed by wrapping it in banana leaves and then wrapping it in bits of my mosquito net. A fair swap, malaria for my foot!

Our job was to prepare a track for the rail but not to lay it. We had to make the cuttings and build embankments and of course clear away the jungle, especially the bamboo thickets. We had to dig round a clump and cut through the roots until the clump could be moved away. Later we got some assistance when a local with an elephant was attached to the squad. That meant our progress was a lot quicker.

There came a time when a guard wanted even more production. The guards were always pressing for more speed;

beatings were the order of the day if they thought we weren't working hard enough. Anyway, this guard poked the elephant with his bayonet, which made the elephant swing his trunk round and knock the guard to the ground. The guard panicked and shot and wounded the elephant, which went berserk, broke free, and disappeared into the jungle. An officer came running over in a high old rage. When he found out the details he pulled his sidearm and shot the guard dead where he stood.

Towards the end I was in a big camp at Tamarkan near the infamous bridge over the River Kwai. The American Liberators bombed the bridge and also our camp with overshoots. We were not allowed to dig foxholes for some reason, but we could, and did, make drainage trenches around the atap thatched bamboo huts we lived in. When the raid alarm went we would lie down in the trenches. They were deep enough but not deep enough to protect two men. Sadly, a man who was late threw himself on top of me as the bombing started. When the all clear sounded I had to call for assistance to get him off me. Shrapnel had taken him through the neck and he was dead. On one raid the Liberators killed 14 of our men and wounded 44.

Reveille, July–August 2004

Roy Kenneth Smith, *was born at Watsons Bay, Sydney, on 31 August 1915, enlisted at Paddington in July 1940. He was discharged, as a sergeant with the 8 Division Provost Company, in February 1946. He died on 11 September 2010.*

Christmas in Captivity:
Three Memorable Days on the Railroad of Death
Author unknown

Christmas and all that it means: the family reunion, the exchange of gifts and greetings, the junketings and good cheer, the feasts and good fellowship ...

Try to imagine the day for prisoners of war in a jungle camp on the Siam Railway. Yet, somehow, we managed to capture that spirit, and for a brief day were able to forget our troubles in our hope for the future.

We had three Christmas Days in captivity, which lasted three and a half years almost to the very day. Much the same pattern of celebration was followed on all three occasions. Carols were practised for weeks in advance, and the special Christmas Day church services were all amazingly well attended — for 'doubt, difficulty, danger and distress' are all conducive to prayer, and this was the atmosphere in which we existed.

Moreover our padres, without exception, were all first class. We had at least two who had discarded their cassocks for combatant uniform and now helped to take services. In the same way, our doctors were also magnificent and inspired.

We were never allowed to sing the national anthem at our services, nor on any other occasions for that matter. So we substituted 'Land of Hope and Glory' and somehow we got particular satisfaction.

Then, after the voluntary Church Parade, we had a sports meeting. How people managed to run and jump, put the weight, and throw the cricket ball in our emaciated condition remains a mystery, but there were always sufficient entries to provide a good show. Football, too, was always popular and of quite a high standard, even if matches were confined by the medical authorities to 20 minutes each way. I recall, incredible as it may seem, that boxing was also popular, and the *pièce de résistance* of an evening's contest might well be a grudge fight, instigated by some hut commander as a means of settling a dispute between two of his charges.

Nerves did not often fray to this extent, but when they did, this proved quite the best means of effecting a reconciliation. Almost invariably the two contestants would start off by thirsting for one another's blood, and then be reduced to helpless laughter by the cheers and comments of the spectators, so at the end of the third round they would walk off arm in arm, the best of pals again.

Boxing helped in many ways, especially in one particular case of a poor fellow (not too bright topsides) who had begun to fret and had even gone off eating what little food was available. In consequence, he was going downhill fast, but he seemed to be interested in boxing, though he had never taken it up. Some of his friends suggested that he really had the physique of a champion and offered to train him. The result was more than gratifying. He started to eat at his rations, to skip and shadow-box, to his great well-being, and his trainers nursed him along, and taught him some of the rudiments. They proclaimed him the 'champ' and issued challenges. Fights were staged, and all the challengers, who of course were in the know, were knocked down like ninepins. The 'champ's' fights became the biggest draw in the camp, and to watch one of his bouts, preceded by all the professional preliminaries, and a succession of challengers all being floored, was one of the funniest things I have ever seen. If, perhaps, the deception was a little cruel, in other ways it was harmless enough, and by providing the 'champ' with an object for living, probably saved both his mentality and his life.

The sports meeting would last until it was time for the midday meal, for which the cooks always made a supreme effort. Even

Christmas in Captivity: Three Memorable Days on the Railroad of Death

the Nips could always be persuaded to release just a little extra, so that for one blessed day we had enough to eat. The basis of everything was rice, but on Christmas Day it was disguised in a half a dozen different ways. One camp reported that with its aid and 24 12-ounce tins of corned beef, they had produced a thousand sausages.

Nearly all camps managed some meat, which was brought in on the hoof. Duck eggs were generally reasonably plentiful, and dried fish, rather like whitebait, were sometimes available. Bananas were responsible for our sweets, and quite a formidable menu was the ultimate result. All our cooks took their duties with a high sense of responsibility — for it was a greatly prized job — and always excelled themselves on Christmas Day. They took a particular pride in their work, which was often interrupted by the too close attention given by the Korean guards.

The pride of every cookhouse was its 'dofers'. Some have this as 'doovers' and believe it to be a corruption of hors d'oeuvres, but my authority, a cook in the officers' camp, maintained that it means 'dofer-termorrow' and consisted of anything that could be saved, disguised and served again. How anything was ever saved is quite miraculous, as, when the ration had been served out, a *lagi* (Malay for 'again') queue formed up on a roster for the 'overs', and if necessary a *lagi-lagi* followed.

My cooking authority was at one time much troubled by a particularly obnoxious Korean guard who was always hanging about for the unconsidered trifle or odd cuppa, and creating trouble when it did not come his way. After one bad session of this kind, and when the guard had moved out of earshot, he burst out with, 'I wish to blazes someone would knock his ruddy head off!' and felt a little better for the outburst.

Now the cook's mate, who happened to be standing by, was a simple fellow, endowed with more brawn than brain, but, as he had always seemed anxious to please, he had been given a nominal job in the cookhouse, mainly as a night watchman.

Just at this time we were getting a number of air raids, and suffered some bombing by the RAF, who were after the railway siding alongside the camp. One night, after a raid, my cook friend thought he would just have a look around his cookhouse, and was met by his mate, the night watchman, who whispered, 'Ah've done it, sir!' 'Done what?' said my friend. 'Knocked his ruddy 'ead off, sir!' said his mate. It was too true. The obnoxious Nip had taken shelter in the cookhouse and had started sniffing around the sacred 'dofers'. This was just too much for the cook's mate, who had dispatched him with a not-so-blunt instrument.

Somehow the cook and his mate managed to drag the body outside the precincts of the camp — which was not difficult as the fence was continually falling down, and we even got tired of reporting it, as the Nips always said, 'Go and build it up again.' Fortunately the raid that night had been a particularly heavy one. Several of the Korean guards had broken camp and a few did not return. Nothing more was ever heard of the incident. The Nips must have presumed that he had been killed in the air raid while outside the perimeter.

After a short siesta on Christmas afternoon — very necessary after our, to us, enormous lunch — it was customary to hold a race meeting. These were quite a feature of camp life, and no holiday was complete without its special meeting. The horses were the burliest men available and the jockeys were the flyweights. Everything else was far more realistic, especially the bookies and the tipsters, and we even had a tote.

The races were rigged in the most dreadful manner by the 'horses' — double-crossing was normal and their form defied the official handicapper. But it was all tremendous fun, and to see the 'horses' being solemnly paraded around the paddock and the jockeys coming with very presentable colours, with the roar of the tipsters and bookies in the background, made quite a scene. The racecourse was any convenient stretch of open ground, and the jockeys were given pick-a-back rides by the horses. Bumping and boring became a fine art, and no race finished without a stream of protests, which was all part of the game.

No Christmas was complete without a pantomime, and *Jack and the Beanstalk*, *Babes in the Wood* and *The Sleeping Beauty* were all staged in their turn. The scenery, the stage effects and, above all, the costumes, all largely made from bamboo and mosquito netting, were amazing. Some camps even had a band. The Nip commandant was always inordinately proud of his camp band, and seemed, particularly, to enjoy their spirited playing of 'Colonel Bogey' whenever he appeared — little knowing the words that the army invariably sings to this excellent march!

Reveille, December 1960

An Elephant Tale
By E.C. Yates

Most working days (or toiling days) on the Siam–Burma Death Railway were similar — backbreaking toil from early morning to night with scarcely a break for rest. We had to carry tons of earth daily to form the flat bed for the railway track. Any change in one's existence would be doubly welcome, but from whence would this come?

On a particular day a bridge-building gang arrived, complete with their workhorse — an elephant. Their job was to span the many small streams on one section of the railway, using green timber hauled from the jungle by the elephant. This gang was strictly isolated from our section of the camp, named Kuei [45 kilometres from the notorious Hellfire Pass]. I was horrified to notice that the elephant had no native mahout; traditionally, an elephant — at birth — is given a mahout, who will remain with the animal until one or other dies, usually the mahout first. They work together as a team, in complete harmony. The mahout for this elephant was a Tommy [British] soldier and he knew little about giving commands to this enormous animal; hence there was often strife between them resulting in the elephant being beaten with a heavy pole, a most demeaning behaviour levied against this child of nature. And so life went on, the elephant being unable to understand why such treatment was meted out to him. Elephants never forget; this is not a cliché but an obvious truth, as we shall see.

One particular day I had the good fortune of completing my task on the railway sooner than anticipated, hence I was back in the camp by 4 p.m. and decided to indulge in a luxury of a swim in the nearby stream where the bridge gang was working. The elephant was hauling tree trunks up the slope to the flat at the top, there to drop them vertically into the river to form support for the deck.

The elephant found it a difficult task, pulling heavy logs up the slippery, muddy slope, and not aided by the Tommy mahout who often resorted to bashing the animal with the heavy pole in order to urge him forward to dump the tree at the top. The elephant was fitted with a heavy leather breastplate, to which were attached chains on the log. I closely watched this procedure as there were portents of disaster to emerge from this operation.

The elephant had hauled the tree trunk to the top, stopped, and the mahout unchained one side; the elephant had his head turned to watch every movement of the mahout. Instead of walking around the front of the elephant to get the other chain, the mahout decided to move under the elephant's belly.

At this instant the elephant urinated about 10 gallons at high pressure, aimed directly at the mahout who was thoroughly drenched in the process.

Several seconds later the elephant raised his head, as if in triumph, and trumpeted his resounding cry of victory.

I must reiterate this story is not a figment of my imagination but true in every respect.

The Listening Post, Spring 1999

Bicycle Camp, Hell Ship and Death Railway
By Dallas Cressey

When WWII broke out, Dallas Cressey was on his way to Europe from his homeland of New Zealand. Stuck in Australia, he signed up 12 months after the war started.

We had only about a fortnight's training and then we were whisked over to Malaya and did our training in Malacca for four months. Then we went up to Ipoh for another five months.

When we got back to Singapore we were among the last vehicles going across before they blew up Johor Bahru. They didn't want us at all on the island and so they decided they'd evacuate us up to the Burma Railroad, which hadn't fallen, or there was no talk of it falling at that time, because of the experience we'd had on the mainland in Malaya.

The lascar crew of the *Kinta* had nicked off as soon as it hit port, so we only had a New Zealand engineer and the captain of the ship. They called for volunteers to work it. And as we were going over in the convoy in this old *Kinta*, the Japs attacked the convoy. So we scattered, and fortunately we escaped, but where we took refuge, in a bay, was a reef, and as the tide went we were left on the reef. So we hung there for a day and they used quick-sealing cement to seal the damage, and we were down to four knots [7.5 kilometres per hour], pumping all the time. The *Jupiter* came along the next day, a big British destroyer.

Everything was megaphoned so we heard the whole conversation. He offered to take every one of us off, just with our pack, no other gear, and he would have us in Darwin that night. The captain said, 'No, I can make port.' You should have heard our officers — they were ropable! So as we were going into Batavia [now Jakarta] Harbour, the convoy that we were intended to link up with was on the way out. And it made your eyes pop out to see the planes and matériel they were taking out to India from Batavia. You see, the Dutch didn't want us at all.

Only days later, the Jupiter was one of 12 Allied ships sunk in the Battle of the Java Sea, on 27 February 1942.

We had trucks issued to every man. So instead of having a spare driver, every man had a truck. And you were driving around the island, all covered and camouflaged, and this gave the impression of terrific Australian movements in Java. And that caused the Japs to divert their landings to Java, whereas they'd had the intention of coming straight on to Darwin. So we were just a sacrifice in Batavia but we managed to hold our own for a couple of weeks, three at the most. We were making for the southern part of Java and the intention was that we were to go off on the beaches down there, be taken off by the *Perth* and the *Houston*. But they were bashed up by the Japs in the Sunda Strait.

So that left us way down in Garut, and we took refuge in a tea planation finally, because they had big factories and that gave us a certain amount of accommodation until the Japs made their minds up and they wanted us marched back to Batavia. Our officers stood their dig and we did get transport by train back to Batavia, and we ended up in Bicycle Camp.

Bicycle Camp was a beautiful camp, better than Changi, and if we'd managed to stay there, we'd have been pretty set. We were there for four or five months. We were really quite favoured. All the huts had big porches, covered, and many of the men slept out there in preference to inside because it was cooler.

Then the Japanese brought us back to Singapore for about four days while they sorted us out. They stuck us on another of their hell ships. They'd put extra decking in, a metre apart, and you could imagine, you went down rope ladders — they were just a death trap, that's why we lost so many men. Even the food used to be dropped down by buckets to the various levels, what food there was. Some of the meat we used to get was Singapore cold storage stuff which had turned green because the power had been turned off. They thought nothing of sending that out as part of your rations. Certainly there was a lot of dysentery that broke out.

Then they changed ships and they took us up to Rangoon. We lay in the Rangoon River for about four days, and you can imagine the heat and, down in those holds, foul conditions. Then they brought us back to Moulmein and then to Thanbyuzayat at the start of the railway. We met the famous Nagatomo[1] — he strutted round and did his speeches and so forth.

From there we were all marched to the 23rd kilometre and that was our first introduction to work. We were fit and well. As you went up on the railway things absolutely deteriorated. Talk about the slops and so forth! They gave us sacks of rice, but, ugh — nothing more to do with it! And the only stuff you could get to cook it in was the night cans — so they washed those out and got them clean. And then there was the matter of firewood. And honestly, we started to pull the building to pieces. How the Japs didn't wake up to it, I don't know. The railings disappeared and if we'd been there long enough we'd have taken the floorboards up. It was a jail that everyone wasn't very happy about sleeping in, especially on the floor, because it had been a syphilis area.

The Aussies were very enterprising in anything they did. And their hygiene was far better than that of the British. And that's why our death rate was better. Even in the cholera camps, the chappies there were just burned. One camp we were in, where we had cholera, we had the fires going without a break for about three weeks, tossing in bodies. Now they wouldn't handle those bodies at all, wouldn't even take the meat ticket off, or identification. You had nothing to disinfect your hands or yourself. The Japs kept right away — they wouldn't even come through the huts if they knew there was cholera. I was a suspect for cholera and the doctor put me on to a mug of Condy's[2] night and morning — either cure or kill. And he forgot all about it. The doctor wouldn't come round and see you every day — he'd only come if the orderly drew his attention. You take Popeye Hunt — his brother Wimpey was sick and he stayed in camp. Popeye came in at lunchtime as he was working close, and he says, 'Where's Wimpey?' Wimpey had died between breakfast time and lunchtime. So you'd just lift the body up on the sack or the rice bag that he was sleeping on, and burn him, rice bag and everything.

I went through it all pretty well, but when the railway was finished, we were graded. The As and Bs practically all went to Japan to work in mines and things like that. I was graded D, right down the bottom of the ladder. I'd had a lot of terrible sickness. I stayed and landed a job in a quarry, cracking stones for the bedding.

I'm trying to crack this bloody stone, with a seven-pound [three-kilogram] hammer. And this bloke's about a metre above me on this ledge. And he's yelling, 'Kura! Kura! Kura!' And I knew I was in for something. And the more he yelled at me the harder I put in the effort on this hammer. The next thing was I felt, or heard, this thing within me like a stockwhip. And I was just left paralysed. And this bloody bloke's dancing round me — that's the last I saw. I can only go now by what Sergeant Armstrong told me in the camp.

Apparently this bastard, Korean he was, did me over. He must have floored me properly. They'd take you from your feet up, and they'd kick your legs, especially if you had bandages because they realised — you have no idea what those tropical ulcers were like, they went right to the bone in you, and you'd be green, you'd have flesh on the end of your toes and nothing between your ankle and your toes, just bloody bone, no flesh. Then they'd come up and do your testes and make sure you'd never be able to use them anymore. Then they'd come to your belly. Now I've had two hernias repaired and the second one, they placed an artificial plastic wall right from my thigh up to my navel.

When the lunch boys came out with the kerosene tins of rice and whatever liquid they could cook up for them, the Japs said, 'Take him away and bury him.' Sergeant Armstrong told me he came along and thought he could feel a pulse. He had me placed in a cubicle next to the dispensary. He used to sit and talk to me. He said, 'After the third day you opened your eyes, and you looked at me as if to say: *Where am I? Who are you?* And then flat out again. And the fifth day you actually opened your eyes and stayed awake with us.' And that's how close I was to just being thrown on the dead heap.

> *After being freed and while recovering from malaria, beri-beri, ulcers, starvation and beatings, Dallas and other prisoners on the Death Railway were asked by an Allied officer at Kamburi to identify any Japanese who had bashed them and to give evidence at war crimes trials.*

To hell with that. I want out. I want home. You see what I mean?

And you shut up. You just put it all behind you. All my discharge papers said was that I had anxiety and back trouble, and I got no pension. I got no pension at all until 1956 when I was operated on for the first hernia: 10 per cent. And then 10 per cent for the second one.

The government warned parents and relatives that we'd be a bit tropical, and not to take any notice of us, and not to remind us of what we'd been through, to forget about it. And you could feel it with your family. You expected to have some support from your family. But they just didn't believe you — and you learned then to shut up. I never got any support from my family, where you really looked for it.

Reveille, 2002, interview with author

Dallas Lowther Cressey, *was born 14 September 1910 at Greymouth, NZ, enlisted at Paddington in March 1941. As a private, he was discharged in April 1946, listed as having served with the 2/3 Australian Reserve Motor Transport Company. He died 23 August 2007.*

Notes:
[1] Lieutenant-Colonel Yoshitada Nagatomo was in charge of POWs at the Burma end of the railway, at Thanbyuzuyat, although he had his headquarters at Moulmein. After the war he was tried in Singapore and sentenced to death by hanging.
[2] Condy's Crystals (potassium permanganate) is used for a number of skin conditions including fungal infections of the foot, impetigo, pemphigus, superficial wounds, dermatitis, and tropical ulcers.

Hail to the Brave Byoki
By 'Banjo' Binstead

The little *Byoki Maru* began life as the cargo ship *Canadian Princess*. Then she became the *Potomac* and, finally, battered and unloved, the *Rushin Maru*. But to the POWs who sailed in her on her last eventful voyage from Singapore to Moji in Japan, she will always be the *Byoki Maru*, the 'sick ship'. She was one of us. Displacing between 3000 and 4000 tonnes, she had been bombed and burnt out in Singapore. Refloated, she had been patched up to carry cargo to Japan, mostly in the form of 1200 POWs who had worked on the Burma–Thailand railway and were now to be slave labour in Japan.

The *Byoki* was not a comforting sight. There was only a gaping hole where the bridge had been and the deck had dropped about 15 inches. The Japanese skipper was to direct her course from a small box-like cabin built over the stern. Two great steel girders welded to the deck were all that kept her from breaking in two. There were no hatch covers for the two forward holds, with 400 POWs in each exposed alternately to rain and the tropical sun. The toilets were wooden boxes lashed to the ship's side with a gap in the centre of the floor to allow us to squat high above the ocean. Definitely 'Not wanted on Voyage' were the lice and bugs that came aboard with us in Singapore. We didn't like the heat and sweat in the holds. They did. They bred as only lice and bugs can.

Our convoy crossed to Borneo and followed the coast north, hugging a chain of islands until we reached Manila. There we waited for three weeks with only an occasional break on deck from the stinking holds. On 9 August we left and it seemed only a few hours before the waiting American subs struck. A large freighter ahead of us was blown clean out of the water. A tanker suffered the same fate. The last ship in the convoy also went down.

It wasn't until an international POW reunion in 1986 that we heard why the *Byoki* might have been spared. A former US submarine commander told about an attack on a convoy near Manila in August 1944. After a look at a 'cruise' ship that may have been ours, he told his men not to waste a torpedo on 'that wreck' and to hit the next ship. It was surely our convoy and 'that wreck' was surely the *Byoki Maru*. Some would say it was just luck. Believers say it was a miracle.

Some days later we were hit by the typhoon. In the early morning when I was allowed on deck to go to the toilet, the sea was dead calm but the crew were lashing down everything in sight. I was told there was 'big wind coming'. Within a few hours what had been a millpond was a violent, turbulent ocean raging against everything in it. The Japanese skipper, generally conceded to be a great seaman, ran before the storm to reach the lee of some small islands. There were no longer guards and prisoners; everybody was working for survival, feeding the boilers with all the coal they could take. At one stage a series of giant waves, 50 to 60 feet high, kept the *Byoki* on her side. But the battling ship righted herself and pushed on to sail into calm seas once again.

There the *Byoki* sprang a kindly leak in her thin plates. It was a heaven-sent opportunity for men stinking to high heaven to bathe in the stream of sea water jetting high into the forward hold before the leak was reluctantly reported. The ship's carpenter arrived with a piece of four-foot by four-foot timber which he whittled down to a point and hammered in.

We made our first landfall in Japan at Kagoshima on the southern end of Kyushu on 3 September, five years to the day since war had been declared. Five days later we reached our destination, the port of Moji. It was 8 September 1944, less than a year before the Japanese surrender. So ended the death-defying voyage of the *Byoki Maru*. And may God bless all who sailed in her.

The Listening Post, Autumn 1996

***Private Francis John 'Banjo' Binstead**, was born on 20 April 1916 in Perth, served as a signaller with the 2/3rd Machine Gun Battalion in the Middle East and Java. From 1942 to 1945 he was a prisoner of war on the Burma–Thailand railway and in Japan. He returned to Perth in October 1945, was demobilised in January 1946, and died 24 July 2006.*

The Specialists
By Hugh V. Clarke

The Japanese wanted some oil-drilling men, so the POWs offered their services. They had never seen an oil well, but the Japanese did not doubt they were experts. Strangely enough I first became interested in oil as a result of my disinterest in coal.

At the time I was working for the Emperor of Japan in the coalmining town of Hakata, on the island of Kyushu. The coal seam was beneath a lake and at the end of a mile and a half tunnel which sloped down into the earth at an angle of 45 degrees.

At first the idea of spending nights so far below the earth's surface had appealed to me as a pleasant alternative to being blown up by American bombs. I was given an ill-fitting hessian suit, oversized sandshoes, and a cloth monkey cap.

Then I was detailed for the night shift. At the pit head I attached to my cap a heavy headlight, apparently designed to develop neck muscles, and fastened to my belt a large wet-cell battery which hung like ballast at the rear. Thus equipped, I became a coalminer.

After the first week certain disadvantages became all too apparent. The lake seemed intent on draining itself into the labyrinthine tunnels and shafts in which I worked, and only continuous pumping kept the coal face above water.

The shafts were walled with green timber props which, bulging alarmingly, creaked and groaned continuously. The roof was given to collapsing. One of my fellow miners died in a roof fall during my very first shift.

In such circumstances I feel I can be excused for ignoring the old soldiers' dictum 'never volunteer for anything' when the camp commandant called for experienced oil drillers.

With two mates, Joe and Slim, I volunteered. Had the commandant called for qualified midwives we would have volunteered with equal assurance. We were interviewed by an English-speaking civilian with a thatch of hair like a magpie's nest, and the eyes of an owl.

'Where did you drill for oil, huh?' he asked me.

I waved my hand vaguely and replied, 'Oh, Western Queensland.'

His eyes seemed twice the normal size through the thick lenses of his spectacles.

'Where precisely, huh?' he insisted.

'Dirranbandi,' I said.

He came at me again. 'What kind of equipment are you used to?'

This was disconcerting, but I mumbled a vague description of the rig used for sinking artesian bores. The oil man listened patiently, and then laughed.

'Most primitive,' he hissed. 'Most primitive. We will give you most modern equipment.'

Next morning, Joe, Slim and I assembled in full marching order by the camp gate, where we were joined by a Malay, two Dutchmen and a small Cockney sailor.

'Any of you blokes know anything about oil drilling?' I inquired.

They shook their heads. Being the only NCO in the party, I took charge of the 'experts' and led them, behind two armed guards, to the railway station. An hour or so later we disembarked at the railway junction of Oreo. On the platform were two other groups of POWs and guards.

In the first group were two more Dutchmen, two Indonesians, and a Chinese. I checked on their qualifications. All except a silent Indonesian confessed total ignorance of oil drilling. The second group joined us, and I was pleased to discover that they were Americans, and even more pleased at the sight of the sergeant's stripes on the sleeve of one of them.

'I hope one of you jokers is an oil driller,' I said.

'Man,' said a long pole-like Texan, 'you sho' took them words right outta mah mouth. Ah figured you guys wus oilmen.'

A train rushed into the station, and the guards, clucking like hens, herded us into a carriage. During the journey I learned that we were bound for the port of Fukuoka, whence we would be shipped to Manchuria. At Fukuoka we marched through the city, past a university, and a huge wind-testing tunnel, and finally came to a camp built in a pine forest near the harbour's edge. The camp was surrounded by a high bamboo fence, and as soon as we entered its gate I realised we were no ordinary prisoners.

A group of Jap guards studied us respectfully and shooed away a few American inmates of the camp who tried to talk to us. It was obvious they knew we were specialists. An interpreter spoke kindly to us and took us to a hut, which we shared with several million vicious black fleas. The camp held mainly American, British and Dutch prisoners, who whiled away their daylight hours in a nearby lumberyard and in dynamite dumps beside the harbour.

During the weeks that followed we waited in uneasy idleness for our ship to come in. At length the commandant suggested that we do a little work in the onion patch to relieve the monotony. We eagerly agreed as the onions were young and succulent. Even the leaves were palatable and we were hungry.

Within a fortnight the onion patch was devastated. Consisting mainly of withered tops — the bulbs having been bandicooted — it looked as though a swarm of locusts had been through it. Wrathfully the commandant drove us from the pastures and put us to work unloading dynamite trains. This indignity we felt most keenly. Not only had we by now come to regard ourselves as skilled technicians, but we regarded our newly appointed task of handling dynamite in the presence of hostile aircraft as downright dangerous.

While on this duty I became friendly with a non-specialist American prisoner named Walt. Walt was a marine who had been captured in Shanghai. He spoke fluent Japanese, and was an accomplished and daring scrounger. It is to my friendship with Walt that I am indebted for an interesting interlude.

Tiring one day of the tedium of carrying and fetching, Walt persuaded our grizzled old *hanch* [Japanese squad leader] to employ us on a special job — spring-cleaning the winter quarters of a horse. It was a sleek and prosperous horse, with a round and glossy belly which filled Walt and me with envy. Its stable was warmly thatched and lined, with a floor of solid hardwood. Compared with our home in Fukuoka, it was a mansion.

I seethed with resentment against the beast and its master, and resolved with Walt to make inroads on its food at the earliest opportunity. The *hanch* told us to clear the winter layer of manure from the floor and scrub the boards clean. Then he went away.

Walt had previously located a bag of corn and two bags of bran in a loft, and the moment the *hanch* turned his back we climbed onto the rafters and began eating. For my first course I selected a handful of rather tough corn. After that I turned to a bag of bran which Walt had already sampled.

I was so occupied with the process of mastication that I did not hear the approaching footsteps of our master. Walt cleared his mouth with a gulp and jumped to the floor in time. I was much slower, and dropped at the feet of our astonished *hanch* as he entered. He stared at me for a moment, and then, with a series of angry grunts, slapped my face. With each slap a fine cloud of powdered bran issued from my mouth.

We were expelled from the stable and awarded the heaviest, dirtiest jobs available in the lumberyard. My status of chief specialist was sinking fast. And then, at noon on 15 August 1945, our guards and *hanchos* suddenly abandoned us to cluster round a loudspeaker which had been erected over the lumberyard office. Their looks were grave and intent as they listened. When the voice in the loudspeaker finally fell silent, tears were running down their yellow faces.

Although we had no way of knowing what had happened, we realised it had been something shattering. Slim looked at me with the light of speculation in his eyes. 'I reckon they should have got us on the job a bit sooner,' he said. 'Something tells me we won't be doin' no drilling for oil, somehow.'

He was right. The atomic bombs had been dropped on Hiroshima and Nagasaki, and the war was over. We were no longer specialists. Our oil-drilling careers had ended before they had begun.

Mufti, August 1956

Hugh Vincent Clarke *was born in Brisbane on 27 November 1919 and enlisted in July 1940 at Kelvin Grove, Queensland. As a bombardier with the 2/10th Field Regiment he was taken prisoner after the fall of Singapore and held initially at Changi before being sent as one of 380 Australians working at Hellfire Pass on the Burma–Thailand railway. In September 1944 he was transferred to Japan. After the war he became a successful journalist and author, and headed the public relations section of the Department of Aboriginal Affairs. He died in 1996.*

Salvation
By Len Ikin

Along with many others I spent some time as a guest of the Emperor of Japan, and the reference to 'Salvation' applies to August 1945 when Japan surrendered, and we reluctant guests were liberated.

I have no intention of repeating the depressing details of the sadistic bastardry that transpired over those years of miserable captivity. I know one or two of my old mates will understand why I practise this restraint. All servicemen in the heat of battle — Australian, British, Japanese or whatever — can understandably be guilty of some atrocity, but the premeditated sadistic torture culminating in so many deaths, as carried out by Japan when it thought it was winning, is not acceptable under any rules of war. They called it Bushido chivalry — what a load of rubbish!

Sufficient to say it was a long three and a half years.

The Death Railway as it was called — Thailand to Burma — was completed and running in late 1943, and most of the surviving POWs were withdrawn south, to camps closer to Bangkok. The cost in human lives was tremendous, but then the Japanese had a complete disregard for human life, just as long as it was not their own.

It was from these camps that men who were reasonably fit were drawn for all manner of work, including parties for railway maintenance, ammunition loading and handling etc. Some parties were drafted for shipment to Japan, where they worked in coalmines.

In early January 1945 I was detailed with a party of 300 Australians, British and Dutch to proceed to a small town called

Ratchaburi, situated on the Bangkok–Singapore railway line where it crossed a large river called the Mae Klong.

The railway bridge was originally a substantial steel bridge built pre-war by British engineers but it had been bombed out by Liberators, which were becoming increasingly active over the whole area. These raids were sometimes so sudden that we often tried to dig ourselves into the dirt with our bare hands. At the same time, we would cheer like banshees while the bombs were dropping and the machine-guns chattering. All hell broke loose — as you can imagine!

Our task was to unload trains travelling between Singapore and Bangkok, ferry the freight across the river on barges, and reload the train waiting on the other side of the river. Our working day, seven days a week, was 7.30 a.m. to 6 p.m., unless a special train at night required handling. There was generally a morning train from Bangkok and one in the afternoon from Singapore.

On 15 August at 3.30 p.m., an agitated Japanese officer arrived at the worksite. After much shouting at the guards and the Japanese NCOs, we were lined up, counted and marched back to camp. This was a complete reversal of usual procedure, and the troops were muttering and conjecturing as to what might be happening ... possibly an Allied landing on the Malayan west coast, and we were to be shifted ahead of a Japanese withdrawal.

Next morning we were lined up for rollcall and told that trucks would be arriving for us within 15 minutes. We were not given any information regarding our destination and were loaded — or I should say, packed (standing up) — into open-tray army trucks with two Japanese guards armed with rifles and bayonets to each truck. We moved off and passed groups of Thais along the way. They cheered and waved to us, much to the annoyance of the Japanese guards. The waving and cheering was a complete reversal of form on the part of the locals, who were generally impassive and always seemed wary of the Japs. For them to show us any friendliness could only mean something out of the ordinary was afoot.

We travelled along a main road, if you could call it that, unsealed and narrow, for about 100 kilometres until we reached a turn-off which some of the troops recognised. It was a track two or three kilometres long that led up to the gateway or entrance to Nakhom Pathom, a base and so-called hospital camp for prisoners.

As we proceeded along this track to the gates, it was obvious that the usual Japanese flags (the fried egg on one side and the rising sun on the other pole) were missing and had been replaced. We finally drew close enough to recognise the replacements and, wonder of wonders, one was the Union Jack and the other the Stars and Stripes. This was the actual moment of the long-awaited and prayed-for Salvation!

It was an emotional moment and I regretfully realise how sadly I lack Churchillian verbosity in my ability to convey adequately how we all felt; but the sight of that Union Jack and all it meant to us will live forever in my memory and, I am sure, in all our memories.

The Japanese guards and their rifles were soon bounced out of the trucks, our own POW Australian and British officers having taken over the administration of the camp. We were on our way home even if it took another three and a half months before I landed in Melbourne on my way to Tasmania.

To arrive home to those who loved us, and whom we loved, was our main objective, our single-minded obsession. Each day, although exciting and full of promise, was frustrating in our urgency to be home — back to all those happy things we'd remembered and dreamed about during those long years.

The Listening Post, Spring 1992

Leonard Leslie Ikin *was born on 17 May 1919 at Launceston, Tasmania. He enlisted at Royal Park, Melbourne, in May 1941 and was posted as a gunner to the 2/15 Field Regiment. He was discharged in January 1946 and died 1 August 2000.*

A Day to Remember
By NX59783

'Yes, mate, it's true. The war finished two days ago.'

That was the answer to my excited plea, 'Has the war finished?', as 25 of us hurriedly scrambled out of a Japanese army truck at the gates of Nakhon Nayok POW camp about midday on 17 August 1945.

Three days beforehand we had been doing concrete work on aerodrome defences some 200 kilometres from Bangkok. It was a concrete-pouring day and work went on from 6 a.m. till the job was finished, somewhere about one o'clock the next morning. All the concrete was hand-mixed and poured. There were no breaks for meals (such as they were). Just one or two men were allowed off at a time to gulp down their mugful of rice.

About 200 Australian POWs had been in this camp about two months. During this time the only washing facility was a drain about 150 yards long, two feet deep and 18 inches wide. The only time off had been a half-day *yasme* ('rest') after each concrete-pouring day. Other days we worked from 6 a.m. till 7 p.m. with two hours off for dinner.

The next day I had been detailed on 'sand party' — loading trucks with sand at the river, about 25 miles away. To our astonishment, at about three-thirty the trucks returned and the Japs said, 'No more work. All men go back to camp.'

Next day, to our further astonishment, when we fell in for our working parties, the Jap sergeant said, 'All men *yasme* all day.' Incidentally this sergeant was the only Jap that I ever knew who made any attempt to keep a promise.

Most of us were so tired that we slept all the morning, but by

A Day to Remember

dinner time we were waking up and starting to wonder at the reason for the sudden rest. Someone then noticed the Japs in their orderly room, tearing up papers and records. We had seen this done in our own orderly rooms three and a half years before. Then ideas started to fly about — ideas became rumours and then they developed into facts — the war was over!

However, we had all been disillusioned by rumours so often, and we had received no authentic news in our camp for so long, that most of us decided that it was just another case of wishful thinking. Late that night we were told by 'Shirley Temple', the Japanese interpreter (he thought he could speak English, even if no one else did), that we would have to pack up and be ready to leave for Nakhon Nayok the next morning. Knowing what conditions were there, this was a move we didn't want.

Next morning about 8 a.m. we were loaded into trucks, about 25 to a truck, and set off for our return to Nakhon Nayok, about 100 kilometres distant. On the way we passed truckload after truckload of Japanese troops, all fully armed and heading up the way we had come. I think that most thoughts were similar to mine — that our forces had perhaps made a surprise landing with paratroops, and that we were being hurried out of the area before we could be rescued. However, there were still a few who clung to the belief that the war was over.

At last we turned the last bend in the road and Nakhon Nayok camp came into view about half a mile ahead of us — the one dry spot surrounded by miles of paddy fields. I was riding in the second truck in the convoy, when suddenly there was a shout from the leading truck. 'The war's over! The Union Jack is flying over the camp!' I got a shock — I dared not look, for fear that someone was playing a poor sort of joke.

Then came a shout from someone in our truck. 'It's true! It's true!'

I looked. Sure enough there were the Union Jack and the Australian flags flying out in the breeze.

I hardly dared believe even then that the war could be over. Possibly it was some new rule that the country's flags had to fly over POW camps — and yet — and yet — could it really be over?

By this time we had pulled up at the gates of the camp and had scrambled out with more haste than we had ever done before. The scene was indescribable. Outside the gates were the Japanese and Korean guards, and some of our own men wearing military police armbands. Inside the gates were some 2000 men yelling and dancing and shouting — I can see the scene now.

We jumped down, and amidst the shouting and confusion — you had to shout at the top of your voice to be heard at all — I at last grabbed one of the MPs by the arm and yelled my query into his ear, 'Is it true?' And his reply came, 'Yes, mate, it's true. The war finished two days ago.'

I couldn't speak. I just turned and grabbed the hand of the nearest one of our party, and shook it and shook it, for how long I don't know. I didn't cry, as many did, but only because I didn't attempt to speak. If I had, I am certain that I would have broken down completely.

Eventually we got more or less counted, sorted out, and allotted to our quarters in the camp. It was not till quite late in the day that I realised we had not even thought about lunch.

After tea that night, the camp was strangely quiet and subdued. Small groups were scattered all about the camp, where, over little fires, they were roasting sweet potatoes, mostly taken from the Jap stores. Friends had got together and were talking over many things — home, girlfriends, wives and families, and their future aspirations.

My own thoughts had turned to home. One of the five letters that I had received in my three and a half years as a POW had told me of my mother's death a few months after our capture.

A Day to Remember

How many other changes had taken place I couldn't guess. Somewhere about midnight the fires began to die out, and the groups dwindled, as we started to turn in. After going to bed it was easy to tell that few slept, by the everlasting glow of the cigarettes.

Our thoughts wandered back over the past three and a half years. The different camps that we had been in — from the hospital in the Cathay Theatre to Changi — back to the Great World — the wharf party and the dog 'Biddy', who'd stuck loyally to us. She steadfastly refused to even sniff at the most choice delicacy offered to her by the Japanese guards, but would relish any scraps offered by one of us. How she growled a warning when the guards started their rounds.

Back again to Changi, and then the nightmare train journey, packed in steel trucks that were like ovens in the daytime and refrigerators at night — then the Burma–Siam railway of death. The many mates that we had lost along the line under unbelievable conditions. Tha Sao, Chungkai, and then back to Tha Muang — up the railway again to Niki. Then the day we'd picked up a leaflet dropped by the RAF. Yes, what a thrill that was! The bombing of the railway — a direct hit on a trainload of POWs just near our camp.

Back to Tha Markam and the mockery of a shrine built by order of the Japanese to those who died or were murdered building the railway. Then away to Kachu Mountain, where the Japanese commandant was so distressed at the number of men who died that he issued the order, 'No more men must die.' Three died the next day. On to Nakhon Nayok, with a nightmare stay for two days on the waterfront at Bangkok, and lastly up to the aerodrome, and our return to Nakhon Nayok.

It was hard to believe, lying there on our bamboo beds, that all the bashings, the filth, the disease and death were over, and that those of us who were left would soon be home. Those of us who were left! What time did I go to sleep? Well, it must have been near morning, but for the rest of my life I will never forget those words which I heard on 17 August 1945.

'Yes, mate, it's true. The war ended two days ago.'

Reveille, August 1963

NX59783 was the service number issued to **Donald William Isles**, *was born at Caulfield, Melbourne, on 29 October 1908. He enlisted at Paddington in Sydney in July 1940, giving his residence as Griffith, NSW, and was discharged in January 1946 with the rank of corporal, having served with the 2/19th Battalion. Don Isles returned to Griffith after his repatriation, became a successful businessman, and drove the establishment of Ningana Enterprises, which provided employment for people with disabilities. He died 22 April 1989.*

The Day the Nips Came In
By 'Krani'

Three weeks after Emperor Hirohito had announced his surrender, we were forward company astride the Beaufort-Tenom railway in British North Borneo. On our right ran the swift muddy river; on our left stood the steep muddy hills.

Beyond a tributary stream, spanned by a bomb-shattered bridge, the Jap also waited. Neither side crossed the bridge; it wasn't done.

Ready for the expected Nip envoys, we had erected a reception tent a few chains forward: our reception party had been issued with nice new jungle greens, which they were ordered to wear continually in order to turn out smart and smartly.

This day, the brigadier and the battalion CO paid us an informal visit and, with the company commander, climbed the high hill where a platoon was posted. The company sig. [signaller] was alone in the orderly room. The phone buzzed and he answered.

An excited voice panted, 'The Nips are coming in!' Shouting the information to the acting CSM the sig. rang the hilltop platoon.

The platoon runner answered.

'Tell the boss the Nips are coming in. Yell it!' was the message.

The runner did as he was told. Everyone heard him!

An ordered turmoil erupted in the company lines as prepared positions were manned. The reception party moved out, but NOT in their spotless new jungle greens. Naturally, these were all in the wash.

The sig. took a hasty look up the track. There, at attention, stood four little men, unarmed, in drab uniforms, beneath a dejected flag, stark white amid the surrounding green. Facing them, with Owen guns at the ready, stood four big men, above whom was flaunted the vivid colours of the Australian ensign.

The sig. went back to his phone; the brigadier and the colonel came in quietly. They waited in silence. The blue ensign returned and the company commander, whose mud-yellow strides indicated that he had tobogganed down the hill, saluted as he handed over a large sealed envelope addressed to GOC, 9th Australian Division. 'A major representing the general commanding 37th Jap Army,' he explained. 'He said his only duty was to deliver this. He then asked permission to return to his own lines.'

We never learned fully what was contained in the document thus delivered, and another 12 long days passed before Major General Akashi[1] handed over his treasured sword at Beaufort, but, factually, on that unforgettable afternoon of 5 September 1945, to one rifle company of an AIF battalion was surrendered a Japanese army.

The Listening Post, October 1948

Notes
[1] Major General Taijiro Akashi commanded the 56th Independent Mixed Brigade which during June and July 1945 was in action against Australian troops in the Borneo campaign. On 17 September 1945 he surrendered at the Officers' Club in Beaufort, handing his sword to Brigadier S.H.W.C. (Bill) Porter.

Caring for Prisoners of War
By June Kerr

My husband and I both served in the AIF in Australia and overseas. My husband was 40 when he sailed for the Middle East and became one of the unfortunate Rats of Tobruk — he then came home and did the Owen Stanley [Kokoda] Track, and all this played havoc with his health.

I was a VAD in civilian life and I enlisted with the AAMWS and served in various Australian general hospitals as a diet supervisor. I eventually went to Morotai with the 2nd AGH, and like some other hospitals we continued to be operational for some months after peace was declared. Ex-prisoners of war were admitted and cared for until they were strong enough for the journey home. This was rewarding — very rewarding — and I had the honour of being mentioned in despatches.

It was shocking — it was heartbreaking to see them. The trouble was we didn't have suitable food for people in that condition. The rations we had were for full diet. They didn't have any soft nourishing types of foods. So I had to use my ingenuity with the help of the medical officer and make up things. We needed protein. We had no protein other than canned bully beef, which was quite unsuitable, and we had lots of powdered egg. That was unpalatable. So I worked out a drink, something like a chocolate smoothie these days. I put lots of this powdered egg in, which was high protein. And I disguised it with some honey, molasses or cocoa, and I used to mix it up. We had a coldroom, and I'd divide it up into the wards, put it in the coldroom overnight and then deliver it in the morning to the wards. So that was one way of giving them a lift in their protein.

Sometimes they were in the last stages of malnutrition and we'd start up giving them just medicinal doses of food: like a medicine glass full of reconstituted milk given hourly, for example. Then we might keep on with that but add orange juice, or broth made from Vegemite. Then I think the first solid food we gave them was a tablespoon of mashed potato, made with dehydrated potato because we didn't have any raw potatoes. Gradually we kept adding so they were getting extra food all the time, until they were strong enough to be sent home.

The medical staff did a tremendous job — the doctors and nurses really did. It was hard work but very rewarding, and I went for weeks without a day off. I was in Morotai for about 12 months, including six months after peace was declared.

Reveille, 2002, interview with author

June Douglas Chancellor (Kerr) *was born in Sydney 2 November 1913 and enlisted 22 March 1943 at Charters Towers, Queensland. She was discharged from the AAMWS with the rank of Warrant Officer Class 2 on 21 June 1946. She died 6 June 2005.*

New Guinea and the Kokoda Track

'The battle rolled on, in our exhausted state each successive attack becoming blurred with the previous one so that it seemed the fight would go on forever.'

— Colonel R.S. Garland

Correspondent's War Diary
By George H. Johnston

In the November–December 1981 issue of Reveille *it was reported that the National Library of Australia had acquired the unpublished diary of Melbourne-born WWII correspondent George H. Johnston.* Reveille *published a number of extracts from the diary, which Johnston maintained while he was based in Port Moresby in 1942.*

Thursday, 15 January
Major John Hudson, who is CO of the anti-aircraft defences of Port Moresby and who has a team of 'kids' — some of them only 16 — has been told that the role of Moresby is to hold the Japs for 36 hours. More than that is not expected of the garrison!

Saturday, 17 January
Every available aircraft is in use, evacuating women and children from Rabaul. Old planes that should have been condemned years ago are ferrying between Port Moresby and Rabaul, and carry loads that just ignore civil aviation regulations. Some planes, built to carry 15 passengers, are arriving with 30 and 40 — standing room only.

Tuesday, 24 February
First daylight raid on Moresby. No sign of panic or anything else but curiosity. With no fighters here, it seems likely that we shall see plenty of daylight raids from now on. When are the promised Kittyhawks coming? Everyone refers to them as 'Tomorrowhawks'.

Saturday, 14 March
Major General B.M. Morris[1] took over full military control of Papua New Guinea. The whole territory thus comes under military administration, and civilian life no longer exists. Those civilians not evacuated or about to be evacuated out of the country are being shoved into the army. Meanwhile a lot of the civilians (who have panicked and got out of the danger zone before there's been any danger) are cashing in on the mainland as real war heroes — talking of their bravery in defying bombs etc. and telling hair-raising stories of the grim hell of Moresby, bombs filled with old razor blades and hacksaw blades etc. Big problem of the changeover will concern the natives more than anybody else, who can't understand — and don't like — war!

Thursday, 26 March
Still looking for pro-Jap agents. The immediate problem is to find the chap who sends up coloured meteorological balloons as a guide every time the Japs come over. They come up from different positions and are usually not seen until they are well up in the air.

Friday, 9 October
The fierce Orokaiva tribe, who had been supporting the Japs, are now openly hostile to them because so many of their women have been raped by the Jap troops. Many of the natives in the coolie gangs also have been bayonetted or left to starve.

Friday, 16 October
Up here everybody is incensed at new censorship bans, including MacArthur's[2] personal censorship of stories of his visit here, which have been slashed to ribbons to convey the impression (a) that he went right up to the frontline (which he certainly did *NOT*), and (b) that this was *NOT* his first visit to New Guinea. Everybody is furious. Censorship now is just plain Gestapo stuff.

Saturday, 24 October

Strange stories are coming down from the track of dead Japanese wearing belts and wristlet watches bearing the names of AIF troops missing in Malaya. There is one signet ring that nobody will ever wear now. It was found on a dead Australian who had taken it from a dead Jap who had got it from a dead Australian!

Monday, 26 October

The hospital ship *Manunda* arrived today with 78 AIF and 18 American nurses. All the public showers have been screened off and the hundreds of Diggers in the baths are now wearing swimming trunks! No army nurses have been here since the second week in March. Moresby at night now has the appearance of a big city — a blaze of lights in every building, crowds of troops jostling in the streets, and every road as far as the eye can see literally choked with interminable lines of motor transports, all with headlights burning. The harbour, too, is crowded with shipping. I am still utterly amazed at the contrast between the Moresby of October and the Moresby of March.

Thursday, 29 October

General Allen[3] was in to see us tonight and he is furious at MacArthur's order to hurry up the advance and his hints that the Australians are not fighting. MacArthur, of course, has never seen the country. Nobody who had not seen the country of the Owen Stanleys could possibly imagine what fighting was like under those conditions.

Monday, 2 November

Kokoda, which has been in Japanese hands for exactly three months, has been occupied by the Australians. Advance patrols went into the village this morning and found it completely deserted.

75

Tuesday, 3 November

The troops up on the track are very weary and were expecting to be relieved at Kokoda. They were all very hungry as the last stretch from Aloa was made with practically no food. It has been a bitter journey, but they have recaptured the whole Owen Stanley Range. At night they slept in sodden clothes in incessant rain with native mountain rats crawling all over them. One man had a great piece of his hair nibbled away by the rats when he woke up in the morning.

Thursday, 12 November

Our casualties, as well as the enemy's, have been heavy. Yet the American journalist Hanson Baldwin, writing in the *New York Times*, described how the Americans saved the Australians from utter defeat. No doubt he based his ignorant statement on the misleading statement issued here by General MacArthur a few nights ago. The fact remains that no American ground soldier has fired a shot in the campaign so far, but there is a widespread tendency among many of the Americans to decry the Australian efforts and to perpetuate rumours that the AIF is opposed only by a handful of Japs — some even say 'only 90', others put the figure at 250! One American was asked today if the hundreds of Australian wounded coming in had been in traffic accidents.

George Henry Johnston OBE (1912–1970) was an Australian journalist, war correspondent and novelist, best known for his novel My Brother Jack. *In 1933 he was employed by the* Argus *newspaper as a cadet reporter. In 1941 Johnston was accredited No.1 Australian war correspondent. He worked in New Guinea (1942), Britain and the United States (1943), India, China and Burma (1944), Italy (1944) and in Burma once more (1945); he also witnessed the Japanese surrender on board USS* Missouri *in Tokyo Bay in 1945.*

Notes:

[1] Major General Basil Moorhouse Morris, CBE, DSO, was in 1942 the Australian military administrator at Port Moresby and although his militia troops were poorly trained and equipped, he managed to delay the Japanese advance along the Kokoda Track until the 2nd AIF forces arrived. In August 1942 he was replaced by Lieutenant General Sydney Rowell, and Morris took responsibility for the New Guinea Lines of Communication Area.

[2] US General Douglas MacArthur was sent to Melbourne in March 1942 and weeks later appointed supreme commander of the South-West Pacific theatre with complete authority over all allied naval, land and air forces in the region. MacArthur controversially questioned the fighting abilities of Australian troops, moved to Port Moresby for the final stages of the New Guinea campaign, and on 2 September 1945 accepted Japan's surrender aboard the USS *Missouri* in Tokyo Bay.

[3] General Arthur Samuel (Tubby) Allen was a WWI veteran who in WWII commanded the 7th Division in Syria before being posted to Port Moresby in August 1942 to take charge of operations against the Japanese attack along the Kokoda Track over the rugged and almost impassable Owen Stanley Range. Despite halting the Japanese, Allen was accused by General MacArthur of not advancing quickly enough. His forces broke the Japanese at Eora Creek on 28 October but Allen was relieved of his command the next day, to see out the war in operational and administrative positions in Port Moresby and the Northern Territory.

Sanananda Epic: Heroic End of Captain Cobb
By Trooper Bob Ebner

On 19 December 1942 we were ordered to make an attack on the Japanese position on the Sanananda Road. We had progressed to within 50 yards of Jap positions when our squadron was instructed to take the right-hand side of the road. As soon as we crossed we met heavy opposition.

Captain Cobb went forward with three men to reconnoitre. All three men were wounded en route by machine-gun fire, so Cobb eliminated two machine-gun nests on his own. You should remember that he was a champion revolver and rifle shot, had been an athlete and was absolutely fearless.

That night we kept our position and early next morning crossed back to the left-hand side of the road and made another advance from this position. In the lead was a Bren gun section, then Cobb, then Trooper Alf Watt with an Owen gun. All unknowing, we came close to a Jap machine-gun post. The Bren gunners actually passed it unmolested. Cobb suddenly saw two Japs on the parapet and promptly shot them with his revolver.

I got hit in the arm when the gun began to splutter. Next, I was conscious of Cobb calling out, 'Into them!' I thought the rest of the chaps were close behind, but I suddenly realised we were alone, except for Alf, who was badly hit in both legs.

Cobb was then unhurt, and dashed at the gun nest with rifle and bayonet. He was a noted bayonet fighter and skittled six of the enemy in this nest. What with the pain of my arm wound and the sight of blood, I was sick. But Cobb was not bothered about it.

Sanananda Epic: Heroic End of Captain Cobb

He then broke up the machine-gun and buried certain parts of it. We thought that hole was unhealthy and we got out. Dropping our equipment off, we made a hole and small trench for ourselves, otherwise we might have been picked off by a Jap sniper.

That night I crawled back to see the whereabouts of the other section, at the same time helping Alf Watt back because of his wounds. After I had contacted the others, I returned to help Cobb back. When I saw him and told him, he said, 'Never mind me — I will look after the equipment — you are wounded,' referring to my arm. He was very careful of my haversack, which contained all the maps of that particular area. So I got back to our first position, Indian scout fashion.

We waited for 10 minutes for Captain Cobb, but he never came. So I made my way back, not knowing what to think, but determined to get hold of our rifles and equipment. Suddenly my foot burned — a bullet had hit me.

Another of the boys went forward and called the captain's name, with no response, except machine-gun fire. While I had been making one of my little journeys, the Japs had opened with a barrage consisting of all they had. They must have got him with this blitz.

Altogether, with revolver and bayonet, and including the men he had picked off with his rifle, he accounted for 17 or 18 Japanese. But for his wonderful leadership, Captain Haydon's section must have been wiped out.

Not until some weeks later, just before we took Sanananda on 22 January, Cobb's body was found. He had been killed by bullets, whether rifle or machine-gun will never be known.

Padre Hartley gave him the funeral honours. VCs mean nothing to him now, but if ever a man won the right to wear the scarlet ribbon on his chest, Captain Cobb did.

The Queensland Digger, April 1943

Edward Robert Ebner *was born on 19 May 1915 at Chinchilla, Queensland. He enlisted at Toowoomba in May 1940 and was discharged in October 1945 with the rank of sergeant, having served in the 2/7th Australian Cavalry (Commando) Regiment. He died 12 March 1994.*

Henry William Albert Cobb *was born on 2 April 1915 at Kandanga, Queensland, and enlisted at Caboolture in July 1940.*

Frederick Bernard Haydon *was born at Murrurundi, NSW, on 26 June 1916 and enlisted at Paddington, Sydney, on 11 April 1940. He was discharged in November 1945 with the rank of captain, having served in the 7th Division Cavalry Regiment.*

Epic Crossing of the Buso River
By Brigadier H.B. Norman, DSO, MC

It has been said that active service is made up of long periods of utter boredom relieved by short periods of intense excitement. That's pretty true. And during those periods of intense excitement a commander is often required to make split-second decisions of great consequence.

Of all such decisions which I had to make during the war there is one which sticks most vividly in my mind: the decision to order 700 men, many of whom could not swim, to cross a raging torrent under enemy fire. Here's the story!

By 20 January 1943 the fighting in Papua had ended and attention was turned to New Guinea. For the initiation of his new plans, General MacArthur used almost exclusively the battle-seasoned 7th and 9th Australian Divisions, supported by Australian and American sea and air forces.

The Japanese expected a frontal attack on Lae, which was garrisoned by 8000 troops in strong defences. Instead the general attacked from each flank. The 7th Division, flown to Nadzab in the Markham Valley, attacked from the west, and the 9th Division landed on the night of 6 September near the Buso River, from Red Beach, 16 miles east of Lae.

After securing the beach head, the attack from the east was made along two routes: 24th Brigade moving along the coast route and 26th Brigade along the inland route. The advance guard or spearhead for the advance of the 24th Brigade was the 2/28th Australian Infantry Battalion, 96 per cent of which were West Australians. I had the honour to command this battalion.

81

On 8 September the battalion arrived at the Buso River, which, with the Markham River, comprises the main drainage system for mountainous north-eastern New Guinea. At the mouth, where the 2/2th Battalion assembled, it is 700 yards wide, broken into several channels by gravelly shoals and a small island carrying tall kunai grass. The channel under the west bank carries the main stream, about 50 yards wide and up to six feet in depth. A shallow bar across the mouth narrows the channel where it enters Huon Gulf.

Heavy rain the previous night had swollen the stream into a torrent which raged through this channel at 10 to 12 knots [about 20 kilometres per hour], pouring into the gulf to form a huge expanse of turbulent yellow. Infantry are not expected to swim into the attack! Before bridging a river such as this, a bridgehead must be captured. To do this, assault boats are used. In this case they were not available. Even if they had been available the current would have washed them down to the bar.

So here was my problem. A fast-flowing river in flood, the enemy on the far bank, no boats, no bridges, no fords. Crossing on foot would be hazardous but not impossible. Not to cross, to stay passively on our side of the Buso, would be to endanger the entire operation.

About 3000 yards upstream the 26th Brigade had also been halted by the Buso, and the brigade commander reported the river to be impassable. It was imperative that somewhere on the divisional front a bridgehead should be established. To complicate my decision I remembered that a little over a year previously, in the desert at Alamein, this same battalion had crossed the minefield at Ruin Ridge on foot, and on the far side had been cut off from supplies. Nearly a whole battalion had been lost in that fateful operation.[1] The same thing could easily happen if we gained the far bank of the Buso. But Ruin Ridge, ending though it did in disaster, had established a unit tradition. I decided that we must cross the Buso.

Epic Crossing of the Buso River

A special officer provided by army headquarters advised the bar to be the only crossing place, but this would so obviously be known to the enemy that to cross there would be to court suicide. Two patrols, each under very experienced officers, Lieutenant Roy Warren and Lieutenant Eddie Benness, both reported 'impassable to loaded troops', and I abandoned continuation of the advance for that night. Patrolling to find a possible crossing was continued throughout the night without success.

Next morning an attempt was made to get a cable across from the island but as the leading man emerged from the kunai grass he was picked off by enemy riflemen from near the bar. The kunai grass on the island gave protection from observation and made possible the only forming-up place near the far bank. Any other crossing meant the troops would be under observation the whole way across the river, instead of for 150 yards or so.

It was obvious all equipment could not be carried if the crossing were to be made. Toilet gear, weapons, ammunition and some rations were all that could be taken. By putting down three-inch mortar and Vickers machine-gun fire along the edge of the far bank, we might drive the observing Japanese further back and gain some respite from enemy fire in the early stage of the assault. Our intelligence told us 5.30 p.m. was generally 'rice time', a propitious time for attack. This would allow time for crossing in daylight and immediate reorganisation, with darkness to cover our consolidation.

The torrent was increasing in fury and to delay longer might mean days of waiting. A drizzling rain was falling as I waited behind the commander of the leading company and heard the orders. 'Three minutes to go. Check your gear.' Then: 'One minute to go. Cigarettes out.' Finally: 'Advance.'

'Rats of Tobruk' and 'Thieves of Alamein', they emerged from their cover, extending to right and left in an almost perfect line as they moved towards the water. A dull gleam came from their hundred bayonets. The supporting fire had ended and the roar of the river in front drowned the sound of boots on shingle as they moved forward to attempt what seemed almost the impossible.

Soon they were knee-deep in water, feeling their way, foot by foot, over the stony bottom. As the water deepened the torrent began to take its toll. Men were being hurled towards the bar, only tin hats and weapons showing. The drift turned many towards the far bank where the strong gained a hold and pulled their cobbers out. The very first man across was the company commander, Captain (James Felix) 'Pat' Hannah. Some were borne headlong to the bar where, in desperation, they clutched to two trees, one dead, one green, that were bent before the flood.

These, pounded on one side by breakers, and on the other by flood, drew the first enemy fire. This was from a heavy machine-gun sited well back to cover beach and bar. From numerous points in the kunai, light machine-guns opened up till at times it seemed lit by tracers. Odd mortar bombs added to the cacophony. Most of the fire was directed at the bar, while the high bank afforded protection to those under or near it.

The second company and battalion headquarters were following 50 yards behind the leaders and took the first casualties from fire. Though men were swept away before their eyes, those succeeding waves of companies never faltered or broke formation. There was no pause. It was a terrifying but truly magnificent spectacle to look back on those waves of men as they moved across the shingle into the water. It was a most classic example of perfect discipline and comradeship.

Once across, officers and NCOs, oblivious of fire, directed the formation of chains. Chopped-down bushes, rifles, human chains with linked arms succoured those hard-pressed. By devious means the whole battalion crossed. Inevitably many weapons were lost and some men went down with their weapons, fighting their momentary enemy, the flood, as grimly as the Japanese.

Reorganisation is always difficult; now it was a hundred times so. Companies and platoons were mixed up, the kunai was up to 15 feet high, and darkness was falling. Yet by 7 p.m. the last company commander had reported he was in position. We had not gained as much ground as we had hoped, but we had a perimeter and were in a position to fight.

The list of 'missing' during the night and in the morning was greatly reduced. One man, Alec Wilson, taken hundreds of yards out to sea, was washed up behind the Japanese lines. He rejoined his company by swimming, wading and crawling back to safety during the night. As could only be expected, some were never accounted for, but considering the number who attempted the crossing, the casualties from fire and flood were remarkably few. Sergeant John Crouchley, of Busselton, swam back across the river to inform the brigade commander the battalion was across and reorganised.

The rain was now constant and heavy. As fast as men dug, the holes filled with water. They had no protection against the downpour, their tobacco was sodden and there was no prospect of a smoke on the morrow. So intense was the cold, men crouched back against back, absorbing warmth from one another.

Three attempts were made to fire a line across, without success, but members of the Pioneer platoon, engineers and a volunteer swimmer from 2/43rd Battalion took across a light cord that hauled a telephone cable over, and for the first time in eight hours I was able to report to my brigadier.

Vivid lightning and peals of thunder interspersed bursts of machine-gun fire and occasional mortar bomb explosions. Daylight revealed our perimeter to be about 650 yards by 200 yards, extending from the beach on our left back to the Buso.

Captain (John Collin) Newbery's company on the beach flank was harassed by grenades, mortar and machine-gun fire from positions in a swamp fronting the company. Lieutenant John Brooks's platoon from this company, supported by another platoon, was ordered to attack these positions. Wading in swamp, sometimes up to the armpits, they inflicted a massacre. Sixty-eight Japanese dead were counted, and many were never seen in the heavy kunai and water. The platoon's casualties, of all kinds, were 14.

This opened the way for our continued advance, which ended six days later in Lae. The battalion throughout was faced by Japan's crack troops, the Special Naval Landing Forces. That crossing of the Buso River paved the way for the advance of the 9th Division on Lae. Many were limping on feet from which the skin had been soaked. All were fatigued, but never was morale higher.

At the Buso, the battalion proved that the fit, well-trained infantryman can go anywhere, under any condition, at any time. Forever the Buso River will be engraved on the battle honours of the 2/28 Australian Infantry Battalion.

The Listening Post, March 1953

Colin Hugh Boyd Norman *was born in Sydney on 20 February 1904 and enlisted in August 1940. He was awarded the Military Cross at Tobruk with the 24th Anti-Tank Company, then as a lieutenant colonel commanded the 2/28th Australian Infantry Battalion in New Guinea. He was discharged in October 1945, but in 1951 was promoted to brigadier and took command of the 13th Infantry Brigade. In December 1952 he was appointed administrator of Norfolk Island. He died in 1996.*

Notes:
[1] The 2/28th Battalion had attacked Ruin Ridge on the Alamein front in North Africa just after midnight on 27 July 1942 but came under German fire from the rear and was cut off. Enemy tanks moved in from three directions, a company was overrun and the battalion commander was forced to surrender. The 2/28th lost

65 officers and men killed or wounded, nearly 500 men were taken prisoner, and of those who took part in the attack only 92 remained. The battalion was withdrawn and rebuilt before being returned to Australia in early 1943 and, after being further reinforced, was posted to New Guinea.

Lieutenant Roy Warren was born 29 March 1914, Lake Darlet, WA, enlisted at Claremont 16 October 1940, was discharged 11 January 1946, and died 13 September 1988.

Lieutenant Edwin Charles Benness was born 18 August 1915, Coolgardie, WA, enlisted at Claremont 16 July 1940, was discharged 3 October 1945, and died 10 November 2008.

Captain James Felix Hannah was born 22 June 1919, Menzies, WA, enlisted at Claremont 22 July 1940, was discharged 6 December 1945, and died 30 December 2003.

Private Alexander (Alec) Vincent Wilson was born 16 July 1912, Day Dawn, WA, enlisted at Rottnest 24 July 1942 and was discharged 24 October 1945.

Sergeant John Crouchley, MM was born in England 13 April 1913, enlisted at Claremont 23 July 1940 and was discharged 11 September 1945.

Captain John Collin Newbery was born 22 July 1911, Perth, enlisted in Perth 20 July 1940 and was discharged 5 November 1945, having been promoted to Major. He died 28 April 1992.

Lieutenant John Wigram Brooks, MC was born in England 16 June 1904, enlisted at Claremont 11 December 1940, was discharged 4 January 1946 and died 19 July 1997.

Ambush Knoll
By 'Commando' (Colonel R.S. Garland, MC and Bar)

The fight for Ambush Knoll took place in July 1943 during the Salamaua campaign in New Guinea. The 2/3rd Independent Company, a commando unit, attacked and captured Ambush Knoll on 15/16 July, without artillery or air support, with a force of about 60 soldiers, from an equal number of well-entrenched Japanese.

In the defensive battle that began three days later, Ambush Knoll was held by about 40 members of the Independent Company. The Japanese launched 20 bitter assaults between 19 and 23 July in their bid to recapture the feature. Known Japanese casualties were 67 killed. The Australians had three killed and seven wounded.

The 2/3rd was organised into three platoons, each commanded by a captain. At this stage of the campaign the strength of each platoon was about 30 soldiers. Each platoon had three sections, each commanded by a lieutenant with an establishment of 18 soldiers. The section which I commanded consisted of eight soldiers. The wastage was due to battle casualties and sickness during the long campaign that had begun at Wau early in 1943.

This account is concerned mainly with two platoons: 'B' Platoon led by Captain John Winterflood; and 'C', led in these operations by Captain Wallie Meares. I commanded 8 Section in 'C' Platoon.

On 14 July the Independent Company was ordered to capture Ambush Knoll. The company borrowed some rations from the 2/5th Battalion and concentrated at Wells Junction in preparation for the attack. There was insufficient time for an adequate reconnaissance as the attack had been ordered for 15 July as a prelude to attacks by the 58th/59th Battalion at Graveyard and Orodubi on the following day.

Only two platoons were available for the attack, the plan for which was simple. Meares would attack at 1330 hours from the south astride the track between Wells Junction and Ambush Knoll. Winterflood would move off at first light and position himself behind the Japanese, astride their supply track on Sugarcane Ridge. Winterflood would also attack Ambush Knoll from this direction at 1330 hours. The attack was to be supported by two Vickers guns and one three-inch mortar from the Wells OP area. My section was chosen as reserve. This left Meares only a relatively small force with which to make the frontal assault.

We had very little ammunition for our support weapons, but (Major) George Warfe made the best use of our Vickers machine-guns — which, by the way, we were not entitled to on our establishment. The Vickers soon shot holes through the jungle canopy and were able to bring enfilading fire onto the Japanese defences at Ambush Knoll, even though this feature was jungle-covered.

Meares commenced his attack on time and by 1400 hours had closed up to the main enemy defences astride the narrow ridge in this area. We had no news of Winterflood's progress, and Meares had to bear the brunt of the brisk Japanese fire. The initial casualties were heavy and the momentum of the attack soon died. Still there was no news from Winterflood!

Thereupon George Warfe ordered me to 'go in and take Ambush Knoll'. I collected my eight tired, sick and hungry commandos and, feeling very inadequate, passed through Meares' force and made some penetration of the enemy defences. We were forced to ground, however, by heavy small arms fire, and the firefight developed again.

Later in the afternoon we were joined by the adjutant, Lieutenant Brian Harrison, and we made some further ground against heavy fire. Brian fought very gallantly and was killed alongside me in the process. The Japanese were well entrenched and had many well-constructed pillboxes. The Jap who killed Brian was dug in on the defiladed side of a large bamboo clump. I was unable to see him although he was so close that I could hear him breathing. I was unable to throw a grenade round the bamboo; his position was well supported by flanking entrenchments and I wasted many rounds trying to hit him by firing through the bamboo.

At this stage Meares ordered a two-inch mortar forward, and by shouting corrections I was able to range it onto the Japanese position. It gave us real satisfaction when the bombs burst in the Japanese entrenchments, causing many casualties.

As last light was falling we heard heavy fire from the rear of the Japanese position, which announced the belated but very welcome arrival of Johnnie Winterflood. Again we pressed the attack, but again the Japanese held. Thereupon George Warfe, who was following progress closely, ordered us to dig in for the night with a view to renewing the attack at first light. We were exhausted!

During the night I took my turn at duty on a listening post with a fellow section commander, who cajoled me into giving him a small tin of honey — the last of my rations. We heard tremendous activity within the Japanese positions and wrongly concluded that they were organising some counteroffensive.

At first light next morning we patrolled to the main Japanese position at Ambush Knoll and linked with Winterflood. To our amazement the Japanese had gone!

The Japanese position was well constructed and had been held by about 60 soldiers — a company of the 11/66th Battalion. They left Ambush Knoll in a shambles, abandoning 10 bodies in the foxholes. Warfe decided to hold Ambush Knoll with two sections, redeploying the remainder of the company on other tasks. The sections were commanded by Lieutenant Hugh Egan and myself: Egan, who was senior, being placed in command. We set about burying the dead, cleaning up the position and making detailed arrangements for the defence. We did not expect that the Japanese would return and regarded our task as a well-earned holiday. However, we placed our standing patrols and listening posts well out, to give us early warning of any enemy approach.

Hughie Egan kindly gave me the southern sector of Ambush Knoll. We were pleased to get a quiet sector and spent the next few days relaxing on fighting patrols and laying booby traps on Japanese tracks. The southern sector, however, did not prove to be quiet. Far from it! The Japanese made their first and main assaults from the south, and it was no holiday for either me or my men.

Then there was the western approach, which the Japanese had not covered in the defence and we had failed to use in the attack. We sited two pits to cover this approach, but the Japanese did not use it. This was very fortunate. George Warfe cut a track up this ridge line, and it was our only supply route during the defensive battle. In addition there was no water on Ambush Knoll; it had to be carried in. The feature was jungle-covered but badly shot up as a result of our attack on the Japanese.

Much later, General Savige [Lieutenant General Sir Stanley Savige, KBE, CB, DSO, MC], commanding the 3rd Division, remarked to me that 'the defence of Ambush Knoll was certainly an outstanding feat, but I will never understand how the 2/3rd Independent Company ever captured the position'.

Our initial layout was based on two defence sectors: the northern covering Sugarcane Ridge and the southern covering the ridge running to Wells Junction. The southern defences included the foxhole behind the bamboo which the Japanese had used to such good effect. I opened a communication trench leading to this position. We deployed two small standing patrols, one on Sugarcane Ridge and one at a track junction on the southern approach. In addition, for close protection, a sentry was deployed forward on each likely approach to act as a listening post.

On the afternoon of 19 July I took out a fighting patrol which laid booby traps to the rear of Orodubi. As the patrol was returning at dusk we noticed that the enemy side of Orodubi was a mass of blinking lights, which I concluded were cigarettes. Obviously a large number of Japanese were concentrated for an operation. I arrived back at Ambush Knoll very weary, made my report on the telephone to company headquarters at Namling, and then fell into a deep sleep. A full moon was rising.

At 2015 hours I was rudely awakened by heavy fire from the standing patrol on the southern approach. The Japanese had moved behind us! Warfe reacted immediately. He ordered one Vickers gun to Ambush Knoll to reinforce my sector. He also ordered Winterflood and two sections to move to Ambush Knoll, with Winterflood to take command.

As soon as the Japanese had overwhelmed our standing patrol they turned and quickly launched a night attack against the southern sector. This was beaten off and the Japanese grouped for a further assault. During this respite the Vickers gun arrived and was set up to cover the ridge approach at point-blank range on loose traverse. I was armed with a Thomson submachine-gun as were most of my men, and we also had a Bren gun covering the ridge. Strict fire control was imposed.

At 2130 the Japanese again attacked the southern sector in strength and a bitter fight ensued. Beyond doubt the Vickers gun saved Ambush Knoll: the assaulting Japanese waves halted before the sustained fire of the gun at close quarters. The momentum of the Japanese attack was broken and a firefight ensued. Our fire was carefully controlled and grenades were used when necessary. Indiscriminate firing at night wastes ammunition, induces panic and reveals positions. The grenade is an excellent night weapon, provided that it is not used indiscriminately. If fire becomes essential, a quick volley from all weapons at identified targets produces the best results, stimulates morale and confuses the enemy as to particular dispositions.

At 0630 next morning John Winterflood arrived to reinforce the defences and take command. We were very pleased to see him and particularly welcomed the ammunition supplies that he brought in. I received some reinforcements to thicken my defences and was left to cover the south and south-east. The Japanese now proceeded to close in, cutting all tracks leading to Ambush Knoll. The telephone line went dead. The battle had only commenced!

Then came the Japanese preparatory fire from the mountain gun, heavy mortar from Orodubi and light mortars from Sugarcane Ridge. Shortly afterwards my listening post reported that the Japanese were coming again. Another bitter fight ensued. Once more the Japanese were held.

The Japanese kept coming back but we were always ready for them. At times ammunition ran very low, so I ordered all my automatic weapons to fire single shots only. As mentioned, a track was opened up on the western approach and supply was maintained by soldier carriers. The late Damien Parer, the well-known war correspondent, acted as one of the porters and inspired us by his courage.

Ammunition resupply was always welcome. I fired an average of 500 rounds a day from my Tommy gun. On several occasions my troops sang with gusto 'Praise the Lord and pass the ammunition' as ammunition was thrown from trench to trench after much-needed supplies arrived.

George Warfe issued his operation order; it was clear and unequivocal: 'I want you to hang on to this piece of ground.' Brigadier Hammer [Brigadier Heathcote Howard Hammer, CBE,

DSO & Bar] the commander of the 15th Brigade, in a letter to General Savige, expressed his pleasure at 'a bit of a real stoush going on now'. He explained that Ambush Knoll was higher than Namling, Namling Ridge and Orodubi. 'That's why the Japs want it,' he wrote.

Hot meals were cooked at Namling and carried up by our secret but very difficult supply route. The meals were very much appreciated by the weary defenders — when we got the chance to eat them. At one stage I had three accumulated meals waiting in my jungle shelter behind the trench.

Mail also came in with the rations. This is reckoned to be good for morale! I received only one letter, from the NSW State Income Tax Department, stating that I owed 4s 7d [four shillings and seven pence] in tax and if this sum was not paid by 1 February 1943 they would take legal action against me. While I was considering an appropriate reply, the Japanese attacked again.

It was at this stage that Hughie Egan, a gallant soldier and good friend, was killed by a mortar bomb. The battle rolled on, in our exhausted state each successive attack becoming blurred with the previous one so that it seemed the fight would go on forever.

Faulty ammunition added to our worries. The Tommy gun ammunition contained a percentage of faulty cartridges that lodged the round in the barrel. This was at times most embarrassing. All of us carried a Japanese steel cleaning rod (from captured Japanese rifles) to punch the jammed rounds out of our barrels so we could continue firing.

On 21 July the 2/6th Battalion commenced their advance from Wells Junction to open up the route to the beleaguered defenders of Ambush Knoll. One company, led by Captain E.W.A. Price, attacked astride the track against the Japanese south of the knoll. They met heavy opposition, had two killed and several wounded, and had to be content with digging in on the slopes close to the Japanese.

The Japanese would not give up, even though one company was sandwiched between Price's company and our troops at Ambush Knoll. They continued their frenzied efforts to capture the knoll and thus prevent a junction between the 17th and 15th Brigades. But they failed, and withdrew after two abortive attacks during the night of 22/23 July.

Ambush Knoll was ours!

At 1330 hours on 23 July I moved my weary but proud section away from Ambush Knoll. We never returned and still had two months of severe fighting ahead of us before Salamaua finally fell. Our force at Ambush Knoll, about 40 strong, had withstood 20 deliberate attacks from a Japanese battalion and had inflicted known casualties of 67 dead. Our meagre losses — three Australians killed and seven wounded — indicate the high fighting qualities of the Australian soldier when his back is to the wall.

Reveille, May–June 1977

***Ronald Selwyn Garland, MC and Bar** (1921–2002), remained in the army after WWII, serving with the occupation forces in Japan, and with 3RAR in the Malayan Emergency, and then rising to be chief instructor at the Officer Cadet School at Portsea, Victoria. He retired in 1974 with the rank of colonel, became public relations officer for the Returned and Services League of Australia, and became editor of the RSL (NSW) magazine* Reveille. *He retired in November 1983 after a series of strokes. He was the author of* Nothing Is Forever, *a history of the 2/3rd Independent Company.*

Note:

Captain John Stuart Winterflood, MC, was born 10 January 1920, Sydney, enlisted in Brisbane 19 May 1941, was discharged 2 November 1945, and died 29 November 1990.

Captain Wallace Archibald Meares, was born 5 September 1908, Strathfield, NSW, enlisted at Caulfield, Victoria. 19 June 1940 and was discharged 2 August 1944.

Major George Radford Warfe, MC, DSO, was born 27 July 1912, Leongatha, Victoria, enlisted 8 November 1939 at South Melbourne, and was discharged 28 February 1946 with the rank of Lieutenant Colonel. He died 5 November 1975.

Lieutenant Frank Bernard Harrison, was born in Sydney 21 June 1917, enlisted at Armadale, Victoria, 9 July 1940, and was killed in action 15 July 1943.

Lieutenant Hubert Leo Egan, was born 8 September 1918, North Melbourne, enlisted at Royal Park, Victoria, 14 July 1941, and was killed in action 21 July 1943.

Captain Ernest William Alfred Price, MC, was born 22 September 1913 Abbotsford, Victoria, enlisted 14 December 1939 at Puckapunyal, Victoria, was discharged 13 October 1945 and died 21 August 1969.

The Bulldog Road
By George Macris

During 1943 I was in a Dragon Rapide somewhere between Moresby and a place called Bulldog. I was 26 and full of confidence, going to take over as lines communications officer between Bulldog and Wau. I knew nothing of my destination or what the job entailed. I was soon to find out!

The pilot of the Rapide told me the trip would take about 90 minutes if we could land at Bulldog. In answer to my query he told me that the strip was usually hidden by low cloud and when you could see it you landed as quickly as possible in case it misted over again. When planes landed, they rumbled along the stubble of what had been jungle not so long ago, and if they didn't blow a tyre or run off the strip, continued to the end and delivered their cargo, usually mail and small stores.

Vince Crowe,[1] the chap I was to relieve, met me and took me to my quarters, then immediately began to brief me about my duties and what was in store for me.

As the fighting moved from the Wau area towards Salamaua, the need was felt for an alternate supply route to Wau and to the Markham River area. In pre-war years there was a track through the area from Bulldog over the mountains, and the preliminary surveys were not optimistic about building a road. The Americans said it could not be done. No way!

However, the Australian decision was to go ahead, and the immense task started. Equipment was moved from the south coast at Terapo by barge upriver to Bulldog, where the river became a shallow mountain torrent. The road, at first, was pushed through with pick and shovel and with the help of native labour from ANGAU (Australian New Guinea Administrative Unit). Then the bulldozers were brought in.

The river was called the Lakekamu, and the road crossed and recrossed it many times, and was bridged in several places. As I recall, the area around Bulldog was one of the wettest in the world and every afternoon the rain came across the sago swamp, drumming its signal long before it arrived and blasting across our camp like a firehose. Snakes abounded; the myriad insects were overjoyed at our presence; it was hell!

Due to the heavy rainfall the surrounding hills were always soggy. There was a single earth-return 200-pound copper phone line run from Bulldog to a place called Centre Camp at the foot of the mountains. From there the line followed the road at infrequent intervals, only because the road zigzagged around the contours so much. Little could be done about the conditions. Regular tours were made along the phone line, clearing creepers, mending breaks etc.

Almost at the highest point was an area of perpetual rain. It was called Ecclestone's Saddle. The trees had no foliage, only a type of moss on them. They looked horrible. Beyond this was the highest point of the road, over 9000 feet, and at the time was regarded as the highest made road in the world. At Steele Falls, the road crossed a face made of very soft stone. I once went through there at about 2 a.m. and had to clear fallen rocks from the roadway before I could get through. By the time I reached Wau, I heard the road had disappeared at Steele's. It just slipped away.

The road ended at Kaindi, just above Wau. There were made roads in the area that had existed pre-war. They went on through Wau and Bulolo, and then the new road was continued north towards the Markham River, to a place called Zenag. From Bulolo northwards the conditions were completely different from the Bulldog section.

I came onto the road when it was finished and convoys were using it. It is still very clear to me. I am still amazed at the engineering skill and the determination of the men and natives who built it.

I have seen very little reference to the road in war history and feel a deep sense of regret that more prominence has not been given to the achievement. There are plenty of ways that men can have their share of danger, and believe me, the men who built this road had theirs.

Reveille, January–February 1981

George Macris was born in Sydney on 8 February 1917 and enlisted at Bonegilla, Victoria, in December 1942. He was discharged in November 1945 as a lieutenant with the 9th Australian Line Maintenance Section. He died 14 October 2012.

Note:
[1] **Captain Vincent John Crowe**, was born 21 July 1919 at Rose Bay, Sydney, enlisted 21 July 1942 at Dundas, Sydney, and was discharged 18 October 1946, his last post being HQ New Guinea Lines of Communication Signals. He died 3 May 1990.

That Big 2/33rd Battalion Tragedy
Author unknown

The following piece, its author unidentified, describes an incident that occurred at Jackson's Airfield, Moresby, on 7 September 1943, when a fully loaded US Air Force Liberator crashed among trucks which were carrying troops waiting to be airlifted to Nadzab. Sixty-two Australians were killed and 90 injured, a third of the 2/33rd Battalion's fatalities for the entire war. All 11 American crew on the aircraft Pride of the Cornhuskers *were killed.*

It was 0415 hours and 'A', 'C' and 'D' Companies were assembled in trucks in the marshalling area on a small hill overlooking the airfield.

A deep-throated blast and roar of aircraft engines was heard as a four-engine bomber, its lights bright, left the strip and became airborne, passing over the heads of the convoy at perhaps 100 feet. One or two men shivered nervously. One remarked, 'Christ! He was close. I hope we don't stay here too long.'

Five minutes later another roar was heard and the lights of an aircraft could be seen, and the thing kept coming. It eventually became airborne but seemed to hang just above the ground. Bill Crooks was talking to Corporals Frank Smith and Billy Musgrave, two 18 Platoon section leaders. All three watched as the bomber came on. Somebody yelled, 'Christ, it's going to hit us.' Crooks was aware of somebody running down the hill past him on his right screaming, 'Look out! Look out!'

The bomber at that instant came crashing through the trees, its engines roaring. The left wing sheared off and the fuselage smashed down like an arrow into the trucks. A great explosion rocked the area and a vast brilliant yellow flash lit up the surrounds brighter than day. For a moment only the sounds of falling parts of aircraft and other debris and the crackle of flames could be heard, and then almost together there broke out the screams and moans of men.

In a second, all about the scene of this frightful disaster could be seen running men. All round the little gullies and re-entrants, petrol was aflame. The dreadful sound of agonising screams of despair seemed to drown out all else. Within minutes the flames had reached the ammunition in the trucks and it began exploding. Men, charging about on fire, would suddenly disappear as either the grenades or two-inch mortar bombs they were carrying in their clothes or equipment exploded.

So much was happening to so many people within seconds after this calamity. I was in a commanding position on the tailgate of the last truck to see it all, and was much later to give evidence at the Army Court of Inquiry. At the scene of this inferno so many brave things were being done by a great number of men that it is impossible to record them all. At the time no one knew the extent of the damage. It had happened in an instant.

Certainly none of the survivors of the six trucks of 'D' Company, which caught the complete fuselage or parts of the bomber, can recall the explosion of the first two 500-pound bombs. Some remember the third exploding some minutes after the crash. The blazing aircraft had hit five of 'D' Company's trucks, four of which were completely reduced to molten metal. Flames, debris and flying metal caught the men in the back of the last truck of 'D' Company and the last truck of 'C' Company, which contained mainly 15 Platoon and some men of HQ Company and was ahead of the first truck of 'D' Company. A number of men were hit with petrol or metal in the second-last truck of 'C' Company, which contained 10 Platoon of 'B' Company.

The Listening Post, Summer 1992

River of Death
Author unknown

A true experience that befell two sections of men from a machine-gun platoon (2/3rd Australian Infantry Battalion, 16th Brigade, 6th Division) early in 1945 during the advance on Wewak.

There were 18 of us on the island. The CO had made his tactical appreciation and issued his orders and, as a consequence, we found that our task was to protect the battalion's right flank and enfilade the water approaches. For this assignment we had two Vickers medium machine-guns, rifles, grenades and Owen guns. To date, no contact had been made with the Japanese on the first leg of that thrust from Aitape to Wewak, but we were getting near them now.

It was the CO's intention to establish a firm base and patrol offensively forward. The island was small: some 20 yards in diameter. It was situated at the junction of the Danmap River and Mimi Creek. Behind us those waterways met and delivered their muddy tribute to the sea, some five miles down jungle.

At the top end of our island was a collection of huge boulders. We did not take much notice of them when we arrived, but we had occasion to think a lot about them later. A couple of them were massive, standing six or seven feet above water level, and about as broad and long as they were tall.

There were a few trees on our island, of varying sizes. The largest had a hole about one foot through. In all it promised an agreeable enough bivouac.

The island was about 15 yards from the mainland and connected to it by the trunk of a huge tree that had been felled at the river's edge. It made a passable enough bridge. When the time came, the quartermaster, or one of his men, would give us a call and we would go severally across the bridge to the mess parades.

On the second afternoon it rained. No one is ever surprised when it rains in New Guinea. Our recollection of it, as soldiers, was of fierce humidity and torrential rains. Those who weren't on duty near the guns lay beneath their tent-halves and listened to the rain on the canvas. Our stretchers were poled and lashed above ground level, clear of any of the mites that carry the scrub typhus germs. The point was that nobody took much notice of the rain.

When night came there was a darkness on the jungle. Only from the river an eerie and unreal light gleamed; not that it was really light, just a less-black strip upon a field of indescribable gloom. The weapon pits were full of water. The disconsolate gunners sat with their glistening groundsheets about them, staring out into the rain, seeing nothing and hearing nothing but the rain splashing on the leaves, and the noises from the river. Those off-duty crawled on to their wet bunks and tried to sleep.

About 8 p.m. the sentry aroused the bivouac. He had alarming news. He said the river had come up at an astonishing rate and was still rising. The lower portions of the island, he said, were already awash. Most amazing of all was his disconcerting statement that the bridge connecting us with the mainland had been washed away.

When we crawled from beneath our tent-halves and stood up, water was swirling about our ankles. The platoon commander asked the sentry why he hadn't roused us earlier. The sentry replied that he had seen no point in doing that — it had been raining like the devil all through his watch, but no more so than during the afternoon. Only when the bridge went did he consider that matters were getting out of hand.

In the pouring rain we gathered our weapons and accoutrement into soggy heaps and splashed towards higher ground. The 15 yards between our island and the battalion's flank were now

30 yards of boiling, swirling, rushing water. It seemed the only sensible thing to do was to stay on the high ground and wait for the river to subside. Even then, and certainly later, nobody thought he could have reached the mainland. We could hear the fury of the river as it roared and boiled through the defile.

Torches were used as the men acquainted themselves with the desolation about them. Over on the mainland we could see other torches moving about as our comrades backed away from the ever-rising waterline. We tried to hail them, but above the roar of the river and the drumming of the rain, we heard no answering call.

The lieutenant ordered that the guns, tripods and stores be lashed up in the forks of the trees, and this was done. There was small talk, of course. No one was to know that within a matter of minutes seven men would be dead. Someone asked where young Curly Bridger was. Curly, we all knew, couldn't swim. Another remembered seeing him hugging the bole of a tree on that side of the island nearest the mainland. That meant he would be in water up to his waist, but maybe he felt safer there; he was that much nearer the mainland.

One of the smaller trees on the island went down with a crack; then another.

Peters said the situation was getting a trifle serious and took off all his clothes, throwing them, in an odd fashion, into the torrent. It was an extraordinary thing but we all followed his lead. All except the lieutenant. He divested not one item of his apparel. He carried his compass and pistol and had his boots on.

About that time, when the water had reached near our waists, we became aware of a greater peril. Against the boulders at the extremity of the island, upstream, had accumulated tons of timber that had been ripped from the margins of the jungle. The pile grew quickly, to immense and terrifying proportions. We could hear the slap and shudder of logs as they crashed into the heaving obstacle. It outlined itself against the river as a rearing black pile that crackled and groaned like a thousand wooden ships in a tempest.

When that pile broke, when those boulders gave, an avalanche of timber would be swept down upon 17 naked men and one man who chose to keep his clothes on. We scrambled up into the trees: helpless, primitive creatures suddenly brought face to face with the fury of nature. We knew we would be embroiled in a maelstrom and powerless to help ourselves.

The lieutenant, shouting to make himself heard for those troubled few yards, called that it was every man for himself. It couldn't have been otherwise, but that made it official. Someone noticed that Curly had gone.

One by one the trees were eased over into the torrent. Naked men were circled slowly back into the water, only this time they couldn't touch bottom. They clung desperately to the trees that still stood, their naked bodies pressed against them like driftwood. There was an ominous crackle as the great pile of timber at the top of the island waddled forward. Hundreds of tons of green timber were being pressed forward against the resisting boulders. Then those boulders groaned and moved forward. Once they moved, the torrent changed the pattern of the timber; the monstrous pile heaved convulsively and the timber scattered, flying into the torrent like a shower of heavy assegais.

On the instant, our island was engulfed, and we were flung pell-mell into the torrent — or some of us were. Some were killed instantly in that avalanche of timber, behind which the boulders lumbered as in a frenzy; others were swirled beneath the press of timber and drowned; others were knocked unconscious and their bodies snatched into the torrent and sent racing downstream. We were no longer a military group acting in cohesion but individuals acting for ourselves.

I found myself far out in the river proper, straddling a log that sped forward like an express train. I looked back to the island, but there was no island — no trees, no boulders, no men, only a heaving, sickening darkness into which the rain poured. Immediately ahead there was another pile of timber rearing in the river. I braced myself as the log on which I sat cannoned into it. I remember the physical pain, the consuming panic, and turning over and over in the water, down, down, down.

I tried to fight my way to the surface but my legs were held fast by the timber. There was a loud ringing in my ears and it seemed as if some force was welling upwards through my chest. All I could think of was that my wife was pregnant and would have her baby soon. Such is the inconsequence of thought.

I knew the force and the fury of water then, as I had never known it before. *This is it*, I thought. *There is nothing you can do to save yourself. This is it.*

The agitation of the water, and in no way my own efforts, freed me, and I stood, miraculously, in the shallows. I was snarling for breath but strangely exhilarated. The water raged about my waist and the force of it sent me stumbling forward. At some point I was drawn into a backwash of boiling water and tossing logs. I climbed into the branches of a giant tree that had been dragged down by the river and thanked God for my deliverance.

It must have been only minutes later that Crowhurst joined me. I heard the commotion beneath the branch on which I sat and reached down and helped him up. He had a great cut over his eye; even in the half-light I could see the blood streaming down his face. He was suffering badly from shock. A few days later he went completely troppo and used to sit on the end of his bed in the hospital at Aitape and 'fish' into the aisle.

Peters was washed up nearby. We climbed the biggest tree we could find — three naked, exhausted men — and waited for the dawn, about six hours away. When the rain stopped the mosquitoes came about us in swarms and bit the hell out of us. The river went down. We could see the waterline receding as the mud traced an even line along the jungle's foliage.

River of Death

When dawn came the line stood high above the water. For as far as the eye could see, great trees lay motionless, their branches torn and twisted. Only the water moved about them, muddy and racing. We climbed down and waded waist-deep through mud to firm ground, with the conviction in our hearts that we alone had survived that dreadful night. We found the quagmire that passed for a track and followed it upstream.

It was soon established that we had lost seven of our comrades — the remainder had been washed up, or had struggled ashore, at varying points along the river. The lieutenant was safe, dressed as he had been when last we saw him. He had also managed to hang on to his pistol and compass. Only his boots were missing.

We were to learn that part of the mountain had plunged into the river soon after night had fallen. It had dammed the river until the weight of water had burst its containing wall and the torrent had been unleashed along the riverbed.

Eventually all the survivors from our island went back to hospital. One fellow contracted scrub typhus; two finished up in mental wards; the rest suffered from malaria, the effects of immersion, shock and exhaustion.

When, later, a few of us got around to rejoining the battalion, we stopped by to look for our island. Only there was no island. Two small black stones marked the spot where it had been — two small black stones about which the muddy waters of the Danmap rippled on their way to the sea.

Reveille, August 1962

The author was unidentified and appears to have used pseudonyms for other members of his platoon.

Attack on Hill 710: Wewak 14 to 24 May 1945
By Lieutenant Colonel B.S. O'Dowd MBE

In this operation I commanded 17 Platoon, 'D' Company of 2/11th Battalion. Officially I was the company sergeant major, but a few weeks earlier the previous commander of 17 Platoon, Lieutenant Abbott, was promoted to captain and appointed to second-in-command. To replace Abbott, the officer commanding 'D' Company, Captain Bayly, instructed me to take over his platoon. 17 Platoon was recognised as a very good outfit, carefully trained and nurtured by the conscientious Bill Abbott. It had a highly developed spirit of mateship, so essential where men are required to share dangerous situations.

On the afternoon of the first attempt to take Hill 710 we marched to the foot of the feature where Bayly informed me that 17 Platoon was to lead the attack. We had no information about the enemy strength on the objective and, to gain some idea of what we were up against, the commander of the nearby native unit, John Godwin, brought two of his trusted New Guinea scouts along to reconnoitre 710. After a lot of jabbering in pidgin the boys dropped their lap-laps [loincloths] and took off. After what seemed like an eternity the scouting party returned to be thoroughly interrogated by Godwin. One did not require a comprehensive knowledge of pidgin to get the message they had for us:

'Ed belong this fella hill how many Japaniman e stop?'

'Too many Japaniman e stop ed belong this fella hill.'

This destroyed my hopes for a cardboard pushover. I assumed 'too many' to mean they ran out of fingers and toes.

Attack on Hill 710: Wewak 14 to 24 May 1945

I patrolled the platoon up the narrow ridge leading to 710 until I estimated we were close enough for ranging and sent for the forward observation officer. He went through the ranging procedure until we considered it was as close to the target as we were going to get it. I then pulled the platoon back and arranged it in attack formation, bayonets fixed, and waited for the guns to fire for effect. When the FOO advised, 'Last rounds on the way', I got the platoon on their feet and they charged up the hill until brought to a halt by an unexpected obstacle.

The artillery had done an excellent job except that the 25-pounder shells had landed between the enemy and our start line, smashing treetops, strewing the ridge with debris and laying a tangled obstacle in our path. The men ignored the fire and took many casualties trying to scramble over and through this mess but it was an impossible task right under Japanese fire. I put them to ground to work out the next step.

The gunner registered again and, having little trouble adjusting his shot from the previous registration, put one right on the nose. It was now getting towards late afternoon and too close to dark to attempt another attack.

Early next morning we were back at the obstacle course area, deployed with bayonets fixed and ready for another attack. The gunner opened fire and blasted the objective with a very comforting, thundering barrage. When the FOO advised, 'Last rounds on the way', the Diggers charged up the hill towards the objective but from the jungle line across the gully. To avoid the barrage the Japanese had retreated to the safety of the wooded area to wait it out. Now they were firing on us from there while some were attempting to make their way back to their weapon pits on the knob.

At this stage 17 Platoon was only partly on the objective and taking heavy casualties from the enemy while returning fire to keep the Japanese back in the timber line. I saw that it was safe to approach the objective via the brow of the feature on our left and shouted for 16 Platoon to come through by that route. For whatever reason they started to come up on our right and under the enemy fire across the gully. It was at this time that 16 Platoon commander, Lieutenant Harding, was shot in the lung and subsequently died. I yelled to get 16 Platoon shifted and they swung across to the covered approach, successfully making it to the north end of 710 where the two platoons were connected. Captain Bayly came through with 16 Platoon (with Harding killed he probably took it over) and called 18 Platoon forward to make the company complete on the objective.

From their position of advantage in cover from the jungle edge, the enemy had an excellent clear field of fire and continued to harass with intense fire at any movement or exposure by 'D' Company. Bren gunners and riflemen returned fire whenever they thought they had a target. Two-inch mortar bombs were sent down at low-angle trajectory but still the enemy fire did not slacken. Out on the right flank either Paddy O'Neill or Pat Winter was alongside a tree and doing an effective job sending grenades into the timber from an EY rifle [Lee Enfield .303 rifle modified to fire grenades]. Unfortunately he poked his head around once too often and took a bullet in the face. The enemy attention made it impossible to put weapon pits down and with night approaching the company was in a very vulnerable position.

It was at this time that the battle took a dramatic turn. Inexplicably, enemy fire ceased, and an eerie silence settled over the contested ground. The Diggers, curious as to what was going on, began to look around and half stand to better study this unexpected situation.

Then it came! From out of the timber arose a blood-curdling scream of 'Banzai, Banzai!' and a line of Japanese soldiers, bayonets fixed, charged us down the intervening stretch of ground. They were led by a sword-wielding officer; everyone gave him one, then settled down to killing off the remainder, some men kneeling, some standing, pouring fire into the

Attack on Hill 710: Wewak 14 to 24 May 1945

advancing line. I remember out on the left flank Joe Middleton, a recognised good shot, standing in full view having the time of his life pumping rounds. Some Japanese actually made it into our forward defences before toppling over dead. Now the irony of the situation was clear; we had laboured away unsuccessfully for two days to get at these Japanese and now they offered themselves up.

Next morning it was clear that the enemy had reinforced his position and once again any movement or exposure received instant attention. We settled down to a protracted period of patrolling. Patrolling became a regular activity in search of some way to get at our enemy but reports only confirmed that he knew about all-round defence in depth.

One patrol Bayly sent me on was to discover the snipers' secret. I took down a dozen men and one of Godwin's native scouts and dropped over the east side of the hill. We worked our way around the flank until the patrol was just below the Japanese position and climbed to where we could see the edge of the enemy defences. There I turned the New Guinea boy loose to take a closer look. On return he guided me to where climbing spikes could be seen running up the back of a large tree. There was no way a man could be observed climbing the tree and little of him would be visible while he monitored our activities or when he decided to take a shot.

The remarkable capacity of these native boys to operate in enemy territory was demonstrated when our scout produced a bandoleer of rifle ammunition he had stolen from a Japanese weapon pit. Imagine the consternation of the Japanese soldier as he searched for his ammunition!

Next morning the attack got underway exactly as planned. The platoons silently stole from the defensive area to cover beneath the brow of the hill. Stretcher-bearers were in position to look after casualties, and 7 Platoon of 'A' Company was ready to occupy our defences. In the first light gloom there was perfect silence while we waited for the umpire to bounce the ball. Then it came! Continuous ear-splitting thunder of hundreds of 25-pounder shells smashing into the enemy defences. To be so close to such savagery was an awesome experience.

Immediately the barrage ceased; Bill Abbott led 18 Platoon in the charge on the Japanese defences and with determined aggression completely overran it, killing every Japanese there.

Then by Murphy's Law things started to go wrong. Abbott was killed, the attack stalled and an enemy started firing from somewhere outside the position just taken. To start the operation moving again, Bayly told me to take 17 Platoon in and continue the attack. We rushed to the far end of the position 18 Platoon had just taken and discovered that a track ran off it from the left, over a small creek and up a rise the other side. It was here that a delaying force of some sort had set up business and was doing a good job of harassing. There was only one way to go at it and that was a frontal dash. We exchanged fire while the platoon got organised and then moved in, but it was an anti-climax. The enemy must have considered their job done and departed without taking 17 Platoon on.

And so ended the battle for Hill 710. What was intended as a one-day show on 14 May took until 27 May, and in the process cost us many good men, killed and wounded. Somewhat hard to justify in the context of the Pacific War at that time: the Americans in the Philippines, next stop Tokyo. Nevertheless the 'D' Company soldiers conducted themselves in the best tradition of the Digger, with determination, guts and aggression. 2/11 Battalion can be proud of its achievements on that hill. The bill in terms of lives was two officers and six other ranks killed, while 28 other ranks were wounded.

The Listening Post, Spring 1997

Attack on Hill 710: Wewak 14 to 24 May 1945

Lieutenant Colonel Bernard Shelley O'Dowd (2 June 1918 to 29 February 2012) enlisted in Perth in November 1939 and served until July 1973. He was awarded the MBE in 1946, after serving in Libya and Syria, and in New Guinea where he was commissioned in the field as a lieutenant. With the rank of captain, O'Dowd commanded 'A' Company of 3RAR during the Battle of Kapyong in the Korean War, planning and leading the withdrawal of the Australian forward companies, an effort described as a superb military feat.

Midnight Marauder
By Leading Aircraftman A.D. Darby

The following amusing incident occurred in a Vultee Vengeance Squadron a few days after arrival at Nadzab in the Markham Valley, New Guinea.

During the day there were rumours abroad that a few stray Japs had come in from the jungle and had been fired upon by guards. The conversation that drifted between the mosquito nets in the hessian-covered hut centred on these rumours before the boys dropped off to sleep. The talking gradually dwindled till, save for the slight stirring of the coconut palms outside and the rhythmic breathing of slumberers inside, there was silence.

At about 2 a.m. I was awakened by wild yells and the sound of a scuffle on the bed next to mine. Sleep left the hut and pandemonium broke loose. What was happening? Surely a Jap commando had entered the hut! So thought the minds whose last waking thoughts had been of skulking Japanese. With whom was he grappling now? Cries of 'Get him, somebody!' and 'Did anybody get him?' alarmed the tropical night air. Then came the click of rifle bolts as leading aircraftmen prepared to sell their lives dearly. Fortunately, no shot was fired. Had anybody fired a shot, bullets would have flown everywhere in the next second. One man said afterwards that he was sitting up in bed, rifle ahead of him, ready to shoot anybody who crossed his path.

The confusion died down, order was restored, and gradually the cause of the disturbance became known. It happened that one man had a nightmare. He dreamed that there was a snake in his bed and, in his sleep, jumped out of his bed, crashed into another, ricocheted from it to another, and fell, clawing and yelling madly. The man so rudely awakened joined in the scuffle, not knowing what was attacking him, and the noise of the struggle startled all who were awakened by the nightmare yells.

As a sequel, some wag drew up a 'newspaper' edition entitled 'Thunderbox', which depicted a Jap commando armed to the teeth in full flight from the heroes of the squadron, and, under startling headlines, told a graphic story of the epic courage exhibited in our first 'brush' with the enemy.

Mufti, December 1956

Alvin Drummond Darby *was born 17 June 1915 in Tasmania and enlisted in Melbourne in September 1942. He was discharged in October 1945, his last posting as a leading aircraftman having been at 7 Operational Training Unit, Tocumwal. He died 30 May 2005.*

Butchers of Milne Bay
By G.F. Donohoe

My story starts in the Middle East, as I was in the 11th Reinforcements for the 28th Battalion. We were camped at Mughazi, November 1941, with the 2/32nd and 2/48th. The 2/28th had come out of Tobruk and were camped at Gaza, awaiting reinforcements, early in 1942.

A Captain Gregory came to our camp and asked for all personnel who had butcher's experience to report to the orderly room. He told us he was forming a butchers' unit, to be the 2/1st Field Butchery. It is history how we came home with the 2/16th Battalion and all other troops — 13 boats in all — from Bombay. Arriving in Fremantle on 15 March 1942, our butchers' unit numbered about 150 from Western Australia, South Australia, Victoria and Queensland, and slaughtermen from Alligator River and other places.

We went on to Adelaide, where we were billeted privately for about four weeks, before going to Charters Towers. We took over the slaughterhouse in the town, and there was a big freezing-works where we kept the cattle and sheep that we slaughtered. There were numbers of troops camped there and we supplied them with fresh meat.

In November 1942 our captain selected 30 of us, under Warrant Officer Vic Thomas from Victoria, Sergeant Jackson from Mackay and Corporal Wolfe from WA, all butchers and slaughtermen, together with Sergeant Townsend, a meat inspector from the Midland Abattoirs. We set sail for Milne Bay on the old *Islander* that used to ply up and down the coast and around to Darwin, arriving to the tune of rain and mud, and made camp about 10 miles from Gili Gili Wharf. Gradually we made stockyards and a slaughterhouse. A corporal from Harvey, WA, and I checked on the horses that the pack transport had left behind because they were too light for them, so we used them for stockhorses. What a job!

The cattle in the area — half Zebu, half Australian — didn't like to be driven anywhere. We killed 25 every time and would get only 20 that were edible; the rest usually had TB. Because of the humidity the hides could not be cured, so they had to be buried.

In 1943 we shifted camp to about a mile from the 2/1st Field Bakery. Our new slaughter yards were more modern and our camp was good, with a games room and a cookhouse. I got a generator and voltage regulator, switches and globes from the wrecked cars, wire from the signal unit, and an old clutch plate, and I made a pulley and set it all up in the coolroom engine-room. I fitted the clutch plate pulley onto the axle of the diesel engine, set the generator to the floor, and ran the wires to the cookhouse, the games room and our tents across the road. It all worked fine.

We had a pump and a shower at the yards from the river nearby; clear water was no problem. We also built a couple of stables from coconut logs for our horses. Our only saddles were army style; put them on the horses and you could see through them from back to front, between the horse's back and the saddle. They took some getting used to.

Our boss, WO Thomas, asked if I wanted chaff and oats and shoes for the horses, and I agreed. We were getting 1000 sheep a month from Australia and had to kill them quickly because of footrot. We had to bury the skin with the offal — full wools, quarter wools and shorn. It was a terrible waste and I wrote to Elders about them after the war, as dead wool was bringing a good price, but they never answered. I could have gone back and dug them up.

The chaff, oats, bran, shoes and nails arrived. There must have been 25 tons of chaff and oats, and five hundredweight of shoes and nails.

I was also looking after the rest of the horses — about 20 — all different shapes and sizes. I let the Yanks have them at weekends and gave them shoes and nails. As they went past our camp they would throw a bag of cigarettes and call out, 'Ted the Drover.'

We also shot and cleaned wild pigs, which the Yanks bought from us. The droving took its toll on me — wet one minute, dry the next, then wet again.

I caught malaria as well as tinea and was sent back to the mainland as doctors would not take responsibility after three weeks. But Blamey[1] flew in for half a day and said it was all right for troops to remain. Pity he did not stay for a couple of months.

I will never forget seeing Milne Bay again from the ship as I went back in 1945 and, once more, I was wet, dry, wet! But it was not for long, as the war with the Japs was over and I came home to good old Australia.

The Listening Post, Autumn 1990

Private George Frederick Donohoe *was born in Perth in July 1920, enlisted at Victoria Park in July 1941, was discharged in December 1945 and died 21 February 2001.*

Note:
[1] Thomas Albert Blamey was a WWI veteran of Gallipoli and the Western Front who later became the chief commissioner of police in Victoria. After rejoining the army at the start of WWII, Blamey reached the rank of general by December 1941. Under US General Douglas MacArthur, Blamey was appointed commander of Allied land forces in the Pacific.

The Bridge
By NX145805

It happened shortly before the war ended. Our battalion had marched across New Britain from Wide Bay to Open Bay, to relieve the unit which had been in occupation there. Our primary job was to hold the positions they had captured.

Our platoon was in perimeter some miles north of battalion headquarters, back beyond the Sai River, and an hour or so, by foot, from the nearest platoon. We had dug in near a stream a little in from the coast, surrounded by heavy jungle, the type which lets in very little light, so that when the Emperor threw in the towel, and we withdrew jubilantly from our positions, our once brown skins were an unhealthy-looking white.

Across the stream lay a large tree which had been felled for use as a bridge. The top was roughly levelled off, but what with mud and the rain, the trip over had to be taken with the utmost care.

We used our 'bridge' (as we fondly called it) for crossing the stream to go on duty at the listening post alongside the track which led to Rabaul. This was perhaps the most nerve-wracking part of any infantryman's life; knowing that somewhere beyond the blanket of jungle lay sudden death in the form of the Japs and their renegade native cohorts.

Every snap of a twig or distant thud echoing in this otherwise complete silence brought the safety catch of the snug little Owen gun forward from the 'safe' position, and ready for immediate use. Our bridge, therefore, became a symbol of security — not merely a means of going out to the listening post, but also an avenue of a quick getaway back to our positions in case of attack.

After two years in the islands in such headline places as Milne Bay, Lae and Finschhafen, the platoon again found itself subjected to attacks by the Japanese, and on this occasion by their black companions, who, it was said, were a fierce type imported from the Sepik River area of New Guinea (one of the bodies we buried had a crocodile scar on the back, from shoulder blades to waist).

Each night they prowled, unseen, outside our perimeter, stumbling over our tripwires, resulting in a great loss of sleep on our part, and a great loss of morale on theirs, as each grenade exploded with a noise that sent one flying to the trench, thinking an artillery barrage was in progress.

After much of this, the enemy became, not unreasonably, a little coy about such devices as tripwires, and on this particular moonlit night (their favourite hunting time), led by an officer, about 10 or 20 stepped cautiously over the wires and committed an act of desecration by walking on to our masterpiece — the bridge.

Their leader was nearly over when an alert sentry destroyed the man's dignity by tossing a hand grenade under his august person, thus dislodging him from our pride and joy. The rest of the party thundered through the scrub yelling and firing at will, dropping such interesting trinkets as 'Made in Rabaul' landmines as they went.

After burying the dead next morning, our attention turned to the bridge. Here, stretched right across from bank to bank at about waist level, was a handrail of jungle vine. One of our thoughtful mates had placed it in position the previous evening, just before nightfall, and hadn't bothered to tell us about it. His intention (an honourable one) was to make it a little easier for us to cross, but the first to use it had been the Japs!

There was a very red face that morning!

Reveille, July 1950

*The service number NX145805 was issued to **Maxwell William Edward Lynch**, was born at Warialda, NSW, on 29 May 1918. He enlisted in January 1943 and was discharged in April 1946, listed as a driver with the 90th Australian Transport Company. He died 16 August 1997.*

Underage but Signed Up
By John Montgomery

So I went into the Showgrounds and walked in. There were all the tables with signs — artillery, infantry, signals. I wanted to join the sigs because my dad said I might get to Middle Head where he worked. So I sat down at the table and the sergeant said, 'Where's your birth certificate?' I said, 'I haven't got one.' He said, 'Well you'd better go and get one and come back tomorrow.' So I went home and my mother was pleased because I didn't get in, but I said I'd go back tomorrow. She said, "What are you going to do about your birth certificate?' and I said, 'I'll see.'

So I went in and they were all around the tables again, and the same sergeant was sitting at the signals table and there were about six fellows down at the artillery sitting round the table on a form [bench], and I went and sat at the end of the form. Filled in the papers and the sergeant spoke for a while, and said, 'I've seen all your birth certificates so now we'll go and do our medical checks.' So I was in — just walked in. The only thing they gave me was a pair of boots. And I wore them home, and when I was walking up the side passage, my mother heard the noise and she started crying before I got in.

I went to North Head where the artillery was and did training there. In the training battalion, if you spoke when you were walking around on parade, they pulled you out and sent you over to the mangle machine. Well they sent half a dozen blokes over to the mangle machine because they were speaking in the ranks. This mangle had wheels on it, I suppose about four feet high, and they put sandbags through the mangle, put them in the wash so they wouldn't rot, and then you'd have to work the

Underage but Signed Up

mangle, and being the youngest, I always seemed to be on the handle of the mangle.

After about a fortnight I said I'd like to join the sigs. So I trained with them in the 29th Line Section, and left there as a corporal. I got on the boat in Brisbane and went to New Guinea in April 1943. We landed at Milne Bay and went from there to Goodenough Island, and we laid phones for the airstrip they were building there. Then we went to Buna and from there to Dobodura, to Lae, then to Labu and started laying a telephone line up to Wau. So we got that finished and they put us into Jacquinot Bay — they got some infantry in there and we went in straight after them.

I was in Lae when the first lot of ladies came in — AWAS — and everybody was busy building their accommodation with a big barbed-wire fence around it. We in the sigs got the job of digging latrines. We had to dig these big pits — and I mean, they're enormous pits — and we took it in turn. The radio fellows went in the last bit and they were there just finishing off on the day the girls came in. They thought they'd have a joke with them so they put a speaker down the bottom of the toilet and they had the microphone over where they could see. When the girls pulled in on the trucks some of them went racing to the toilets. The fellows said, 'Hey, cut it out! We're still working down here!' There was a scream and all the girls came out. The fellow who did it, he got six months' hard labour — they didn't like that at all.

I got back on the boat on 23 April 1945 so I was out in New Guinea about 25 months. We were lucky, I suppose, because we used to get close to the infantry when they were coming back, and that was pretty awful to see them — they were just buggered and they'd lie down on pieces of iron, anywhere to lie down and have a rest.

Then I went up to Darwin and stayed there till December 1945. I came back with Bell's palsy. I came back on the *Manoora*, which had called in to Darwin to pick up some supplies and a load of fellows who had syphilis and things like that, and they said they had room for six others, so they took me. With Bell's palsy, your face drops and your eye drops with paralysis, and it comes with a shock.

One of the boys rang and told my family I was coming back on the *Manoora*. So they all came down to see me.

Those in charge told us the six of us were going straight out to Yooralla, while the rest, with syphilis and so on, were going to Little Bay. They put us straight in an ambulance and out to Yooralla.

My family didn't see me so they walked down to the provost on duty and my dad said, 'I can't see my son. He's got a sore eye.' And the fellow said, 'Oh yeah, I know he's got a sore eye. They're all out at Little Bay!'

So my family all went home, and I rang up and my dad said, 'Why didn't you tell us you had something wrong with you? I'm that embarrassed. I found out you're at Little Bay.' But I told him I was at Yooralla and I was coming home on leave.

Reveille, 2003, interview with author

John Arthur Montgomery *has his date of birth recorded as 14 December 1923, having enlisted at North Head, NSW, in August 1942. He had earlier joined the militia at the age of 16. He was discharged in May 1946 with the rank of sergeant, having served with the 29th Australian Line Section. After the war he played rugby league and became a referee and first-grade touch judge. He died in 2011.*

Nursing in New Guinea
By Hazel Dalton

When war broke out we all went mad and joined up. My father was a policeman, stationed at Mascot. We were all sitting round, and bang! He said the war was on! My mother started to cry and I said, 'Well, we'll all go off to war.' I was in my early 20s and was an office worker. I signed up in the Red Cross, and then they changed it to the AAMWS [Australian Army Medical Women's Service] and we came under the control of the army. We got paid five bob.

We used to go up to Sydney Hospital of a weekend, and train there, learn first aid and the rest of it. We were mad, working up there for nothing. But it was interesting because we were learning things. That was in 1940.

The army certainly gave us training. I don't think any of us were model soldiers but there weren't enough trained nurses so we did things we never thought we could do. I started out at the blood bank, and then went to Goulburn, which was an asylum. After I'd been in the army about 18 months we had to learn how to be soldiers. We had to go to Ingleburn, and we played up, I must admit! We didn't want to go on a route march, so we'd start off and get up where there were a few hills, and we'd fall off and wait for them to come back, and join up again. It was fun though, because we were getting ready to go away.

Then they recruited us for New Guinea. We went up on a train to Brisbane and were equipped with all our tropical gear. Then we got on another train and went up to Townsville. Then we got on the *Canberra*, and the worst part was that the sailors went on strike, and it was the dirtiest, filthiest ship that you've seen in your life. There was nowhere to sleep and it took a couple of days to get to Port Moresby, just at the start of 1943.

So we stayed about 12 months there while the Kokoda Track campaign was on. We looked after a lot of injuries, with fellows coming back sick and wounded, gunshot wounds and a lot of malaria. Scrub typhus — a friend of mine got that and she was terribly sick, poor girl. She recovered but not many of them did, not from scrub typhus. There were mosquitoes, and awful malaria. We put up mosquito nets every night, and it rained — how can people go to the tropics? I don't ever want to see the tropics again.

The hospital was just stretchers and tents, and there were rats running along. And there was no help — you couldn't just get on the phone and say you wanted some more staff or more dressings. The showers and toilets were pretty rough too. You had to wear anti-malaria clothes at night, get your slacks and long sleeves on, so there was no relief from the heat. And you had to do your share of night duty, which wasn't very pleasant — you'd try to get some sleep during the day.

We couldn't go out unless we had six girls and guards with us, and the Americans would invite us to their mess — they always looked after us and fed us well. We used to go swimming during the day — the water wasn't too cold. Then we all got sunburnt.

The worst part for me was my sister. Her fiancé, George, was one of the Rats of Tobruk. Then he came home and they decided to get married. They were married for six weeks, and then he was sent up to Armidale. And the day we arrived in Port Moresby, George landed in Milne Bay. He got killed. They only had six weeks of marriage.

Then we were sent to Morotai. We arrived at night — no tents, no beds. We had to put our own tent up — that was awful. It was only a very small place.

We had a very bad crash. A group of our fellows lined up, ready to be flown back, and a big American plane was taking off and it crashed into our fellows. It was terrible. You couldn't do anything. We didn't have penicillin in those days, no antibiotics. The plane caught fire and there wasn't much you could do for them except pour saline over them.

Then we had the ex-prisoners of war come in. They were so thin and miserable. We did what we could for them. Some didn't get back, after all that — it was very sad to see those poor devils like that. We didn't get home for three or four months after the war because we had to get those people home first.

Reveille, January–February 2004, interview with author

Hazel Dorothy Kimber (Dalton) *was born in Sydney on 30 June 1918, enlisted at Goulburn on 27 October 1942, and was discharged as a private with the AAMWS on 18 February 1946. She died 4 July 2010.*

Tarakan and Sandakan

'Could anything remain alive through that hell of searing flame and raining fire?'

— Sergeant Emmett O'Keefe

Tarakan Island:
The Death of Lieutenant T.C. Derrick, VC
By Emmett O'Keefe

I met him once. Just once. But that was when he died.

Lieutenant T.C. Derrick, VC, DCM, of the 2/48th Battalion, 9th Division, had fought his way from the deserts of North Africa, across the razor-backed ridges of New Guinea, to the jungles of Borneo. It was on the island of Tarakan, off the Borneo coast, that he met his death in the final year of the war.

It was quiet in the pre-dawn off the coast of Tarakan on that morning of 1 May 1945. We lay off shore in convoy. The flames from burning oil tanks blazed like beacons in the darkness on the shore. The dawn came up in silence. No, this could not be a war; the low, flat shore emerging now in half-light; the rolling, densely wooded hills; so still, so quiet.

In full light now, we stood at battle stations on the decks. There was movement on the water. Destroyers were moving shorewards and their five-inch guns were blazing. Gunboats moved in close and hurled their rockets at the shore. The world was noise and clamour now, rising smoke and dust haze shot by leaping flame. Above it came the Liberators, the heavy bombers. Flight followed flight of silver lethal cylinders up and down the beach. Tarakan had gone from view, lost in the smoke and dust and flame.

The smoke was lifting; the dust was settling; the planes had gone. The naval barrage was directed further inland. The assault craft were carrying troops to the shore.

Somewhere down there in the boats was the No. 1 soldier of the 26th Brigade: T.C. (Diver) Derrick. He had known the bombardments of the Middle East. He had won his DCM at Tel el Eisa for leading a successful charge against three machine-gun posts, resulting in the capture of 100 of the enemy. He had been through it all before, but never a barrage to equal this, on that May morning when Australians, for the first time in history, invaded Dutch territory.

We met no opposition on the beach. Could anything remain alive through that hell of searing flame and raining fire? The worst was yet to come.

The Japanese fought desperately for every foot of ground. They contested each ridge and feature from a complicated system of tunnels and trenches. The ground was dotted with booby traps and mines. Tarakan was the most heavily mined area encountered by Australians in the Pacific theatre of war. Any step could bring sudden violent death.

Within 14 days of landing, the AIF had made an advance of merely two miles; two miles of blood and sweat and pain. By day the enemy fought ferociously; by night he waged a war of nerves. A master of infiltration, he would make nightly sallies behind the Australian lines, armed with bayonets tied to bamboo poles, or carrying shells and grenades to hurl amongst sleeping troops. Each day would dawn to the smack of snipers' bullets from the trees behind the lines. Suicide troops, these, who had infiltrated through the night to attack from the rear at daylight.

The 26th Brigade was not lacking in decorated soldiers, heroes of other campaigns. Amongst these men, Lieutenant Derrick had a special place of honour. At Sattelberg, New Guinea, he had won his VC when the position had been declared hopeless. Alone he had scaled the slopes of a cliff and, throwing grenades, had knocked out 10 enemy machine-gun posts, capturing vital ground for the final, successful attack on Sattelberg.

In warfare each man has his part to play; his own small part that uses all his time. He cannot see the pattern in the action all around. From time to time you would get some news of Derrick from a soldier who had passed his way.

Tarakan Island: The Death of Lieutenant T.C. Derrick, VC

We were at a feature known as Freda, a ridge held strongly by the Japanese. For three days it had remained unconquered in the face of heavy attack. Liberators and artillery had smashed it with high explosive; Lightning fighter planes had set it afire with flaming belly tanks dropped from low-level runs; yet still the Japanese came back with screaming, suicidal counterattacks.

Derrick commanded the 7th Platoon of the 2/48th Battalion. His platoon had occupied a knoll on the feature. It was 3.30 a.m., 23 May 1945. The night was quiet, and Derrick was on the most exposed position of a jungle path leading to another knoll. A short burst of machine-gun fire from the Japanese preceded what was to be a strong counterattack. Derrick rose and was hit in the abdomen by a second burst. He continued giving orders until he was evacuated some hours later.

I was working at the casualty clearing station when they brought him in. All that could be done for him was done, but his wounds were such that God alone could have saved him. He survived that day and night and the morning of the following day. During the afternoon of 24 May, I was attending to him. I knew I was attending a dying man. What makes us still persist when even hope has gone? He died while I had a needle in his vein. If Derrick spoke the last words heroes are said to speak, I did not hear them.

Such are the ways of war that his bed was then occupied by a Japanese sergeant major, badly wounded. He died that night.

By 15 June 1945 all organised Japanese resistance on Tarakan had ended. By the end of the year we had left the island. Lieutenant T.C. Derrick, VC, DCM, remained.

Reveille, May 1964

Emmett Walter James O'Keefe, *born 29 November 1917, was 26 when he enlisted at Kings Cross, Sydney, on 4 January 1944. He served with the 110 Casualty Clearing Station and was discharged in December 1945 with the rank of sergeant. He died 11 July 1998.*

Brothers Inseparable Until Death
By Mark Wells

Mark Wells was a teenage jackeroo in NSW; his older brother, Frank, a talented musician, composer and arranger of orchestral recitals. Together they went looking for action in the Pacific; Frank was blown up by a makeshift Japanese grenade and died in Mark's arms. It was a devastating blow for Mark, who carefully preserved his brother's diaries and presented them to the Australian War Memorial.

I had been a jackeroo on the north-western plains, at a little town called Rowena. I started life there at 13 because I was a problem child — I wouldn't go to school. I was then offered a job at twice the salary, which took me to 30 shillings a week, near Moree as a cowboy. It was very rough living, and the day that Japan hit Pearl Harbor I got a ride on the mail truck into Moree and enlisted as an escape route. I was 17 then.

I duly got to Sydney and went in for my testing, and promptly got chucked out as being underage. What I didn't realise was that anyone of 19 was already in the army. I tried again and the same thing happened. And eventually I took a cut lunch up to the drill hall at North Sydney and just got on the queue of the conscripts — and I was in the army.

My brother claimed me in May 1942 — an older brother could claim a younger brother — and we sailed out of Sydney the day the submarines came into Sydney Harbour. Frank had been conscripted, being 19, and we were bound for parts unknown. The Coral Sea Battle was going on, and we were diverted to Townsville and ended up at Charters Towers, which was then a frontline airstrip. From there we went to Cairns and sat on the airfield for the best part of a year, defending Cairns, which was never attacked, and then to New Guinea.

We went to Moresby first and then to Lae, and again sat, doing nothing. During this time my brother and I had applied to transfer to my father's unit, which was the 2/1st Infantry Battalion, 6th Division, and they weren't calling for reinforcements at the time, so we didn't get in there. He had already come back from the Middle East — he'd put his age down to get in, and he went to Greece and Crete, came back and was discharged as unfit. Later he became Assistant Crown Solicitor for South Australia.

Anyway our unit came home to Australia and was disbanded. We applied for infantry, to do something worthwhile, and were duly awarded the 2/48th Battalion. We had to do infantry training for about two months at Bathurst, and then jungle training, and then we went up to Morotai and eventually into Tarakan. It was one of the worst campaigns of the South Pacific, because they couldn't justify why we went in there, other than that they wanted the airfield. The intelligence the unit received from the Dutch was mostly wrong. The airfield couldn't be repaired because there were no facilities. It wasn't what they expected because it was just a coral strip, and the bombardment the Allies had given it had totally ruined and waterlogged it. I think we were successful eventually and got a DC-3 in there — but that was about it. So it was a useless campaign with very heavy casualties.

We went in as a very big convoy, due to land on 1 May. We were on the *Manoora*.

Frank was killed and I was blown up on the 24th. The Japanese always worked at night — we worked in the daytime. They had two favourite weapons. One was a bayonet blade on a length of bamboo — if they could entice you to put your head up by calling, 'Are you all right down there?' you got the blade through you. The other was a six-inch naval shell which they used as a grenade with a sling attached to it, and a fuse in the nose which they'd ignite from a piece of smouldering bamboo. They'd just ignite it, stand up and *banzai!* And hurl it over the perimeter. That's what killed my brother and got me.

I'd been lying down, not in my pit but on the ground, and when all hell broke loose I jumped into the wrong pit and the fellow thought I was the enemy, fired his rifle at me, burnt my shirt, went between my chest and my arm — panic!

Bear in mind this was at one o'clock in the morning. The shell killed three of them, including Frank. It [temporarily] deafened me and I was evacuated the next morning.

We'd been on patrol virtually every day, with very little sleep. Seven days without sleep, or sleep where you could. At night we'd tie ourselves to telephone cable, and the section would dig in and attach the cord to the next fellow's arm, and then we'd pull it to make sure he was awake and to keep ourselves awake through the night. From artillery bombardments and shelling and what-have-you the trees would be cracking, and you'd hear these sounds at night. You didn't trust any sound, and if it got too close to you, you'd toss the grenades over. We never used our weapons at night — the grenade was the most important weapon we had at night.

One of our officers went berserk on one occasion. He'd come up from headquarters, and he wasn't quite used to these sounds at night. He was firing his pistol at whatever he thought it was and gave his position away — which was our position. The tension was enormous at night. During the day we'd go on patrol and we'd be active — we would see things. We went a great deal on smell. I only saw two or three live Japanese — lots of dead ones. I don't know if you've been in the bush but if a fox went past your chicken yard, you'd smell the fox the next day. We could smell the Japanese if they'd been nearby, or were nearby. You couldn't see more than 20 or 30 feet in front of you. We'd have a forward scout, and he was the poor bloke who would cop it first, which many of them did. But the lack of sleep and the tension at night were the hardest things to cope with.

Frank and I had been inseparable. We'd been together for nigh on four years and we'd shared everything — our girls, our food, our water (because water was a big problem there). Our platoon leader wouldn't allow us to pick up water from a stream in case it was poisoned. So we survived on whatever water could be brought up to the frontline for us. Needless to say, given the opportunity, going through a creek we'd defy regulations and gulp water while we could. But that was hard — the shortage of water — because we poured more out than we put in — very, very hot and tremendously humid. You were saturated all day and you'd sit through the night thirsty. For food we had bully beef — no, it was K-rations[1] then. Three meals from a can, wrapped in sealed, waxed cardboard. It wasn't bad, actually. And bless their hearts, the Salvation Army would come up to the frontline when they could and bring food and socks and the odd shirt, whatever they could carry. They were wonderful.

So I was evacuated by hospital ship to Morotai and stayed there a month or so, and then sailed back into Sydney on, I think, the *Kanimbla*. I got in the day the first atomic bomb was dropped on Japan and I came out of the army in October.

Reveille, November–December 2003

Mark Ernest Wells *was born in Sydney on 3 February 1924 and enlisted at North Sydney in February 1942. He was discharged in October 1945 after serving as a private with the 2/48th Australian Infantry Battalion. He died 25 April 2009.*

*His brother, **Frank Morris Wells**, was born on 20 March 1922 and enlisted at North Sydney in October 1941, serving as a private with the 2/48th Australian Infantry Battalion. He was killed on 24 May 1945.*

Note:
[1] The K-ration was the individual daily ration of the American soldier during WWII. It was developed in 1941 under the direction of the physiologist Ancel Keys (hence the name K), who aimed to produce a non-perishable ration ready to eat and able to fit in a soldier's pocket.

Mopping Up at Sandakan
By Tom Turner

I have read several articles written recently regarding Sandakan and Australian prisoners of war held by the Japanese, and also the death marches carried out.

Never once have I come across any mention of the further Australian action concerning our landing on Sandakan in September to October 1945. I was one of about 1000 Australian soldiers, together with a small group of British Borneo Civil Administrative Units (BBCAU), placed aboard two Australian corvettes, HMAS *Deloraine* and HMAS *Latrobe*, in Labuan, Borneo, and landed in Sandakan several days later. Our job was to round up the Japanese soldiers and place them in the compound, which had been specially built.

Each day, Australian troops would leave the ships around 4 to 5 a.m., after a meal, and would march to a certain destination, where a number of Japanese troops would be waiting to surrender and be taken to the compound.

One of my jobs was to attend the compound each morning and arrange to pick up Japs and march them to work. So many had been captured that when I asked for 15 or so, I would be forced to accept double the number, whom I would march back to the ships and put to work cleaning. I can assure you that these people were not gently handled.

A most surprising thing happened to me, in that one of my prisoners approached me every day a number of times, speaking in Japanese, but all I could understand was 'tomorrow, tomorrow'. After I had procured an interpreter, I learned that this man wanted me to pick him up every day. Several days later we had a visit from a person who, I was informed, was a doctor, who had originally lived in Sandakan and had been taken prisoner by the Japs. He had come aboard the *Deloraine* to identify Japanese soldiers. When he came to my 'tomorrow, tomorrow' man, he called out to me to 'Arrest that Jap!' When I asked him to explain, I was informed that my prisoner was responsible for killing Australian prisoners of war.

I immediately tied up 'tomorrow, tomorrow', placed a noose around his neck and stood him against a stanchion with certain intentions which we were unable to carry out.

Later, during one of my searches, I came across a Japanese soldier who was a member of a marine kamikaze unit, recently arrived from the Philippines. This person was the coxswain of a timber vessel which had the bow loaded up with explosives and was to attempt to collide with one of our vessels. One of the Japanese timber vessels was brought back to Australia, and is at present in the National War Memorial in Canberra. I relieved the coxswain of his flag, which is at present in the Victoria Barracks Museum, Sydney.

The doctor was one of several persons who were able to identify Japanese connected to the Sandakan POW camp.

A number of Japs were charged at Labuan between 3 and 5 January 1946. There were over 5000 charged with crimes against humanity and tried by courts established in Singapore, Morotai, Rabaul, Darwin and Hong Kong.

A Jap force several hundred strong showed no sign of surrendering. An Australian force unofficially organised the Dyak natives, who were known for their chopping off of heads, to follow the Nips along the Trusan River area, from Brunei Bay. A force of 346 led by their Captain Fujino surrendered several days later.

In November 1945, I was flown back to Labuan by a Catalina plane, and remained at the aerodrome whilst awaiting a ship to Australia. I eventually arrived in Brisbane in December 1945, and finally arrived in Sydney on Christmas Eve. I was discharged in 1946.

Reveille, July–August 1999

The Sandakan Underground
By Paddy Funk

This is a true story of my experience during World War II. We were three Sandakan brothers captured by the Japanese Kempeitai in 1943 for being members of the Underground that helped Australian soldiers in captivity. We were brutally tortured and imprisoned for years, and our brother Alexander was executed, with eight others including Australian Army Captain L.C. Matthews, GC, MC,[1] an 8th Division AIF officer.

We supplied food, medicine, radio parts, Japanese shipping and troop movements to the Allies, and helped prisoners of war to escape to the Philippines.

It was dusk on 19 July 1943 and I had just finished my meagre dinner when there was a bang at my front door followed by a kick. I knew they were coming for me, because my younger brother Alexander and a handful of my comrades had been taken by them about a fortnight ago.

From my window I could see a truckload of Japanese soldiers with fixed bayonets waiting at the roadside. I unlocked the door and saw an officer from the dreaded Kempeitai with two burly soldiers. Without warning, he gave me one big slap on my face followed by a kick to my stomach. He nodded to the two soldiers to take me to the waiting truck right away.

I pleaded with the officer that I may be allowed to take some clothes along with me; this was refused. They even forbade me to say goodbye to my wife and two children, Gabriel and Olga, who were crying at one corner of the house.

The Sandakan Underground

House of Torture

I was taken to the House of Torture: that was the name we gave to the Japanese military police headquarters at Sandakan. This building was the official residence of the general manager of Bakau and Kenya Extract Company. The Japanese had turned this once-beautiful bungalow into their military police headquarters.

For one whole week I was left alone in a dark room below the building. I could hear the shouting, yelling, groaning and beating almost every night and day of my friends and Australian soldiers who were interrogated by the Japanese military officers. After one week, they took me upstairs to join the rest of the people who were arrested in connection with the case. There were more than 100 of us in that big room, and there were Japanese guards all around with fixed bayonets. No one was allowed to talk, smile or even look at each other; only to look at the floor in front of you, where we all squatted.

Anyone who just smiled was mercilessly beaten up by at least three to four guards. These guards really enjoyed doing this. My elder brother, John, was there and so was Alexander. The Kempeitai and the burly guards hated the three of us most, because we were three brothers who had committed the same offence against them.

The officers said that they had witnesses who were willing to testify against us, that the three of us had threatened and forced them to help the prisoners of war or else reprisals would be taken against them when the 'whites' returned.

We were subjected to the diabolic water torture (filled with water and rice, then Japanese guards marched over our swollen stomachs); the bakau firewood torture; burnt with fag ends; whipped and bashed — but we did not give in.

On 25 October 1943 the Japanese took 53 of us (the rest were released) from all walks of life: doctor, dental surgeon, *towkays* [business owners], manager, traders, *jamadar* [Indian army officers], police inspector, sergeants, policemen, detective, clerks, forest ranger, overseers, farmers, watchman and boatmen. We were an international group composed of Chinese, Europeans, Eurasian, Kadazans, Sikh, Muruts, Malays, Filipinos, Suluks and Javanese.

We were shipped like cattle by a small coastal boat to Kuching, Sarawak, and imprisoned in the Penjarah Orang Sangsarah military prison for final judgment to be passed on us by high-ranking Japanese military officers.

On 1 March 1944 John and myself were each sentenced to nine years' military imprisonment, and my younger brother Alexander and seven others were sentenced to death.

Firing Squad

The seven condemned were shot by a Japanese firing squad on a hot noon on 2 March 1944, together with the gallant Australian, Captain Matthews, who was posthumously awarded the George Cross in March 1944. This brave captain could have easily escaped, because we had wanted him to be in the Philippines so that he could negotiate for guns etc. to arm the 2750 Allied soldiers in the camp. He'd told us that his duty was to stand by with his boys and that he must go through thick and thin with them under any circumstances.

So instead we had contacted Wong Mu Sing[2] — a Chinese-Filipino barter trader who held the rank of lieutenant with the Filipino guerrillas — to get the arms. This barter trader, who was introduced to me by Quadra, another Filipino guerrilla, was one of those executed on 2 March 1944.

The prisoners of war in the camp had told us that if we could supply the arms, they could easily overpower the Japanese Army stationed in Sandakan. The majority of us who were involved in the case knew about this. The Japanese military police even came to know about it; because someone who could not stand the torture had spilled the beans to the Kempeitai. This had spread some fear among the Japanese, plus the fact that seven prisoners of war had made good their escape to the Philippines by our Underground.

The Kempeitai at once transferred 250 POW officers from the Sandakan Camp to Kuching, leaving [almost] 2500 prisoners of war behind at Sandakan (1800 Australians and 700 Britons). At the war's end only six of them [the only escapees] were still alive. The great majority died or were brutally bashed to death on the 1945 Sandakan–Ranau death march.

On 19 September 1945 we were liberated by the 7th Australian Division. On 20 September they sent us by Catalinas to Labuan where we were all looked after by the convalescent camp at Timbali. On 23 November 1945, being fully recovered after the best treatment received from the Australian Red Cross, I was sent back to Sandakan, my home town.

Rewards

From 1946 to 1947, the Australian government assigned Major H.W.S. Jackson[3] — the man who hunted head-hunters — to find and identify all those in North Borneo who had assisted Australian prisoners of war. Altogether about 285 names were on his list, and he paid out rewards which were calculated on a definite formula of risk bonus plus a specific amount for harbouring and feeding one POW for one day. He had to trudge 200 miles over the Sandakan–Ranau death march route to complete the final chapter of his assignment.

On 16 November 1951 the eight heroes of the Sandakan Underground were exhumed and re-buried at the Roman Catholic cemetery, Kuching, Sarawak, in a common grave, with this inscription on the slab:

In memory of the eight gallant men of all races who, loyal to the cause of freedom, rendered assistance to Allied prisoners of war at Sandakan camp, and were executed in Kuching on 2 March 1944, and also the five who died in prison for the same reason.

This was done personally through the efforts of my brother, John, who, after the war, decided to do something for them. He appealed to the people of Sandakan, who generously donated the required sum; and he approached all relatives concerned, who finally agreed to his idea that they be buried in one grave.

My parents and my family lived in fear of reprisals right through the Japanese occupation but came through safely thanks to providence.

In May 1946 I was selected by the British government to represent North Borneo in the great Victory Parade held in London on 8 June.

In recognition of his valuable services to Australian prisoners of war, John was given honorary life membership of the RSL and the Ex-POW Association. He was granted Australian citizenship and left Jesselton with his family on 7 November 1951, and now lives at Holland Park, Brisbane, Queensland.

Reveille, July 1969

Notes:
[1] Captain Lionel Colin Matthews, GC, MC, of 8th Division Signals, was executed by a Japanese firing squad at Kuching, Borneo, on 2 March 1944 after being pronounced guilty of espionage, rebellion, violation of prisoner of war regulations, and spreading of rumours. Matthews was born 15 August 1912 at Stepney, S.A., and enlisted at Caulfield, Victoria, 10 June 1940. He was awarded the George Cross posthumously.

[2] Wong Mu Sing was a prominent Chinese-Filipino civilian who traded between Sandakan and the Philippines, and was a key member of the underground in Borneo, bringing in weapons and assisting with plans for POWs to escape and rise up against their

Japanese captors. Wong Mu Sing was one of the civilians executed with Captain Matthews.

[3] Major (later Lieutenant Colonel) Harry Jackson was assigned after the war to investigate the facts behind the Sandakan–Ranau death march in Borneo. The purpose of the exercise was to contact natives who rendered assistance to Australian and British POWs and to obtain additional information regarding the event.

Repatriating POWs to Australia
By Joan Dowson — Red Cross Field Force Officer

We had been very busy at the Redbank Military Hospital in Queensland preparing to move, with several other AGHs, to form one of the largest hospitals in the southern hemisphere at Holland Park, through where it was expected that all released prisoners of war from the north would pass to be 'seasoned', as they termed it, before returning to their home states, when suddenly I had notice to pack and move to Sydney to a posting on a Royal Naval ship.

Everything happened so suddenly that with the wild rush of having more injections, obtaining a passport and tropical clothing, and not knowing either our destination or length of stay in the ship, we did not fully realise our unique experience of going on one of the Royal Navy's largest aircraft carriers. On 19 September we joined HMS *Formidable*, which was to be our home for the next three months. We drew all our Red Cross supplies for the POWs from Sydney, consisting of toilet gear, towels, pyjamas, slippers, socks, pullovers, sunglasses, cordials, peanut butter, barley sugar, honey, tomato juice, whitebait, chocolate and cigarettes, as well as games, books, deckchairs and tables, and that morning's issue of Sydney papers, plus three portable gramophones and 500 records, bedside lockers, bed rests, walking sticks, crutches and material for handcrafts.

We left Sydney with very mixed feelings, as our destination was in the air and we knew no one on the ship; however, we were instructed to stand to on the flight deck to dress the ship as we left Woolloomooloo. It was a grand sight with the Royal Navy smartly standing to in their blues and the marine band playing in the centre of the flight deck. We were drawn to attention by the bugles when we returned the salute of the smaller ships on the way out of Sydney Harbour. The admiral came out in his small motorboat to see us out of the 'boom', and he must have had some qualms at seeing women on board his ship for the first time in the history of the Royal Navy.

The four British sisters had comfortable cabins off the quarter deck, and the 12 British and Australian VADs had the admiral's quarters and their own dining room. The two British and two Australian Red Cross officers had the captain's 'shore' cabin and, with the English sisters, dined in the wardroom. The men put up with women entering their wardroom, or 'holy of holies', with great tact. The ship had its own broadcasting system and some excellent programs were arranged by the entertainments group — music, plays, quiz sessions and lectures.

On our first day at sea the crew began a complete reorganisation of the hangar, which was to be the hospital and quarters for the POWs, and it was strange to see the trucks and jeeps running up and down the huge hangar carrying stores and clearing it out, and then hoisted and stored away in the bulkhead. Next the whole hangar floor, 500 feet by 62 feet, was scraped and painted by the ratings while coloured bunting was erected to hide the bulkhead storehouse and make the hangar bright and attractive. The hospital section was screened off and made into wards, and then the duty room, dispensary, kitchen and bathrooms were arranged. Meanwhile, we began unpacking and organising our Red Cross stores, and we made comfortable our Red Cross welfare room which was to act as a library and office for the POWs.

We called at Manus and everyone was allowed to go for a swim overboard — gangways were let down 'forward and aft'. It was a most unreal feeling swimming off an aircraft carrier with several hundred others in the middle of the Coral Sea! Next we refuelled at Leyte, which was hot and steamy, and the harbour was crowded with ships. On arrival at Manila, our destination, the commander of the ship and a small party went ashore in the captain's motorboat; one English and one Australian Red Cross officer were allowed to go to contact Red Cross headquarters for extra stores.

The Australian Red Cross representative called for us and took us out to the 5th Replacement Depot, where our well Australian POWs were waiting to come home. There, we met the British Red Cross, Australian sisters, and Red Cross Field Force and American Red Cross girls, who were living in adjoining huts. The girls at this depot had a bare minimum of comfort, having with them only what they could take when they flew up. Their time was very busy and they were all terribly happy to be able to do so much for the POWs. Their recreation centre was filled from morning to night, and the girls who worked at the replacement depot took it in turns for canteen duty and chatting to the boys who did not give them any opportunities to rest from talking.

The passengers, as we called the POWs — who included Australians, Englishmen and New Zealanders — finally began to embark. The first landing craft arrived alongside the forward boat deck with stretcher and walking patients, who immediately were taken down to the hospital at the end of the hangar. At the same time, the second landing craft was alongside the starboard boat deck. The men came straight into the forward lift well, where they passed in turn by tables, receiving several pamphlets, including a card designating them into Red, White and Blue watches and saying where they were sleeping in the hangar, at what hours they ate etc. They also received a free chit for use at the NAAFI canteen[1] — all from the Royal Navy. We followed up with our distribution of cigarettes, chocolates and newspapers.

Royal Navy men, acting as guides, carried the men's 'heavy' baggage and showed them to their bunks. The entire embarkation of more than 1200 men took little over two hours of steady and cooperative work.

The relief of the passengers to be at last on board and on their way home on what they termed 'a luxury hotel on the seas' all boiled down to one verdict — the Royal Navy was 'tops'. The men's entertainment was fully organised by the ship and the men said they didn't have a spare moment. They were welcomed on the first evening by our concert. The lift well, which only a month before had been conveying planes, was raised to make an ideal stage. The beds were moved back and the men sat on cushions on the floor. We repeated the concert one afternoon for the 250 bed patients. Picture shows were on several times a day, and the boys would 'book' their seats early in the afternoon for the evening session, and leave them for their tea only if someone would stand by and guard them while they were away. The POWs had the bare minimum of restrictions, even to 'lights out'. The Red Cross deckchairs were placed all around the flight deck, giving the impression of a large lounge.

The wards' provisions were supplemented by Red Cross supplies, and the sick men were visited in the morning and any request attended to. There was a morning issue of cigarettes, toilet gear and extras such as whitebait, tomato juice, sweets, salted peanuts, asparagus, parcels, socks and books, including a cool drink. One afternoon we gave them a party, dividing all the states into separate groups, plus one for the United Kingdom and one for New Zealand. The officers joined in, and so quite a number of men met friends they hadn't known were on board. One of the passengers played the violin, with a ship's officer accompanying him, and the party ended with community singing.

On the eve of arrival in Sydney, shoe brushes and polish appeared from nowhere, and there was a wild rush as colour patches had to be sewn on. The men dressed the ship on arrival in Sydney Harbour and looked a grand sight. It was amazing how smart these weary men of only a week ago could appear. Small ships tooted around the *Formidable* and large banners, waving welcome signs to the boys on board, fluttered in the breeze. When the ship neared the wharf it proved too much for their self-control and they all rushed over to the wharf side where a band played 'Waltzing Matilda'.

Many and varied were our jobs on this trip, with Red Cross stores to distribute and personal contacts to be made, library books to select for the sick and messages to send on their behalf, patches to be sewn on and various other work for 1300 men. It was certainly a big undertaking but we felt that no matter what we did for them, it was too little in repayment for what they had done for us.

The Listening Post, Autumn 1999

Dorothy Joan Dowson *was born 4 June 1918, enlisted in Perth in October 1941, served with the 110 Military Hospital, and was discharged in March 1945. She died 11 October 2006.*

Note:
[1] NAAFI: The Navy, Army and Air Force Institutes, created by the British Government in 1921 when the Expeditionary Force Canteens (EFC) and the Navy and Army Canteen Board (NACB) were combined to run the recreational establishments needed by the Armed Forces, and to sell goods to servicemen and their families.

The First Japanese POW on Australian Soil
By Sergeant Leslie Powell

I was assigned with the 23rd Field Company, Royal Australian Engineers Militia, camped at Winnellie, about eight kilometres from Darwin. Early in January 1942 I was detached to headquarters, Larrakeyah Barracks; from there I was flown to Bathurst Island. My instructions were to assist in preparing the aerodrome area for demolition in case of a Japanese attack. Most of our work had been carried out by one of our officers, assisted by the natives, and a corporal and LAC from the RAAF who were stationed on the 'drome.

My orders were, on completion, to maintain and test the circuits twice daily for continuity, and, in the case of a Japanese landing, wait until they had landed, then blow up the landing area. Then I was to make my way back to the mainland the best way possible — pretty expendable, I would say.

On the morning of the first raid on Darwin we were startled by the sound of many aircraft — seemed to be hundreds — heading in that direction. We took off as three Zeros broke formation and attacked. They fired on the radio shack where Father McGrath was sending the warning of the impending attack on Darwin, which, we believe, was ignored. Then they machine-gunned a US Air Force transport plane that had been damaged on landing, where it had hit one of the poles holding up the demolition wires.

The planes made three passes and then rejoined their group heading towards Darwin. I headed for the firing point — never got there — managed to lie between the cement that was used to tie down the aircraft in a storm. Actually, I lay under my rifle — not impossible. The two air force chaps, they climbed down a well.

The next day, after it was all over, Father McGrath evacuated the mission, which was situated alongside the aerodrome. It was also decided to move the radio into the bush for security reasons. It then became routine for us; the two air force fellows would stay with the radio in the bush during the day, and I at the firing point. We would return in the evening to eat and sleep.

One morning, after the two RAAF fellows had gone into the bush with the radio, I was preparing to go when three natives came running around to our quarters singing out, 'Japanese! Japanese!' I grabbed my gear, water, food and exploder, and took off across the 'drome, the natives running after me. They finally got through to me that there was only one. They then told me how he had walked into their camp on Melville Island and started playing with the children.

I must point out here that the natives had had a lot to do with Japanese pearling luggers that called in at Melville Island before the war. I knew these natives — they had worked on the 'drome — so I told them to bring him over. They refused, saying he had a gun and they would only bring him across in their canoe if I brought my rifle down to the beach and hid behind a tree. This I did.

As he stepped out of the canoe I came forward and told the startled Japanese to put up his hands, and disarmed him of a .32 automatic pistol. He then became a prisoner. I took him around to our quarters, then sent a native to fetch the two air force fellows. They turned up some 20 minutes later; we then took off his flying overalls and fixed up the wounds he had sustained crash-landing. He evidently took a bullet in the engine and lost oil, and his engine seized — the reason he crashed. I then took him outside and had my photo taken.

The natives later included in their story that the Jap had the camera; not so, it was mine. They also said he had fired a pistol; not true. The pistol had never been fired; it had a full clip and the barrel was clean.

Later a message was coded and sent to Darwin requesting an aircraft and informing them of the prisoner. The plane came two or three days later. During this time, waiting, we would, at night, sit around the table with a pidgin-Japanese book and interrogate him. He was quite a nice type of bloke; he ate the same food as us and slept in the same type of bed. We did a couple of hours on and off at night guarding him with his own pistol. He also acted as our mess orderly — under supervision, of course. It was suggested to give the natives the credit for his capture so we could make a big splash of food and tobacco, supplied from Darwin, thus ensuring their help and silence if the place was occupied, as we would have to rely solely on their help. To this I agreed, as survival was the name of the game.

On another occasion the natives came running around to our hut calling out, 'Japanese! Japanese!' This time I had a companion, an American off the aircraft that was on the ground; he had returned to salvage some parts. So the two of us went down to the beach, then the natives brought the Japanese men over in their canoes.

The American and I stepped out to the surprise of five very weary Japanese. As in the first instance, the natives had told them there were Japanese on the island. We then told them to put their hands up over their heads and stop talking — they were jabbering away. To make them stop I fired a bullet at their feet, the only shot that was fired during the two episodes.

They told us they were off a cargo ship, the *Nunken Maru*, that was sunk off Melville Island. In fact they were from a bomber that had come down off Melville Island. There had been six in the crew — one did not survive.

Later I was relieved by another sergeant from our company and returned to the mainland.

Reveille, May–June 2002

Leslie Joseph Powell *was born 8 May 1920 at Karinga, NSW, and enlisted at Morphett Creek, NT. He was discharged 18 December 1945 with the rank of Staff Sergeant, and died 3 July 2003.*

The first Japanese pilot to be taken prisoner was ***Sergeant Hajime Toyoshima****, from the aircraft carrier* Hiryu. *Toyoshima was to die in the breakout of Japanese POWs at Cowra in August 1944.*

In 2016 a statue was unveiled on Bathurst Island, commemorating ***Matthias Ulungura****, the Tiwi Islander who first captured Toyoshima and handed him over to Sergeant Powell.*

The War in the Middle East

'We are working furiously, firing as fast as possible. We haven't even time to duck some of the "Itie" shells which land dangerously close — within feet of us.'

— Sergeant Albert Hertzberg

First Stop, Bardia!
By NX2621

The nuggety New Zealand transport major scanned the line of crowded Bedford trucks. Then, like a puppet in a dumb show, he went through the motions of cranking an imaginary engine, and clambered aboard the leading vehicle. All along the line starters whirred, and cold motors spluttered into life.

The trucks, driven by New Zealanders, were crammed with troops of the 16th Australian Brigade. The time, early morning 17 December 1940; the place, Sidi Haneish, midway between Alexandria and Mersa Matruh [an inlet]; the occasion, the first movement towards the coming battle of Bardia.

On 12 December our battalion had moved up to Sidi Haneish from the El Amiriya aerodrome on the outskirts of Alexandria. That night we had our first taste of enemy offensive action when a draft of tri-motored Savoias [Savoia-Marchetti bomber aircraft] droned over and straddled the railway station with a stick of bombs.

For the few days that we were there, trainloads of Italian prisoners from the current actions at Sidi Barrani and Sollum passed through on their way to Suez and final pilgrimage to labour-hungry Australian farmers. When we finally moved up towards the battle area, our Kiwi drivers, who had done the trip before, proved to be stores of misinformation, telling fantastic stories of flame-throwing tanks and massed squadrons of Senussi irregulars who did everything short of eating any of Mussolini's enemies foolish enough to fall into their hands.

The first night out, the long convoy of trucks camped a few kilometres beyond Sidi Barrani; its shattered buildings and bomb-cratered hinterland were plain evidence that there had been a war on there at some time. Now it was deserted. Piles of captured rifles, machine-guns, and other martial odds and ends lay guarded alongside the road, and the ubiquitous truckloads of prisoners continued to pour back from the west. At Sollum we left the trucks and dug in above the battered little seaport, its whitewashed houses, now roofless, nestling down to the Mediterranean.

Behind us the escarpment of the Libyan plateau rose up like a wall. It was only two days since Sollum had been captured by the British, and the town yielded well in souvenirs — tinny, red-painted hand grenades, neatly turned mortar bombs, toy-like rifles with folding stiletto bayonets, and a remarkable variety of the tinsel badges and trappings with which the Italians loved to decorate themselves.

In the afternoon, 17 Savoias with fighter escort lumbered across our encampment from behind the escarpment. They dropped four sticks of bombs across the area, destroying a bit more of the town but doing us no harm. There was some excitement when they were jumped by a squadron of Hurricanes right over our position, and for a minute or two after the whole mess of aircraft had passed from sight we could hear the muffled chatter of machine-guns.

We revised our opinion of the ease of infantry life that night. Mustered together, in silence we marched in full kit (somewhat weighed down with souvenirs) up the tortuous slope of the steep Halfaya (afterwards, with justice, Hellfire) Pass — camping towards the early hours near the ghostly ruins of Fort Capuzzo. Despite the bitter cold of the night we were running with sweat by the time the hourly 10-minute spells arrived; by the time they were over our teeth were chattering with the cold.

In the early hours of the morning we were bombed from the air, and later in the day we resumed the march to our positions about six miles from the Bardia perimeter. Conditions were grim during our 13 days' wait for the offensive to begin. Midwinter cold in the desert was intense and men wrapped themselves in any odd bits of clothing; with scarves and balaclavas round our faces, two sets of underwear, pullovers, uniform jackets, greatcoats and flannel-lined leather jerkins, we were still bitterly cold.

We had anticipated an attack before Christmas, but Christmas Day came and went without it. On Christmas night (popularly voted the coldest night to date) we received Comforts Fund parcels[1] and, tantalisingly, a bottle of beer to every four men. Hardened drinkers as most of us were, we fortunately saw the funny side of it, and nostalgically swilled the stuff around in our throats before swallowing it.

On the 27th we had another large-scale air raid and were entertained by the spectacle of one of their ungainly old Savoias coming down in flames. Three of the crew bailed out but the parachute of one failed to open. We all experienced the common fear that the big plane, well afire, would crash right on top of our individual funkholes. As a matter of fact, it went down half a mile from our company, and frightened hell out of battalion HQ.

On New Year's Eve we went through a dress rehearsal of the coming attack, and again the next night. By this time the troops were so heartily sick of the desert, and of waiting about, that they would gladly have undertaken an attack on the combined strengths of the Italian and German armies. But the static part of the campaign was finished, and in the early hours of 3 January the battalion moved up to the vicinity of the start line, and bedded down for a couple of hours' rest.

Just before 5 a.m. we were directed by guides to a white tape. It was all very unreal and unwarlike. In the darkness there was no sound save the jingling of equipment and low-pitched whispers as the troops arranged themselves for the hop off.

At 5 a.m., on the dot, our artillery opened up behind us, and we moved away at a strictly regulated pace. The horizon towards which we were heading was like a colour picture of the solar prominences, as shells from the 200 British and Australian guns crashed into the Italian defences, raising luminous pillars of smoke, flames and dust. Over our heads the noise of the shells cutting through the night air added to the shock of their detonations to our front. From the sea, some miles to our right, we could hear the muffled boom of the 16-inch guns on the naval monitors.

We had our first casualties when the Italian guns opened in reply, their shells lobbing amongst the advancing troops in the semi-darkness. One shell dropped into the company on our left, where there had earlier been some hilarity. It stopped after that.

Our company was not held up by any of the first isolated outer-defence posts but went straight through to the main bastion, a long stone wall lined with artillery pieces, machine-guns and small Fiat tanks. As we went, we cut the telephone lines over which we passed, and budding marksmen took some long shots at the position looming up ahead through the dirt.

The fight for our main objective was short. The enemy had been badly shaken by the barrage and cowered in his dugouts. He failed to use his superior weapon strength against us when we approached at close quarters (in daylight now); and once his defence wall had been pierced, contented himself with sporadic rifle fire and throwing his ineffective grenades. After only a few minutes of close quarters fighting, 600 of them surrendered to our company and were sent back under guard.

As soon as we had rid ourselves of our prisoners we occupied the positions they had vacated, and the second wave of the Australian attack passed through us to grapple with the inner enemy fortifications. By this time the tanks were on the job, providing good cover for the troops who followed behind them.

Soon after the second wave had passed through, the Italian artillery and machine-gunners further in opened a sharp fire, aiming with commendable accuracy at our newly won positions and inflicting casualties on us. Some were killed, and one of our most valuable NCOs, an old British soldier who had fought throughout WWI with the Highland Light Infantry, was stitched by a burst of machine-gun fire. He received five bullets in the chest, leg and arm, but had recovered sufficiently to rejoin and serve in Greece and Crete a few months later. The long lines of prisoners heading towards the rear suffered most from the counter-artillery fire because they had to be kept on the move for security reasons.

Sunday 5 January completed the action, and by that night nearly all prisoners had been removed to the POW cage back near Fort Capuzzo. On 6 January a small party of us went a short distance up the coast to intercept the few enterprising Italians who tried to escape westwards to Tobruk. The prisoners themselves seemed to have no sense of military disgrace after their mass surrender, and apparently considered their defection quite natural after the artillery pounding they had taken on the first morning. It was impossible to work up any sort of hatred against them: they were so eager to talk except for the few sullen senior officers who resented being bundled into the backs of trucks with the erstwhile followers.

The Italian equipment was like the curate's egg — all right in parts. Their rifles were crude in comparison with our Lee-Enfields, but their light Breda machine-guns were superior to our Brens under desert conditions. They had fixed magazines and were loaded with chargers, which didn't seem such a good idea. Some of their heavy water-cooled machine-guns were of Australian make and had been captured during WWI or surrendered at the Armistice.

After the tedious weeks in the desert, Bardia was a little heaven for the few days we rested there. Tinned fish and unlimited supplies of cognac (mixed with equally plentiful supplies of lemon syrup and Vichy water, it made a good drink) helped to make life pleasant. Ever souvenir conscious, we browsed over the spoils we had won, some finding cameras and jewellery, and all making spoil of decorations and other finery. On the utilitarian side we added trucks and staff cars to our company transport.

On the afternoon of 8 January we moved off on the west road towards Tobruk, not as raw troops but as seasoned campaigners.

Bardia was not a hard-fought action in the Western Front sense of the words. The enemy, never good collective fighters although capable of outstanding acts of individual bravery, had been demoralised badly by the effects of our artillery and the inhibitions of a siege. But it was an important victory at a time when the Allies were being defeated on all other fronts.

Sidi Barrani, Sollum and Fort Capuzzo were mere outposts compared with Bardia. It was Graziani's [Rodolfo Graziani commanded the Italian 10th Army in Libya] first strongly held bastion on the road to Benghazi, and with its fall he lost 2041 officers and 42,827 men, 368 field guns, 26 heavy anti-aircraft guns, 130 tanks and 708 transport vehicles. The effect on already weak Italian morale was considerable.

Reveille, April 1952

NX2621 was the service number of **Private Iain Donald Hay McDougall**, *was born 6 September 1921 in Christchurch, New Zealand. He enlisted at Millers Point, Sydney, in October 1939, serving with the 2/1st Battalion. Wounded near Tobruk, he was discharged in September 1941 and became a regular contributor to the pages of* Reveille *and the* Bulletin. *His service record shows his date of birth as 1917, but his daughter, Christine Colley, explained that McDougall put his age up by four years in order to enlist. He died in Townsville, Queensland, in September 2000.*

Note:

[1] The Australian Comforts Fund was run largely by women volunteers who undertook the majority of administrative and manual work, and was recognised by the Australian Government to support and assist Australia's servicemen and women. The aim of the ACF was to provide free 'comfort' items that were not supplied by the services, such as singlets, socks, pyjamas, cigarettes and tobacco, razor blades, soap, toothbrush, toothpaste, newspapers and magazines. The ACF also provided troops with recreational facilities, rest rooms, sporting equipment, gramophones and records, as well as pencils, paper and postcards so the soldiers could write home.

The Battle of Mahomed Aly Square
By H.J. Moore

It was September 1941 and the Wogs of Alexandria were showing little signs of affection for the Allied forces, who were at this time entrenched on the El Alamein defence works.

Pictures of Winston and FDR, with their British and American flags, had disappeared from most bars and their places were to be taken, no doubt, by Adolf, Benito and Rommel, who, the locals reckoned, would be in Alexandria at any time.

I was on HMS *Jervis* at the time and after a night of revelry in the Fleet Club and several 'Beer Street' cabarets, about 10 of us had reached Mahomed Aly Square around midnight.

Six of us were walking when the other four matelots [sailors] arrived in the semi-blacked-out road to 'Sister Street' in a gharry, an open horse-drawn buggy.

'Bluey' Green, who had elected himself 'captain', offered the driver 10 ackers (about 2/-) for the short ride, but the Wog brushed it aside and let out a stream of 'Gyppo' lingo, which no doubt meant: 'Don't come the raw prawn, Blue, that's not enough!'

Now this sort of argument was standard practice, and Blue patiently offered the 10 piastre note.

But our dark friend snarled and brushed the note aside with one hand, brought the butt of his whip across Blue's face with the other, at the same time screaming out what sounded like 'English custards!'

It was on! Blue was sent sprawling, his face cut; but in a flash he was joined on the ground by the Wog, who was sent flying through the air, propelled by the bony fist of one 'Shorty' Shaw, a five-foot six-inch bundle of fury from Sydney.

The Battle of Mahomed Aly Square

But Egyptian 'courage' rose to the fore, and in a matter of seconds we were surrounded by about 30 to 40 assorted gharry drivers and civvies, who arrived on the scene screaming abuse, and waving long-handled whips, sticks and little but deadly coshes.

Dick Baber, a sailor from Sydney, took charge of the Allied group and ordered a retreat across the square, where we regrouped at the corner of 'Sister Street'.

After a brief pause we charged across the square again and into the bewildered Wogs, who had thought we had gone away. After a short flurry, in which we inflicted severe casualties on the Gyppos, we retreated again, and again after a pause attacked once more.

This tactic we employed several times, each time striking fear into the hearts of the Wogs!

After about 10 minutes Dick decided to deliver a last crushing blow, so, halving our force (we had been reinforced by two Diggers and a Scot sergeant), he sent one half charging across the square, and when they were engaged at close quarters he ordered the other half in from the rear. One Wog, his back against a tree, was swinging a half-full bag of empty bottles around, and with a definite threat.

One of our boys waited until he swung and while he was off balance ran in and delivered a terrific right swing to the jaw, and the Wog slid down the tree, out to the world!

With the Scot doing great work in the clinches with his head, the Wogs finally broke and ran for cover. The battle was won!

Tired and a trifle battered, we retired to the Black Cat Bar, across in 'Sister Street', and revived with a bottle or two.

Monty [Field Marshal Bernard Montgomery] attacked the following month, and finally cleared the Hun out of North Africa, and all the Allied flags and pictures were shown once more in the bars of Alexandria. Peace reigned in Mahomed Aly Square once again.

Mufti, 2 August 1958

Diary of a Digger of Tobruk
By A. Hertzberg, Sergeant, AIF, Abroad

At 2000 hours on Monday, 20 January, we move up to our battle position for the final assault on Tobruk.

We pass many infantry boys, lying low, on the way, and we wish each other good luck. The enemy bring down harassing fire close to our position, but it does not last long. We drop our trails, fill sandbags, and place them around the gun. We can plainly hear enemy machine guns stuttering their cry of defiance as if the 'Ities' scented that a battle was about to begin. If this be their assumption, we will verify it.

We stack about 300 shells around our gun, then decide to have a rest till zero hour, which will be just before dawn.

About 0100 hours I am awakened by gun reports and explosions. Listen to that terrific rumble! We all know that it's our navy once again in action, and they send salvo after salvo crashing into the enemy defences.

Gee! I'm glad the navy is on our side. The 'Ities' are certainly getting to know what our big stuff is like.

At approximately 0300 hours everything is quiet again; but only for a few minutes, as we can hear a plane roaring overhead. It must be ours — we haven't seen an enemy plane for about the last 10 days.

Here is proof as to its identity: *Crash! Crash!* and many more following as sticks of bombs fall into 'Itie' positions.

The enemy reply with AA [anti-aircraft] gunfire and spray the sky with their Breda tracer bullets of red, green and yellow; really a very pretty colour display, but that's about all, as our bomber is continually diving through their barrage and machine-gunning; we can plainly see the white tracer bullets.

The bomber then drops a parachute flare, lays one more egg, and then roars overhead back to its base. Almost immediately another bomber has arrived and is guided to its position by the parachute flare dropped by the previous plane.

Well, the fun starts again. This goes on till 0500 hours when all is silent once more.

So far the Jack Tars and 'Blue Orchids' [Royal Navy and RAF] have done their bit; so just to make the attack a combined service affair, the army of 0535 hours opens up to finish the enemy in no uncertain manner. Our infantry move forward behind our terrific barrage. It is still dark and the flashes from our guns illuminate the battle area with a rather ghostly effect.

We are working furiously, firing as fast as possible. We haven't even time to duck some of the 'Itie' shells which land dangerously close — within feet of us.

If they were British shells I would not be here to relate this narrative; but, fortunately, their shells have a very poor fragmentation effect. Often the shell breaks up into only three parts. Also the rocks that the explosion throws up go practically straight up and not sideways.

We are firing on our final lift a few minutes before dawn. And with the dawn comes the great news that the infantry has broken through. Hurrah! It's over.

We have a sip of rum and a smoke, and I receive two letters from home.

Although most of us are temporarily deaf we discuss the battle — our lucky escapes — and the next item on the programme.

Soon we see hundreds of prisoners file past us.

There is still enemy artillery fire coming from the heavy guns just outside Tobruk. However, our Lysander (plane that does our spotting) soon ranges our guns on the enemy gun positions and after a short duel we put them out of action.

We then range on to an enemy warship that has the audacity to try to escape from Tobruk Harbour. We later see this cruiser burning furiously.

All enemy activity is now silenced and we are complete victors of Tobruk.

After a short rest we push on to Derna as fast as possible. Our morale is very high because of our successes and it is generally thought that this campaign will be over shortly.

With the boys so keen and full of fight, I know that the life of Italian Libya is very limited.

From what I have seen in this campaign, the feature responsible for our success is the coordination of the navy, army and air force. The precision, the force and daring of the coordinated effort displays all that is best in modern strategy.

Please excuse the roughness of this letter as I wrote it in the desert (where there are no tables and chairs).

The Queensland Digger, April 1942

Albert Abraham Hertzberg *was born on 6 May 1917 at Waverley, Sydney, and enlisted at Ingleburn in November 1939. He stayed in the army after the war, was discharged in January 1963 with the rank of Warrant Officer Class 2, and died 20 May 2011.*

Incident in Cairo: 1942
By F.C. Turner

Early in 1942 six Australian Army sisters, during a week's leave in Cairo, went to the cinema. When the film finished, in the gloom, rush and push of a packed crowd, two of us were separated from the others.

Eventually we found a taxi and gave directions to the driver 'George'. He seemed to turn a great many corners and, perhaps foolishly since we were ignorant of the areas, this was mentioned.

Abruptly he was confused. Then suddenly we were in a slum-lane with the taxi up against a dark wall! A crowd of shouting men immediately surrounded the car, pounding on the roof and smacking at the windows. The din was terrific. We sat stunned, and George crouched out of sight. A door was wrenched open and an English private tumbled into the car, slamming the door shut as he fell. He was astounded. 'I heard yelling and saw a taxi in the middle of the mob. What the *hell* are you two girls doing here?'

We explained that we were lost (and so was George), and that we wanted to get to the bridge and the Australians' houseboats. Our welcome guest turned on George who, roused from his terror, backed rapidly out from the dead-end, and with bodies falling or brushed off, we were soon free and in the open road.

We soon reached the bridge, and our hero hurried us along the riverbank, watched us up the gangway and onto the deck. Then, turning smartly, he ran back to the waiting George. Almost there, he looked back, and seeing us still on the deck shouted in despair, 'I'm AWOL and over an hour late. They'll kill me for this.' And the two were off at speed.

Stupefied, we had not thought to open our purses and grab a handful of money for the unfortunate George, nor to ask our rescuer his name. Inexperienced then, we could have still, somehow the next day, contacted a British senior authority to explain the situation and saved our splendid soldier from harsh treatment, or we could have written an explanation as he would have been easily tracked down.

Jess made the only comment on the night's event. 'We didn't even say "thank you".' Nothing was ever again said of the affair during the years we were together. Last Anzac Day I recalled the details of that evening in Cairo.

Fifty-three years later I write about that brave young man who saved us in our hour of need.

I hope the following will convey a little of what so many sisters and VADs felt for soldiers. It was recognised that if a sister (English or Australian) ventured alone into crowds or dubious places, a khaki-clad soldier would always be near her to make sure she was safe. Then he/they would wander off.

Many young girls would have received similar prompt and selfless protection to that given to two Australian sisters in danger, when a young English private 'did not walk by, on the other side'.

To all servicemen of dreadful times, and those who stoically endured pain and lengthy rehabilitation, who in their glorious, crazy youth unknowingly inspired those around them, and for all armed forces — especially the largely unsung, quiet men of the merchant marine service — I have unfailing respect and affection.

The Listening Post, Winter 1996

Florence C Turner (Maletti) *was born 2 April 1913, served in the AAMWS with the service number WFX11187, and died 23 October 2001.*

Ajax Won at Cairo Race Meeting
By Rex C. Testro

Gezira, Cairo's fashionable racecourse, which, until two years ago, was patronised almost exclusively by Egyptians, Greeks and a sprinkling of staid Englishmen, now echoes with the wild shouting and urging of Diggers, as they 'ride' their fancies in true Australian style.

The multimillionaires' playgrounds of Hollywood have nothing on the island paradise of the Gezira Sporting Club, whose square mile of beautiful lawns and meadows is valued at £4,000,000 for the land alone.

An 18-hole golf course that would compare with many of Australia's best, a racecourse, a luxurious swimming pool adjoining an open-air café, a cricket field redolent of a bit of Old England, and some 20 tennis courts comprise some of the attractions of this peacetime retreat of Egypt's wealthy English.

And now, in wartime, all this is open not only to the officers of the Empire forces, but also — with a few reservations — to the troops. Every day you will see British and Dominion troops mingling in play on the football field, playing tennis, taking a welcome dip in the pool, or munching cakes and tea under the shade of the peaceful trees.

At weekends they roll up in force to the races. Unlike Australian courses, Gezira has no bookmakers and betting is confined to the tote, which pays 1, 2, 3 in a field of six; 1, 2 in a field of four. Eight is the average number of starters in a race, and the average distance is seven furlongs.

Almost every European nation is represented among the jockeys, including Italians, French, Greeks and English. The track is very heavily grassed, and the run home from the turn is a little over a furlong [200 metres]. A mystery is the ability of the club to keep the track so well grassed. In Cairo, rain falls only once or twice a year, so artificial watering has to be resorted to.

One of the different ideas at Gezira is the human roller that carefully and correctly levels out the turf after each race. The native turf treaders, about 30 of them, get to work immediately after the race, and every sod that has been disturbed is replaced and trampled into the pattern of the track with an exactness that no machine could equal.

It's primitive but good, and although the Arab nags don't break records, it helps them to cover six furlongs at a shade under 1.22. Who said records!

The Australian national game of two-up rivals the horses for popularity on race days. The Egyptians were mystified at first, on seeing Diggers standing around in a circle throwing pennies up in the air. They caught on, however, and as one Egyptian, who played with the old Diggers of the last war, put it, 'I only go to the races to play pennies with the Diggers.'

Recently, to the delight of the Diggers, a horse named Ajax won a race. Most of the boys backed it. 'With a name like that it just couldn't lose,' said one Digger.

All kinds of pranks are played by the Diggers, and two infantrymen were discovered one day in the jockeys' room, trying to persuade one of the hoops [jockeys] to ride in a race wearing a Digger hat.

Horseracing is much the same the world over, except at Gezira, where, nowadays, the tarbrush and the slouch hat, getting together for the form of the Tobruk Handicap (the main event on the card) is as common as the Pyramids of Giza.

The Australian's thirst for gambling is certainly satisfied by an afternoon at Gezira. It is the nearest thing to Flemington in these parts. But Middle East form has its upsets no less renowned than Australia, and many a Digger walks home to his leave billet with a sad tale of the 'good thing' that just got pipped!

Reveille, May 1942

Rex Clifford Testro, *born on 2 July 1917 in Brisbane, enlisted at Fitzroy, Melbourne, in March 1940. He was discharged in September 1945, with the rank of sergeant, having served in the Australian Entertainment Unit. He was renowned as a comedian and juggler. He died 12 August 1988.*

Ajax *was a champion Australian racehorse in the late 1930s who won 18 consecutive races before being sensationally defeated in a three-horse race in 1939, still the shortest-priced favourite ever beaten in Australia.*

They Dived in with Messerschmitt-Like Accuracy
By 'Dan R' (AIF)

Four lascars squatted on their haunches, their inscrutable brown eyes focused on the vacillatings of a fly. Four copper coins lay on the deck, and suddenly the fly alighted in the centre of them.

A gleam came into the eyes of one of the dark men as the fly sniffed at a coin, then backed away, to return two seconds later and crawl across the copper. Then came an audible sigh from the group of Australian soldiers surrounding the lascars and watching the play.

The lascar owning the coin on which the fly had shown favour collected the other three coppers, while his countrymen each placed a coin once more on the deck, and the game recommenced.

The above incident occurred on the troopship that brought us back from the Middle East. This game did not find favour with the impatient Australians, although a gang of us did make one attempt to popularise it.

'Bluey' won four games in quick succession — the flies invariably attacking his copper with the deadly precision of a Messerschmitt dive-bomber, perhaps because he had immersed his coin in a liquid comprising sugar and water.

But the main relaxation of Australians is two-up. We played two-up on four continents. Every 6th Division soldier will remember the two-up schools at Mersa Matruh.

Before the entry of Italy into the war, some of the early games in Palestine were conducted per medium of empty bottles (redeemable 5 mils, the equivalent of (Aust.) 1 1/2d) or picture tickets worth 20 mils. The game was the thing.

Tel Aviv

There was another big school opposite the Australian canteen in Tel Aviv; New Zealanders, Tommies, Polish, Palestinian and Greek soldiers and airmen, and even civilians were initiated into the mysteries of Australia's national game.

And it was not uncommon to hear a shrill voice belonging to a Yemenite shoe-cleaner mimicking the raucous appeal of the ringkeeper: 'Come on — a coupla quid in the "guts" — a coupla to see him go.'

Original 6th Division men will also remember the big two-up game at 'Madam's' near the seafront in Benghazi.

Inflation

Egyptian money, Italian currency, a bit of English and Palestinian coinage supplemented with discs sold by 'Madam' were used to gamble with, and set a problem in finance which not even a Montagu Norman could stabilise.

Despite the busy time we had in Greece and Crete, at many off occasions 'drachma' would pass hands whenever a two-up game could be arranged. Then came the Syrian campaign and a few days in Beirut, and we were introduced to baccarat.

Favourite

In the pine forest at the rear of the Beirut racecourse were set dozens of small folding tables on which lay greasy packs of well-used cards, with shrewd, keen-faced Assyrians waiting to fleece the unwary.

Housie-housie, minahdinah and a host of other gambles were indulged in, including games of 'crap' with the Americans, but the good old two-up still is and always will remain the favourite of the Digger.

Mufti, 4 January 1958

With the 7th Division Cavalry Regiment
By Norman Grinyer

I was in Sydney when the war started, living at Ashfield, and a member of the Australian Tank Corps at Randwick. I was lying in bed when the announcement came over the radio, and I went and told my father.

We were called up for a 30-day camp and then we did a 90-day camp up at Greta. It was up there that we heard they were forming the 7th Division Cavalry Regiment, and a group of us just went and put our names down. A little man said, 'You can't sign up — you're too young.' So I told him to turn his back for a moment and changed my year of birth from 1920 to 1919. So I had my NX number and we just waited for the call-up, which came in May 1940.

We'd had a lot of experience on tanks by that time — I was a gunner operator, but I could handle anything from driving tanks, to guns, to radios, the lot. The 7th Division Cavalry was comprised mainly of light horsemen from all over NSW and Queensland. I had never handled a rifle in my life. I had handled machine-guns, three-pounder guns and Webley .45 pistols, the whole bit, and I joined a unit, the light horsemen, who were fully rifle-trained and I had to learn it all from the ground up. And learnt by copying, rather than being trained.

We went to Trincomalee [Ceylon/Sri Lanka] because the *Queen Mary* couldn't fit into any other harbour and they transhipped us onto smaller vessels. Ours was the Bibby Line's *Lancashire*. We went from Trincomalee to Colombo, and then formed a convoy and went across to Port Tawfiq [Suez Canal, Egypt]. There we got our first air raid. I was posted onto the anti-aircraft gun — 3.7-

inch gun on the poop deck of the *Lancashire* — and we camped around the gun on a 24-hour watch.

I woke up to the sound of a thunderstorm — looked around and thought we were in for a bit of rain. The thunderstorm continued, and I looked out and an air raid had developed. There were flashes in the air, and shells exploding, and aeroplanes flying over. I immediately climbed out and got the gun into operational position and looked for the crew. I rang the bridge and said I had the gun elevated and a shell up the breech, and 'What do I do now?' They said, 'Don't fire the bloody thing!' It transpired that the gun crew on duty had gone down below for a quiet smoke. There was an anti-panic squad on board, to stop anyone panicking in the event of an air raid, and their task was to keep everyone below decks. So there was the gun crew down below, trying to get back up, being told by the anti-panic squad to get back downstairs, and the gun was unattended!

We couldn't go any further so they sent us on by train to El-Qantarah — we crossed the Suez Canal there — and up by train again to Dimra outside Gaza. It was a lovely night — we arrived at two o'clock in the morning, it had been raining, and the whole place was a sea of mud. You'd throw your gear down in the mud, wrap a groundsheet around you, and sleep for the rest of the night. Introduction to Palestine! Why we were fighting over it I don't know.

We were equipped with light-horse equipment — light-horse bandoliers, light-horse water bottles; we were fully equipped as light horsemen. We had no webbing equipment. We had no pack. We had a sea kit bag, and our kit bag, and a haversack. We were completely unprepared for war. Within 24 hours they'd sent an emissary to us, asking for volunteers to go up into the desert. I think there were 400 captured Italian tanks up in Tripolitania. Nine of us volunteered to go up and take over some of these tanks and use them because we had no equipment. So we chuffed off by train down to Amariya, just outside Alexandria, then by road up to Mersa Matruh, then a bit further up to Charing Cross — some of these were British names dubbed into various areas up there. We were going to pick up those tanks, then they wheeled us back to Amariya and slapped us on 24 hours' notice to take these tanks to Greece in the *Illustrious*.

We were anchored in Alexandria for a while. Then they withdrew that order, even though we were all packed and ready to go to Greece. They handed the tanks over to the Greek Army because they had nothing either, and they told us we'd better get back to our own unit. Then the regiment was moved to near Cairo and we were sent to a school at Abassia — the Royal Tank Corps headquarters was at Abassia so we bowled in there to do a couple of courses on tank gunnery etc.

The 6th Division Cavalry Regiment had been up in the desert, and they'd been shoved back. We were fully equipped but the decision was made that 6th Division Cavalry would take all our equipment and go back up to the desert. So they threw us on a rotten old ship, the *Warsaw*, and headed us off to Cyprus because the threat was Greece, Crete, Cyprus, Palestine, Turkey, Syria — they were after the Suez Canal. So we went to Cyprus with broken-down tanks that we'd picked up in Abassia — some of them wouldn't steer, some wouldn't go — and we went to Nicosia, and by this time we were picking up a few survivors from Crete.

While we were on Cyprus the Jerries took over Crete and Rhodes, and they used to visit us regularly and bomb the airfields. There was a squadron of torpedo bombers that came off the *Illustrious* and was stationed on a secret hidden airfield on Cyprus. I verified this after the war as best I could. These Swordfish aircraft were equipped with radar and they'd go out at night and locate targets, and sink them. Of course we always knew if they'd had a successful night because the next morning we'd cop all the bombers coming over looking for them but they'd bomb the wrong airfield. One of these Swordfish came in early one morning and pranged into a swamp. Our blokes raced out to help them and there was a small explosion in the cockpit, which alerted us that there was a radar screen in there that they'd destroyed. The bloke in the observer's seat had the radar and was directing the pilot.

We were four months on Cyprus, expecting a landing. We knew that in Cairo, unofficially, they'd put a red line through our unit — we were expendable. I was a radio operator in regimental headquarters by now, and we knew semiofficially that there was a three-month supply of food for us in the mountains and there was an area that was very heavily defended with wire etc. I was one of a group of 20 whose task was to blow seven bridges as we retreated up into the mountains, and we were to play guerrilla warfare if the Jerries landed.

We didn't know what commandos were — this was all foreign to us. So we formed ourselves into what we called 'Ned Kelly' gangs — a group of four or five of us. I had a 100-round bandolier slung round my neck, 40 rounds in my basic pouches, a pistol, my rifle, three Bren gun magazines in panniers each side of my pack, my blanket, a couple of pairs of socks, two or three tins of bully beef, some biscuits — we were Australians. And we had been trained to be self-sufficient, and we knew what we would take. We stood by for this — but it didn't happen.

They threw us on a destroyer, HMS *Havock*, and high-tailed us across to Haifa and up to Mount Carmel — this war was a story of unpreparedness, of panic stations, the whole thing! We got up to Mount Carmel — a regiment of 500 blokes, and they didn't know we were coming. They had nothing prepared for us, no transport or anything else.

Eventually they got us up to Tripoli and sorted us out, and we went into Syria, right up to the Turkish border. The road up along the coast was built up against the sea — there were mountains on the right, the sea on the left, and the one road. We were coming back — a division of 20,000 men being brought down that road — and the 9th Division, 20,000 men, going up the same road. Couldn't organise a bunfight at a Sunday school picnic!

I did a long-range patrol up to the Turkish border, preparing or nominating positions to hold the German Army. We were expecting the Germans to break their truce with Turkey and we were expecting them to come down, so we were picking positions where we could hold the German Army. We had tanks — mostly captured French tanks, Renaults, and some of our own. The plan was to make a second Tobruk at Tripoli, to guard the coast road.

Eventually the Germans didn't break through, and they withdrew us. We went back to Port Said or Port Tawfiq, arrived back at night, and all the ships were lined up, and they more or less said, 'Well, there's all the ships — get yourselves aboard — get yourselves back home.' So we went along the wharves, and questioned all the ships — was there space for us? No. Packed tight. Can't get aboard. So we broke into a warehouse and made ourselves comfortable. The British redcaps, military police, came in and ordered us out, and we ordered them out and told them what we'd do to them if they tried to disturb us. We were fighting troops and they were just a mob of bastards. So next morning we went out and went along the line of ships, and were told we could come aboard one ship — this was the *Sophocles*. There was accommodation for 20 men aboard, the troops' accommodation was full, they were sleeping anywhere they could on the deck, and provided we could bring some food with us we could come aboard. So we went back to the warehouse and kicked open some crates of bully beef. We bought our passage out of there with food!

We arrived back in Fremantle, and we had all the equipment, guns and the headquarters of the 2/3rd Machine-gun Battalion. They landed the 2/3rd Machine-gun Battalion with no guns, just a rifle and 20 rounds or something, and we had their headquarters and all their guns aboard the *Sophocles*. A couple of our blokes volunteered to transfer to them and help them rebuild it.

Then we went to Adelaide. We came off the ship after being at sea for 10 weeks, and stooged around Morphettville for a while. The regiment had been on nine different ships. So they sent search parties out all round Adelaide — there were some people quartered in private homes, some sleeping in parks, anywhere at all in Morphettville Racecourse. They told us there'd be trucks to take us to Sandy Creek, near Gawler, and the trucks would have a sign saying 'showground'. But the trucks were all lined up and not one of them had a sign saying 'showground' so we all headed to the nearest pub.

But we got to Sandy Creek and reformed there — and did some long-range patrols around the vineyards. Met quite a lot of the locals and drank a lot of the local produce. Of course you'd go out for a route march and when it got hot and dusty, someone would lean over a fence. 'You blokes thirsty? Yes — come up here and we'll find you something to drink!'

Then someone obviously knew we were going to the tropics. We were ordered to cut our blankets in two — take half a blanket, your groundsheet and a mosquito net. The tropics, you know it's hot up there, and don't need a full blanket! We didn't realise it became very cold at night. My first night in New Guinea, we were taken off the *Katoomba* and put on trucks, and taken out to Wards Strip [military airfield] and dumped. There was a Mitsubishi fighter up the end, half buried, and bits of bones scattered around, flying boots with skeletons of feet in them, and that was it. No amenities, not even a tent. I remember my first night I tied my mosquito net between two trees and camped there on the deck, and I woke up in the morning and the whole of my net was covered in caterpillars about two inches long. A nice greeting!

I finished up getting malaria, amoebic dysentery, the lot. So I was brought home in February 1943 and spent three months in hospital in Bathurst sorting myself out.

Reveille, 2003, interview with author

Norman Robert Grinyer's *date of birth on his service record (22 July 1919) does indeed show he made out he was a year older than he really was. He enlisted in May 1940 and was discharged in September 1943 as a trooper with the 7th Division Cavalry Regiment. He died 16 June 2009.*

Rats with Guts
By 'Poopdeck', ex-2/13 Battalion

After being rats in a trap — according to Lord Haw-Haw — for seven months inside the Tobruk perimeter, we were to be relieved and returned to Palestine to rest — and we sure needed that rest. Tobruk, with close proximity to the enemy at all times, had no safe areas, and those seven months had been long. We needed something more than a rest, I guess.

All units of the Australian 9th Division except ours were gone; we were the last to be relieved, and in the darkness of night we clambered aboard trucks with our equipment and were driven to the harbour.

Ferried out to the *San Giorgio*, the burnt-out hulk of an Italian cruiser resting on the bottom in shallow water, we were told that a British destroyer would lift us in the vicinity of midnight. Cheered by this information, the lads lay back in the darkness of the foul-smelling 'tween decks, smoking, sweating, searching by Braille for our lice — unimportant details at this stage, we thought — and talking; about women. About everything that one could expect to find and enjoy in a country that had a lot of the good things of civilisation.

'Whacko!' we said. For a couple of hours it went on. When the hands of my luminous watch registered 1.30 a.m. we had been silent for a long while. No one was really surprised when the OC came down and told us — you could see that he hated to do this to us — that the destroyer had been sunk, the operation was cancelled.

Silently we made the return trip to the beach and into the same trucks. As we turned the Eagle corner, dance music from

Cairo could be heard coming over the radio in the provost control post, and some cow laughed — said a funeral march would be more apt.

To some of the lads who died on patrols, and the 74 killed at El Duda within the next few weeks, it was in fact a funeral march. The sweet music seemed to write *mafeesh* ['nothing'] to all our hopes, and as the trucks rolled on through clouds of sand towards the line, nine miles up the Derna Road, I'll swear that no man gave a thought to Alexandria or Tel Aviv, to beer or to bints.

Thoughts of all sped back to Australia, to home and to all the things that go with home, and those thoughts were urgent on account of the fear that this might be the last chance to reach out mentally, back to our world before Hitler.

No one could reasonably expect his luck to last forever.

Reveille, December 1948

El Alamein: Gate of the Road to Victory
By A.E. Bannear

On 23 October 1942 a battle began in the Western Desert that, with Stalingrad, turned the tide of fortune for the Allies. This battle, now known in world history as the (Second) Battle of El Alamein, began at 9.40 p.m. and continued without a stop until approximately 5 p.m. on 5 November 1942.

We who were there remember that day. We also remember the months before that day. The grim, bitter struggle for Tel el Eisa, and the many white crosses on that bare and barren slope. The Battle for Ruin Ridge, and our failure. 'Bulimba' Raid and the costly but valuable lesson learnt. The tenseness when the German Panzers punched solidly down behind Ruweisat Ridge, and the dull mutter of guns and bombs that meant the death of 300 German and Italian tanks.

There followed a period of quietness while the reinforced 8th Army prepared for the great day. We remember that day, hot and sultry and a mass of towering storm clouds. A day of no movement, save for one fighter-bomber attack on the enemy positions on the Clover Leaf feature.

Then came that night, with rapidly clearing skies. A brilliant desert moon rose at eight o'clock. An evening of silence, save for the occasional burst of machine-gun fire or the discharge of a field gun. Night birds called eerily from the swamps near the coast; otherwise an uncanny silence in the tense atmosphere.

At zero hour, 2140 hours, nearly a thousand field guns thundered the opening chorus and turned night into day with their stabbing lances of white flame. Their target was the German and Italian field guns. Under the overwhelming weight of bursting shells the enemy gunners perished or fled. Then came another 10 minutes of 'cease fire' while guns altered range to enemy infantry positions. Our infantry moved forward with naked bayonets, and amid them rumbled the tanks, in close support.

At 10 p.m. the real fighting began as the two great armies locked, and throughout the night the 8th Army advanced.

In the Australian sector, the 20th and 26th Brigades moved in while the 24th Brigade staged a great firework display on the coastal strip. The engineers cleared the deep minefield with thresher tanks — known to us as the Scorpions. Above us the RAF bombers droned ceaselessly, and their heavy weight of bombs fell on the gun positions and strong posts of the dazed enemy.

We remember those 12 days. The infantry who fought stubbornly into enemy positions in the smoke-stained moonlight, and by day held their thin line against the savage counterattacks of the Afrika Korps. Those 25 full-blooded attacks that hammered 'the thumb' up above Point 29 in the daylight hours of early November. The RAF that did a magnificent job in close support. Their famous 18 light bombers crumbled the enemy morale with their perfect formation, their regularity and their faultless bombing.

Behind the lines, the artillery, the medical and service corps kept the shells flying over, the supplies and water coming forward, and cared for the wounded. The gunners slept for brief periods in their gun pits, ready at a moment's notice to answer calls from the hard-pressed men out in the front.

We remember the vicious tank battle that developed in front of the New Zealand division's lines, and the black columns of oily smoke that marked the death of men and machines. Then came the night of 3/4 November, when the armoured divisions got through, and the tide slowly turned in our favour.

Out of the blue came the intelligence report that the Germans were mining their dead. This was an indication to us that it was nearly all over. Grim news, but welcome.

We remember the end of the battle that came about 5 p.m. when every aircraft under the command of the 8th Army went over to be in the kill and to harass the fleeing and confused enemy. Rommel was defeated, and in his defeat he abandoned the Italian Army and escaped with what was left of the proud and arrogant Afrika Korps.

On this day we who were there pause for a moment of thought for the many comrades who lie in the ridge under the hot Egyptian sun barely a mile from El Alamein railway station.

Back (South Australia), October 1947

Albert 'Alby' Edward Bannear, *born on 19 December 1915, enlisted at Wayville, SA, in July 1940 and served as a bombardier, being discharged in 1945 with the rank of corporal. He became a noted local historian in the Clare Valley and died 18 December 1986.*

Mussolini's Way
By John M. McWilliam, MM

During the chase to Benghazi, our mechanised unit was held up at the village of D'Annunzio [known as El Bayyada, 140 kilometres east of Benghazi] owing to the retreating Italians having blown all bridges on the pass. I was sent out with 50 sappers to make a detour round one of the gaps.

I went to a farmhouse to borrow a barrow.

'Can you speak English?' I inquired of the farmer.

'I can speak Australian,' he replied. 'I come from Southern Cross, in West Australia, where I make farm,' he continued.

'After seven years, I think I go to Italy to get my wife and two boys. My neighbour look after farm till I come back.

'When I reach Italy, Mussolini he send for me and say, "What do you do here?" I tell him I bring the money to get the family. I had £600.

'Mussolini he take it and give me £80, and say, "You be down at the boat tonight and take your wife and boys to colonise Libya."'

That was seven years ago, and that poor old peasant still dreams of getting his freedom and returning to Australia!

Reveille, February 1942

John Mathew McWilliam *was born at Merrylands, Sydney, on 28 December 1908. He enlisted at Paddington and joined the 2/1st Field Company. In 1941, as a lance sergeant, he was awarded the Military Medal, and he was discharged in October 1945 with the rank of lieutenant. He died 9 November 1995.*

The War at Sea

'When you've got four destroyers coming at you and they all let go torpedoes, there's not much chance of you dodging the lot of them.'

— Fred Taylor

HMAS Yarra: A Survivor's Story
By Alfred George Orton

On 4 March 1942 HMAS Yarra *was in the Timor Sea, escorting the tanker* Francol, *the depot ship* Anking *and the small motor minesweeper No. 51 from Jakarta to Fremantle. The convoy was confronted by a Japanese fleet of three heavy cruisers and two destroyers.* Yarra's *captain, Lieutenant Commander Robert Rankin, positioned his ship between the enemy and the convoy, fighting to the end. All four ships were sunk and of the* Yarra's *crew of 151 officers and men, only 13 were to survive. Alf Orton was one of those.*

On breaking daylight we were confronted by a task force of three cruisers and some destroyers coming at us fast. Our captain immediately laid a smokescreen to protect the convoy and ordered ships to scatter in all directions.

We were soon under heavy fire as the Japs had us circled. We were taking so many hits that it was only a matter of time. We were being blown to pieces and the captain gave the order to abandon ship.

I left my gun and proceeded to my station post Carley raft, which lay at a 45-degree angle on a chute with a wire rope connected to a slip. I slipped the raft and with superhuman strength landed it over the side. I proceeded to the starboard and slipped the other raft over. I then made it back to my gun to report to Commander Smith that the rafts were over the side.

My life jacket was already blown away and then there was a terrible surge of air and noise and I was blown over the side.

When I came to, the *Yarra* was on her port side, with the twin screws still turning. A tin of biscuits floated past and I managed to grab it.

I had lost my boots, a sock, a glove and half my overalls, and I was bleeding from the nose and ears. I made it to one of the rafts, put the tin of biscuits aboard, and hooked my arm through the life ropes. There were a lot of wounded people in the water, and we gently lifted them onto the raft and continued to hold on for our lives.

The Japs then circled us looking for officers, but we were all dressed in the same battle station rig. A large cruiser came alongside and I'll never forget looking up at the Jap sailors grinning down at us.

The cruiser made a 160-degree turn, swamping the rafts in its wake. We righted them and scrambled back, losing quite a few men in the incident. The rafts and a plank that had drifted off the timber rack were filled to capacity and we were all up to our necks in the sea.

We spent the first day silent and dejected. We had not had a decent sleep since the fall of Singapore and, having no food, we were not in a very good position to survive what lay ahead of us. We lost men that day as some were too weak to hang on and we were powerless to help them. You'd be surprised at the number of sailors who can't swim.

The sun was very hot and we were relieved when it went down. But we shivered that night and waves were continually breaking over our heads. That night we lost 26 men and prayed for the sun to come up as we were chilled to the bone.

When it eventually did, to our horror, we were surrounded by sharks. Huge brutes they were, continually circling us but not attacking. Only when we lost a man over the side would we look away. It is in such predicaments that men turn to religion. The Catholics on the rafts crossed themselves continually. The worst time for shark attacks is dusk. That evening, as the sun went down, they came in to attack. One would make a pass and then the others followed.

That night they tore away the men hanging over the sides. All we could do was smash the water with paddles. We lost another 14 men.

After that terrible night we faced a new day in rafts more buoyant because of the loss of so many men. I learnt that I was the leading seaman aboard and had to get some routine going if we were to survive. At nine o'clock in the morning, by my reckoning, I thought it appropriate to say the prayer we all know in the navy. So I got the men to hang their heads while I conducted a service in what was a very strange place indeed.

'Protect us from the violence of the enemy (which He did) and the raging seas, so that we may return to the land, and enjoy the fruits of our labour. Amen!'

A rating then asked where I thought we were, and I lied and said not far from Darwin. I said that if we kept paddling south we would make it, as patrol boats from Darwin would be looking for us. This settled a few of them down and gave them heart. But the truth was we were 250 miles from the nearest land.

We were now into our third day and it was starting to play on us all, some worse than others. The terrible sun was beating down on us. We had no water and the tin of biscuits had drifted away in the rough seas. Some ratings started to drink salt water and some held their heads under. I told them to stop but when I wasn't looking they'd do it again. We were attacked again that night by the sharks and lost more men. There were 17 on our raft, with none over the sides. But we were still up to our necks in water.

By this time we had had no water or food for five days and the men were throwing salt water on their faces and eating seaweed as it drifted past. There were only 13 of us left, and I tore strips off my life jacket and passed them to the men to suck on, to keep the saliva going in their mouths. We ate rubber, buttons, our singlets and seaweed, but the privation was taking its toll. We were burnt black by the sun and froze at night. We cursed the sun coming up and we cursed it going down. We cursed the sharks, the sea snakes and the insects that bit us all night. By this time we were unable to talk, only croak. We sat at a 45-degree angle on the raft and hugged each other for warmth at night and got a few hours' sleep.

Some of the things that happened on the raft are painful to record but I think it is my duty to do so. One rating stood up in the raft and said he could see his wife in the distance and was going over the side to meet her. He swam away, and I ordered the men to look in the opposite direction.

When a warship enters harbour the first man ashore is the duty postman. One man asked us if we had any letters to post as he was going ashore to get the mail. He then swam away. Another rating confided in me that there was a cellar full of food under the raft. When it got dark he was going down to get some and share it with me. I couldn't convince him it wasn't true, and we never saw him again.

I am really convinced that the rating saw his wife, the postie felt his duty was to go ashore, and the other rating had his cellar full of food under the raft.

By this time we had stopped paddling as all our strength was gone. Our buttocks were red raw with the chafing of the canvas raft and covered with huge saltwater ulcers. It was agony to move. All we could do was stare at the endless ocean.

We all had our visions. I used to see a spit post sticking out of the sea. It is clear to this day.

I looked for it one day just before sundown, and sure enough, it was there. I told the other men, 'It seems different this evening.'

Then I saw it move. It wasn't a spit post. It was the conning tower of a submarine, coming towards us.

I stripped off my half overalls and hung them from a paddle. The men held me while I waved. The submarine circled us and

I could see the officers scanning us with binoculars. It must have been obvious from our emaciated appearance that we were shipwrecked.

They came alongside the raft and threw a rope. One by one I put it round the ratings, and the sailors (they were Dutch) heaved them onto the submarine. I was the last to go, but those stupid Dutch sailors — curse them and bless them — pulled me off as the raft was under water. Like the christening of a ship, I hit my head on the side of the submarine. Bloody hell! With all I had been through, now I had a bump on my head. I don't remember them carrying me into the submarine.

The Dutch submarine K11 took the 13 survivors to Ceylon (Sri Lanka) where they were admitted to hospital. After recuperating they were taken back to Fremantle.

The Listening Post, Autumn 1986

Alfred George Orton *was born at Subiaco, Perth, on 16 November 1915. He enlisted at Fremantle in April 1940 and was discharged with the rank of able seaman in December 1943, his last posting being HMAS Leeuwin. He later served in the merchant navy. He wrote this memoir shortly before he died on 4 May 1985 from lung cancer, aged 68.*

Out of School and Under Kamikaze Attack
By Gilburd 'Gibb' Woods

I was at school at Cranbrook, in Sydney's eastern suburbs, when the war started. I was not of a very high scholastic persuasion so towards the end of my time at school in 1943 I thought, *Where am I?* and *What am I going to do?* I knew a couple of fellows who'd been in the navy a couple of years, and I was very impressed with them and their attitude. They said it wasn't an easy life but it was good and a close community. So I went and put my name down for the navy. And when the school certificate was over, I didn't pay much attention to it because I knew I was heading for the navy as soon as I could get there. Also I knew my mother wouldn't sign any papers for the army or the air force, and the navy would take you at 17.

As soon as I could I was down at the naval recruiting depot and they said they'd have to leave it to the first week of January. So I went in the first week of 1944 as an ordinary seaman 2nd class at the age of 17 and a half, and straight off to Flinders Naval Depot — and that started my career in the navy.

I'm very fortunate in many ways because I've lived an interesting life. I came from the land. I know what very hard work is, and as a kid for many years I used to help out in the shearing shed and do anything else that was going — lumping wheat, harvesting — and I knew all sorts of people. I've always got on with people, so I didn't find going into the navy very hard at all — as a matter of fact I was in my element.

I was quite a large person then. I think the last year I was playing football I was six foot two [1.9 metres] and 16 stone [100 kilograms] at the age of 17, so I didn't have too many worries,

Out of School and Under Kamikaze Attack

and until the last few years I've always been physically fit. I think that's a great help.

I met all sorts of characters in the navy, from all walks of life, enjoyed their company, and we got on terribly well. Because I had a broken nose with a bit of a dent in it, a few of the leading seamen thought I must have been keen on fighting. Of course in the navy if you're a pugilist you go up a couple of marks, and I had great trouble assuring them that I wasn't and I didn't even like boxing. But I ended up being called 'The Nose'.

We had no desire to do anything but start off and work our way through and make sure you know what you're doing. This was the impression I'd been given by the fellows I met in my last year of school — don't go to officers' training school, even if you're asked, until you've done a year at sea. And that was the best advice I've ever been given in my life.

From Flinders I got a draft immediately to HMAS *Australia*, and we travelled all the way from Sydney to Milne Bay to see her sailing out as we arrived to join her. So after a few days in Milne Bay, a good friend and I thought, *This place is no good — you could die here in this terrible climate*, so we carefully went down to one of the merchant ships there (the *Merca*, I think it was), and asked them if they were short of any seamen. 'Oh yes — we're short of two stokers [workers who stoke the furnace]. Start tomorrow morning — have your gear on board.' So we didn't say anything to anyone and just walked onto the *Merca* with our gear as stokers. Having been an old salt for six months we knew our way around and found a spare cabin on the upper deck which we occupied until we got to Townsville. So from Townsville we just said we were on draft to HMAS *Australia* and went by train to Sydney and joined her. I remember the officer saying as we reported on board, 'Where did you two come from? There's supposed to be another 10 or 15 of you.' We just said we were lucky and found our way back!

We were in Sydney for a couple of weeks while the *Australia* did a quick update on radar in particular. Then we headed off back to the Admiralty Islands, two degrees south of the equator, which was our base. Seeadler [harbour on Manus Island] was probably the biggest harbour in the world — absolutely full of ships, never seen anything like it.

Then we went to various places, giving support bombardment for Biak, and did the invasion of Morotai.

And then the difficult times started. We did Leyte first and got badly knocked around by kamikazes. The Yanks wouldn't let us go back to Australia, because we were too valuable with the new radar we had, which was superior to theirs, and we did more of the incoming raids, which were numerous, than anyone. And the Japs knew it, so they always had us in their minds. So we went back to the Admiralty Islands and then over to Espiritu Santo. We were put in this enormous dry dock and they completely rebuilt the eight-inch director right on top of the ship, along with a whole lot of other things that had been severely damaged by fire from the kamikazes that had hit us. We were back in the Admiralty Islands by late December, and unfortunately — we didn't know it at the time — they were getting us ready to go to the Lingayen Gulf, which was MacArthur's next step. MacArthur being MacArthur, it had to be done his way!

It was probably an even more dangerous frolic than the Leyte one because we seemed to be mistaken for an aircraft carrier and we had five Japanese planes actually hit us. So we had our share!

It's rather terrifying. The dedication, or the intent, of the pilots was frightening. These were the first sustained kamikaze attacks there'd been and we began to see a pattern. The pattern was always to head for the bridge where all the commanding officers and the brains of the ship were — and of the fleet, in some cases. And the number of hits they made on ships on the bridge was quite amazing.

I'd been rated as having very good eyesight so my day position was up in the air defence position above the bridge. It was fascinating because you could hear everything that was going on, and they relied a lot on us, because apart from the radar, we were the eyes. Because I was also fairly strong, my position in action was in the four-inch shell-handling room, which is damn hard work. You'd be picking up shells and putting them in a hoist, and they weighed a fair bit each — unending, and it was about 105 degrees Fahrenheit [40 degrees Celsius], and they had coir mats on the floor so you wouldn't slip. It was amazing — you're right down in the bowels of the ship so you hear lots of thuds and bangs and you don't know what's going on.

After the Leyte Gulf action I finished up in the air defence position full-time — not a comfortable place to be, I might add. I was lucky because in the time I was up there, they only knocked off one of the three funnels behind us and just missed the bridge, and although we received numerous hits we never sustained them to that area again. We were hoping on a theory of 'once hit, twice shy' as far as the bridge was concerned.

But you know the only way you were going to get the kamikazes was to shoot them. The firepower that was brought to bear upon them was just enormous because there were so many hundreds of ships there, and they used to fly right through it. I think we used to amaze the Americans because they'd never seen a major ship use its main armament for anti-aircraft defence and we quite often used the 18-inch guns for a barrage, calculated to meet the plane on the way in — very destructive. The casualties were fairly high in upper-deck personnel — a few of us were very fortunate. My only wound was from being hit by a flying rivet! And for an 18-year-old, it was a pretty amazing experience.

Certainly I think this helped make me as a person in later years — having seen what went on and how it was handled by the crew. It stays in your mind and you don't give up — it's as simple as that.

HMAS *Australia* was then headed for England for repairs because they couldn't do it here, and we all expected to go to England with her. Unfortunately a lot of us were down on what they called a CW1 sheet, which was the captain's recommendation for officer training school, and they'd been signed, and the next thing we knew we were off the ship three days before she sailed. None of us was very happy about that, and we all ended up staying as able seamen and doing gunnery courses, radar courses, asdic [Allied Submarine Detection Investigation Committee, the first anti-submarine detection device] courses. *Watson* then became my home base.

Reveille, 2003, interview with author

Gilburd William Edward Woods *was born on 11 April 1926 at Baan Baa, NSW, and enlisted in January 1944. He was discharged as an able seaman in July 1946, his last posting being HMAS* Rushcutter. *He died 31 July 2004.*

The Luck of the Draw
By Frank Glover

When I was a boy I was in the Navy League Sea Cadets in Newcastle, and when we came to Sydney I stayed in it. There I first learned about destroyers. The two foundation ships were the *Parramatta* and *Yarra*, and they used to moor in Iron Cove along with the other two ships in that class, the *Warrego* and the *Swan*, and we used to go on board at the weekend and stay overnight to gain experience and training. That was *Yarra* One.

Then war broke out and I finished up being drafted to *Yarra* Two. I became the captain's secretary there, and was also in gunnery control. I spent two years on her — we went to the Red Sea and the Mediterranean, we went to the Persian Gulf, and we were the only Aussie ship ever that went all the way up to Basra. We did the patrol right up to Iraq and Iran with the Gurkhas. Then Iran came into the picture and we destroyed the Iranian navy base at Khorramshahr and destroyed the whole of the Iranian Navy — we did three gunboats and one sloop, knocked them out of action. Then they moved us down around the bottom of Iran and we caught eight enemy ships hiding in there. No one knows too much about the Persian Gulf because it was never elaborated on.

We spent four months on the Tobruk run, taking supplies in and bringing out the wounded. There used to be only one or two ships and us, or we'd do it alone. That's where *Parramatta* was sunk. We got written off there. We got bombed by 36 Stukas [Junkers Ju 87 or Stuka was a German dive bomber and ground-attack aircraft] — they never let up on us. We were written off by the Mediterranean Fleet headquarters and when we got back in we were popping rivets and everything everywhere.

We even survived our first convoy in the Red Sea. We had a big convoy and we were on the starboard wing and we were attacked by two Italian destroyers. We thought they were British until we caught them out on the coded identification. They let a couple of fish [torpedoes] go at us so we came up between the two fish but then as soon as we saw them coming, the skipper got us between them and away went the two forward guns. That bashed one of the destroyers so we got the first hits on that. Meantime the two British K-Class [destroyers] we were expecting arrived on the scene, and they got into the fun and games. One Italian was finally sunk and the second was beached at Masturah. Then we were on mine-sweeping before convoys — as they'd come up we'd let a little two-pounder go, and up she'd go. We did that quite frequently.

We used to call the *Yarra* 1500 tons of fighting fury. We were a very happy ship. We had a very good captain, a very good seaman, Harrington [Lieutenant Commander W. H. Harrington], who became chief of the naval staff. (I later attended his wedding and the christening of his son, who became a rear admiral, Simon Harrington.)

Eventually we finished up being directed to Trincomalee and we went on the Burma run. We were then diverted down through Malaya into the Sumatra Straits, taking convoys into Singapore, and we took the last of the British ships in, like the *Empress of Asia*. We had a convoy coming in and they all got bombed, and we got three Zeros. We went alongside the *Empress of Asia* and took 2000 troops off while she was on fire and being bombed, and took them into the dock. We were assisted by either the *Bendigo* or *Ballarat*. Then we assisted in getting the *Vendetta* out of dock; we towed her out and handed her over to a tug which eventually took her down to Fremantle.

We then were back again and picked up a convoy, which was the depot ship, the *Nanking*, and two other ships, and we had to bring them across to Batavia. We refuelled there and got orders to go home. Then a change of command took place between Rankin [Lieutenant Commander Robert William Rankin] and Harrington, and we were waiting there. *Hobart* was ready to go so we jumped ship with the captain and came home on the *Hobart*, taking four other ships of the convoy, and she got through Sunda Strait. Four days later the *Yarra* and its convoy were sunk in the Java Sea — it's just the luck of the draw.

I was rotten with malaria and a few other things so I came ashore. Then I went to the *Canberra*. I went on a promotional course — then she went up to the Solomons and she went down, so it was one of those things. I finished up on quite a few different jobs, and was with the British fleet on the admiral's staff, and then I went to Seventh Fleet on the admiral's staff, and finished up back again in the navy and became a movements man.

I'm the only bloke left who's been on *Yarra* One and served on *Yarra* Two; I've seen *Yarra* Three commissioned and decommissioned and sent to India for scrap, and now seen *Yarra* Four's keel laid, seen her launched, and I'll be at her commissioning.

Reveille, 2003, interview with author

Francis Joseph Glover, *was born at Newcastle, 21 July 1917, enlisted in September 1939 and was discharged with the rank of leading writer in July 1946, his last posting being to HMAS Kuttabul. He died 5 August 2017, just weeks after celebrating his 100th birthday.*

The Sinking of HMAS Perth
By Fred Taylor

Fred Taylor is typical of so many young men who joined the Royal Australian Navy and found themselves serving on the other side of the world. It was the luck of the draw in many instances as to which ship they were posted to, and what happened to that ship. For Fred, it was HMAS Perth, service in the Mediterranean and South-East Asia, and, ultimately, time as a prisoner of the Japanese.

I was born at Subiaco in Western Australia and joined the navy in 1938 when the Italian turn-up was on. I was on the *Vampire*, and then I went to the *Perth*, across to the Middle East, and we got there the day before Christmas 1940. We did convoys in the Mediterranean, to Malta and all over the place up there. We were in the evacuation of Greece and Crete.

Every time we stuck our noses outside Alexandria Harbour we got pelted. They only had to come from Rhodes — only a hop, step and a jump — and they were on us. The same thing happened at Malta. We were only there for five minutes and bang! They were on us. We were in action against the Italian fleet and the German planes. The British had one aircraft carrier, the *Illustrious* — she had a hole blown in her you could have run a train through.

They dropped a bomb between us and the wharf. The bomb dropped on an ammunition ship there, and they sent out a signal to send help to put the fire out. But the joke was the way the signal was worded: that if you put the fire out, many lives would be saved. But they didn't say if you didn't put the fire out, you'd be blown to buggery.

And there was this cross, of Christ crucified, on the wall of this church they'd bombed — everything was in ruins and this cross was still fixed to the wall.

Then our silly bloody commander and I had a run-in. Malta is all limestone, and I'd lost my cap, and my uniform was all white from this limestone. He put me on a charge for being improperly dressed — for being minus a cap and filthy uniform. As luck would have it, we lost him and we got Waller [Captain Hector 'Hec' MacDonald Laws Waller] as our captain, and he read the charge and said, 'Case dismissed.'

When you were on convoys, you hardly got any sleep. They were on to you all the time. They knew where you were and when you were going out. I was on the bridge — captain's bridge messenger. Then I went for a torpedo rating and got that, and was in the torpedo party. During the evacuation of Greece and Crete, first we took them to Crete, then we had to take them off again. It was one stuff-up after another. Too many bloody heads and not enough chicken to go round!

Then we got hit at Malta and we [HMAS *Perth*] came home and did convoys around the Australian coast. Then when the *Sydney* got sunk we were sent up as a relief and got to Java at the wrong time to take part in the evacuation. We got tied up with the Java squadron, and went round off Surabaya and joined in the fun there until we got hit in the Sunda Strait.

We sank seven destroyers and they sent in four destroyers at us because we were doing the most damage. When you've got four destroyers coming at you and they all let go torpedoes, there's not much chance of you dodging the lot of them. We dodged half of them, but there were too many. I reckon we were hit by about six.

Those silly bloody life jackets — they were inflatable. You had to strap them on, partly inflate them and jump over the side. But the silly part was if you inflated them and jumped over the side you'd break your bloody neck. They were useless bloody things! I just stepped over, from one landing to another. I was a good swimmer and had no trouble keeping afloat until I was picked up by a rubber boat, hauled across by a boat-landing hook. It was bedlam. It was fairly calm, as luck would have it, but there was a three- or four-knot [about seven kilometres per hour] rip going through there. That's how we lost half our men — they were drowned.

I attached myself to a piece of Oregon, about 18 or 19 feet long and 12 inches wide, and I used it like a surfboard. I came ashore on that. Then in the morning I had a look at the island we were on and we found this steel lifeboat. The fellows who could row went around the island and found a few more blokes, and a few of the others who'd come ashore on one of the other islands turned up later in the day.

About 20 of them were going to make Cilacap and then go on to Fremantle. I missed out. The rest of us started to walk down towards Cilacap, which was about 10 miles or so. As far as we knew, Cilacap was still in Allied hands. The natives found us and we lived with them for a couple of days — then they said the Japs had sent out a decree that anyone harbouring sailors would be punished, so they turned us in. They had no option at all.

The first six or seven months as a prisoner were reasonable. We were in Pandeglang. There was a Dutch hospital, and a few of the chaps who were taken early in the piece were there. Then we went to Bicycle Camp in Batavia — there were good conditions there. Then they put us on these tramps and took us to Singapore, just as they got the first lot of Red Cross rations, so we were lucky there.

Then they took us to Burma. We had a plan to take the ship over and go up around the Andamans and get to India. The trouble was they had two machine-guns placed on either side of the bridge, pointing back, that made it impossible. It would have been suicide.

On the railroad I was with natives cutting trees down for sleepers, then I was building embankments, pick and shovel work. They had a couple of elephants and you'd say, 'Can't lift this log — it's too heavy — get an elephant.' One time there, one of the Japs tried to get this elephant to pick up a log and it wouldn't, so he jabbed it with his bayonet. The elephant picked him up and threw him against a tree and killed him. We laughed.

I got my share of malaria. You weren't more than a week between bouts. They called it malignant malaria — it would come in and go out, come in again.

Reveille, 2003, interview with author

Frederick James Taylor, *was born 13 May 1920 at Subiaco, WA, enlisted in January 1938 at Fremantle. After being repatriated as a prisoner of war he was discharged in March 1946, his last posting recorded as HMAS Penguin. He died 25 May 2009.*

HMAS Perth, *under the command of Captain 'Hec' Waller, engaged Japanese ships shortly before midnight on 28 February 1942. Of the 681 ship's company, 328 survived her sinking. Four naval personnel died ashore without being taken prisoner; another 106 men died in captivity. After the war, 214 personnel were repatriated to Australia.*

The Tobruk Run
By Lieutenant Fred Gill, RAN

I was just old enough to get into the war as it began, and in very short order I was sent to England to study asdic. I was there for the Blitz and then was drafted to HMS *Defender*, a D-Class destroyer. I was the only Aussie on board, and I knew that whatever happened, I mustn't look scared, for the sake of the name of Australia. It was hard to live up to at times.

We had a rather uneventful few months convoying around the Mediterranean Sea, chasing Italian ships and dodging an occasional bomb. We got sick of it. In Alexandria we wondered when we might get into something really exciting.

We didn't have long to wait. We were put on evacuating troops from Greece to Crete. Then from Crete. We were lucky to get out of it. We began the Tobruk ferry run. That was also quite a warm job, and we weren't so lucky.

On 29 June 1941, we were scooting along in pleasant evening weather, accompanied by HMAS *Waterhen*. I was a rating on *Defender* and it was fun to hail Aussie ships and give them a surprise when they heard the Aussie accent coming from a Limey ship. At eight o'clock that night we were due for a 'turn-out' exercise, but the 'red' went at five minutes to eight, and, cursing a little at what we took to be the eagerness of the officers, we went to our stations — and found there was no exercise about this. It was the real thing!

Enemy planes were coming at us from three directions — from 15 to 30 of them. I was down in the magazine, passing up the ammo. I could tell that the *Defender* was evading and that she would need a lot of luck as well as skill. For the first time in my experience, bombs were coming so close that, although I was not in the open air and there was the noise of the propellers and the vibration of the ammunition cases, I could hear the scream and concussion of the 'eggs' of death.

Then, for some reason best known to themselves, the Jerry planes turned their concentrated attention on *Waterhen*. While turning sharp to port and rolling with the effort, she stopped a bomb on the waterline abreast the anti-aircraft gun which had replaced her after-torpedo tubes. The bomb didn't explode — just tore a hole in her and stopped her dead. The planes called it a day.

The *Waterhen* was loaded with supplies and Diggers for Tobruk. The concussion of that hit on her side burst tins of peaches, and peaches flew everywhere. One fellow felt something hit his face hard, put up his hand and yelled, 'I'm hit — my face is a pulp!' But he was all right when the peaches were scraped off.

As fast as we could, we took everyone off *Waterhen* and ran for safety, expecting the planes back at any moment. But nothing happened, and black darkness came down, so we returned to take *Waterhen* in tow, getting back to her at 9.30 p.m.

One man up on the bows, who was quite alone, was suddenly amazed to discover an Italian submarine surfaced near the deserted destroyer! He shouted his news, then ran to a four-point-seven [4.7-inch/12-centimetre gun] and operated it alone, running like a mad thing — slammed in the load, ran round and laid it, raced back to the trainer's position to fire. There was plenty of firing going on at that time. The sub crash-dived, and the *Defender* dropped a depth charge over the spot and was later credited with a possible [sinking].

Now we wondered: were there any Italians on the *Waterhen*? An armed boarding party was sent onto the Aussie ship but there was no sign of anyone. A towline was made fast, the boarding party returned, and we set off to tow her to port. Unfortunately at 2 a.m. she turned turtle and sank, with her war ensign still flying at the foremast head — and Australia had lost her first warship of the Second Great War. We Aussies hated to see her go.

A few days later, on 3 July, the *Defender* left Alexandria at 7.30 a.m. and picked up HMAS *Stuart* and HMAS *Vendetta* off Mersa Matruh, an inlet not far from Alexandria where we did a lot of loading. That was at 2 p.m. and we made for Tobruk. We sighted one plane at eight-thirty that night; and he sighted us, for he must have contacted a submarine. About midnight the sub threw two torpedoes at us, and both missed. The *Defender* searched for the sub while the others unloaded.

Searching for the sub was not all fun. We knew a torpedo might come at any time. But we didn't find him and he didn't find us. We left Tobruk at 2 a.m. and went back to Alexandria.

The Tobruk run was more or less a routine affair. An example can be taken from the run of 5 July.

We left Alexandria at 8.15 a.m., travelled all day at 23 knots [43 kmh], the last part of the trip with the *Vendetta*. Two ships did the run every day. The idea was to arrive at Tobruk in the dark and get well away before daylight. On that run we arrived at midnight. We would then unload and load in an hour and a half. Barges would swing up to us, and all hands and the cook, including the officers, would work at frenzied speed. We would unload ammo and supplies, and usually take on Italian prisoners and soldiers wounded or going on leave.

We arrived back at Mersa Matruh at 10 a.m. the following day, 6 July, where we dropped the passengers, loaded more ammo and supplies, and went back, leaving at 1.45 p.m. for Tobruk, where we arrived on 7 July. It was exciting enough. We were often under fire at Tobruk. On that run we got back in Alexandria at 2.30 p.m. and had an all-night leave. Back on the job again, we left Alexandria at 7.15 a.m. with the *Vendetta*, not knowing what was in store for us.

We arrived at Tobruk at midnight and left at 1.30 a.m. on 11 July. At 3.30 a.m. we got the 'red' and had a hot time for a few minutes while a plane tried to strafe both destroyers. He decided, however, that he could not do much on his own in the dark, and departed.

The fateful day dawned slowly. I was asleep in the asdic office, just off the mess-deck. Without warning at 5.15 a.m. a stick of bombs straddled the ship! I awoke suddenly. She lifted a few feet into the air and dropped back hard. I thought that her back must be broken. The lights went out and the engines stopped. I knew it was serious then. This looked like it!

I fumbled my way into the open. The only things I could hear were the drone of planes and Limey voices asking questions. We were loaded with Aussie troops returning from Tobruk for leave in Alexandria. The *Vendetta* was with us, carrying stretcher and walking-wounded cases. The *Defender* was listing fast to the starboard. Then held. The *Vendetta*, with a superb bit of seamanship, came alongside in the pitch-dark. The troops and most of the crew climbed from one destroyer directly onto the other, leaving 25 volunteers on *Defender* including myself. I just had to keep up the Aussie reputation.

The *Vendetta* prepared to take us in tow. The planes had drawn off. But now we heard one approaching. One of the ratings said, 'Here they come back!' The skipper, up on the bridge, listened for a moment and said, 'It's all right, lads — it's one of ours!' We didn't believe him, for we remembered he had once said the same thing before, when we were near Malta, and the plane which was 'ours' dropped a bomb, scoring a near miss and wounding about six men. (One of the wounded ratings had been very annoyed because he couldn't show his wound to anyone — it was in the buttock!) But we knew it was a white lie for the sake of morale. We kept one ear cocked on the plane. It did nothing. We were quite aware that our only air cover in the Mediterranean belonged to the enemy.

As the *Vendetta* drew away from us someone remembered the ship's cat. I found her huddled up in the far corner of a gun shield. As I reached for her, she ran up my arm to my shoulder. I thought she was going to tear my eyes out, but she just sat there, trembling. I ran to the side, where a Tar grabbed her from my shoulder and threw her at the *Vendetta*, which was then 20 feet away. She landed safely on the deck and dived below. It was a beautiful throw!

Of the 25 men on the *Defender*, one group worked on the forecastle arranging the tow, while the rest of us set about lightening ship. As soon as the towline tightened the *Defender* couldn't take the strain. She buckled, both ends lifting into the air, the middle going down. Orders were given to abandon ship.

We stood by the side and I remember a big midshipman casually yelling, 'Felucca!' as though hailing one of the native Egyptian water-taxi ferries which plied with sails and oars round Alexandria. The towline parted. We tried again, but once more it parted.

The *Defender* was too twisted and heavy in the water. Our felucca came — a whaler, with orders to get the officers' gear and valuables. Among the valuables were two kegs of rum. While we were unloading the kegs on the *Vendetta*, one of them was dropped on a ringbolt and damaged. The contents had to be consumed before they ran away. The other keg went into the wardroom. The broached keg was placed on a 12-pounder gun mounting, and it was funny to see the men race up to it, get a drink, and walk away slowly and carefully. I was offered so many nips that in about 10 minutes I was out cold.

So I missed the sinking of the *Defender*. I was glad. I had served a long time on her and it would have been like leaving home, knowing you couldn't go back; or the burial of a dear friend. The *Vendetta* put a torpedo into her but that had no effect! So she had to be sunk with four-inch guns.

The commander of the *Vendetta* was Rodney Rhodes, DSC, RAN. I later served under him when he was CO of the *Shoalhaven*, but I had moved up in rank by then.

After the sinking of the *Defender*, the *Vendetta* took us straight back to Alexandria. We arrived at the base, HMS *Resource*, at eight forty-five that night, where we fed, washed and turned in. The next day they sent us to the survivors' camp, HMS *Grebe*. The first men to welcome us were the survivors of the *Waterhen*, whom we had rescued less than a fortnight before!

Reveille, July 1951

Lieutenant Frederick Arthur Gill *was born at Granville, Sydney, on 2 May 1920. He enlisted in January 1940 and was discharged in January 1947, his last posting having been HMAS Shoalhaven. He died 1 June 2010.*

Collision in the North Atlantic
By Frederick (Frank) Finch

The Norwegian oil tanker *Strix* was westbound from England to America, leaving Southend in convoy ON 287 on 25 February 1945. Snow covered the ship from topmast to deck. Icicles hung everywhere. With our tanks now empty of oil, except for that which we kept for refuelling purposes, it was tank-cleaning time. Most of our days were spent deep down in the empty tanks, cleaning the filth and slush from the bottom and sides before passing it up in buckets to men on deck on long rope lines. To be caught down a tank when a ship is torpedoed must be terrifying, and I never enjoyed being down there one little bit.

One morning, all day workers and the watches were down in a tank when a U-boat was detected close by, and so a corvette raced in alongside and dropped a pattern of depth charges. The noise, and the damage to a person's ears, can best be described as being inside a galvanised empty water tank and somebody on the outside belting it with a sledgehammer. We all cleared that ladder out of the tank in record time.

We had now been refuelling our escorts in the Atlantic convoys for the past five months. In that time we were used to running into fog. But now as we were on the Newfoundland Banks, the bloody stuff had enveloped the convoy for the past three days. How ships were able to keep station without radar in those days boggles the mind. But we did with maybe one or two ships straying a little. The fog had reduced the convoy speed down to a crawl. Foghorns, blasting day and night from every ship, let you know just where they were.

There were now 90 ships in this convoy, and to give an idea

Collision in the North Atlantic

of what faced each ship, one only has to know stories of earlier smaller convoys of 50 to 60 ships and their escorts covering an ocean of over 50 square miles. By the end of 1944, most convoys doubled that number, up to 160 ships.

In fine weather it was all good sailing; we just followed the ship ahead. In heavy weather when the seas were really bad and high as telegraph poles, the swell of the Atlantic Ocean would knock the ships around a little. You could lose your position in the column of a slow-moving convoy, with the helmsmen trying to keep a steady course, but the ship would eventually be knocked off course further.

In the death-like quiet of the fog I could plainly hear the engines of a ship to our starboard, though I could not catch the faintest glimpse of it. I rang the bridge, thinking I was going a little crazy, as I could hear farm animals, roosters crowing, and hens making a racket. There were all sorts of silly sounds way out here in the North Atlantic, but the bridge informed me I wasn't going crazy as they could hear it as well.

The engines of the ship became louder and louder, and quite suddenly there it was, a ghost-like shade darker than the fog itself, steaming along, sinister-looking, now about 30 feet from us and closing steadily. Our second mate was shouting to them through the megaphone that we were number 84 in our column. 'Keep the hell away from us and go find your own bloody column.' Slowly the big ship veered away to starboard and faded back into the swirling fog.

As the afternoon wore on we were to lose our position and found ourselves very, very close to a Greek ship on our port side. It was their turn to abuse us, then we veered back to starboard to our lost position. Throughout the many hours of fog it went on, ship after ship losing its way, only to be shepherded back by the help of others.

Looking forward to the rigours of another watch in the freezing conditions on deck, I turned in early. With all the racket that had been going on I would be lucky to get any sleep at all. I switched off the light, hoping to get just a little sleep before going on watch at midnight.

I woke with a start. The noise and thud seemed to have come from the fore part of the ship and the *Strix* had staggered severely under the blow, then engines were stopped. Confusion reigned all around me. Our ship's whistle now blew madly and the alarm bell sounded. Cabin doors were flung open and men streamed out into the alleyway.

'Torpedoed?' a voice said in English.

'No, I don't think so,' replied the Norwegian bosun. 'Get out quick, something has happened up for'ard.'

No sooner had the bosun spoken than I was thrown to the deck by a jarring concussion, and the bulkhead was pushed in with much crunching and grating of steel against steel.

Throwing some clothes on, I ran along the alleyway and up the accommodation ladder at the far end. As I stepped out onto the poop deck, the first thing I noticed was the misty glow of a searchlight trying to penetrate the thick fog. Enough light was showing the blunt bows of an American Liberty ship, wedged hard up against our poop. Many years after the war I was to learn it was the SS *John Trumbull*.

For the time being both ships were immobilised, while others in this column slowly crept past us. When the last ship had passed, the *John Trumbull* rang astern on its engine and vanished back into the fog. Once we were again underway, our captain and chief officer made an inspection of the damage.

We had a hole in the port bow where the Liberty ship had collided with us. Her bow had then slid down our port side, first destroying our number two lifeboat and its steel davits. Her bow had continued its damage as our own vessel was still going ahead until our engines were stopped. Continuing down our port side, the Liberty completely smashed our number 4 lifeboat and its steel davits, on the poop deck above my cabin. Both lifeboats were hanging, dragging in the water, and had to be cut adrift. This left us only the two starboard lifeboats if we needed them in an emergency. All our port rails were bent, and our degaussing cable was compressed and damaged, plus all the ship's port-side steel plates were dented causing leakage in my cabin and two other cabins. As the damage was suffered above the waterline, we were in no immediate danger.

The following afternoon the fog lifted and to our surprise we found that we had actually sailed through one column of ships before being rammed in the next column.

We arrived in New York on 17 March 1945. Two days later, a Marine Court of Inquiry opened in New York, and the captain and third mate were exonerated from all blame. The court took into consideration the weather on the night concerned, and the continuous blowing of all ships' whistles in the convoy. It was also mentioned at the inquiry that two other ships had made the same mistakes as our vessel but no damage had been done to them.

The *Strix* sailed back to Sparrow Point, Baltimore, from where we had sailed six months earlier. However, I signed off in New York before shipping out again.

Reveille, 2016

Frank Finch, *was born 1926, signed on in Sydney on a Norwegian merchant navy ship in April 1942, aged 15. During WWII he served on six Norwegian ships and with the US Army Services of Supply, Small Ships Section. After the war he sailed on Australian merchant ships, retiring in 1988. He is a member of the Kyogle, NSW, RSL sub-branch, a member of the American Legion, and Vice-President of the US Army Small Ships Association.*

Poker Game Went to the Bottom the Day They Sank the Brave Limerick
By Harold 'Snow' Mackrell

This is a true story of the gallant ship SS *Limerick*, 8724 tons, registered in London, and her crew, torpedoed off Tweed Heads by a Japanese submarine. Ours may have been an old cargo ship but she was still vital to the war effort for she had just been refitted to carry frozen meat in her cargo holds.

We left Sydney on Anzac Day 1943. We had no public holiday and we missed seeing the Anzacs march in Martin Place. We could only reminisce. The present war brought home to us the need to get these vital food supplies to England. Our mission now was to pick up meat in Brisbane.

We were empty, loaded in ballast. Two carpenters were still working on the refrigeration rooms prior to loading at Hamilton Wharf. The sea was running a two-metre swell, there were no naked lights, and some of the boys were playing cards in the forecastle (the bosun had the winning hand), when at midnight the Japanese sub fired her torpedoes, which blew the stern and portside right off.

It knocked us off our chairs and stools. Stewie, one of the players (all had similar stories to relate later), said, 'When I got up I made for the deck ladder. I realised I did not have a life jacket so I rushed to my cabin. As I made for the ladder again I passed the table where we had been playing poker. Some money on the table reminded me of 36 pounds in my suitcase, so again I rushed back to my cabin. Then all the lights went out. It was a nasty sensation in the dark, in a sinking ship. *Bugger the money!* I thought. When I got on deck some of the crew were trying to get a raft away but it had jammed. We then attempted to lower two boats but they had swung in on the deck. Eventually we managed to get one away; it saved 38 of us.

One of two brothers from New Zealand who had been playing cards held a full house: three kings, two aces. He really cursed that submarine.

Shandy was celebrating the first few minutes of his 21st birthday asleep in his bunk, clad only in his underpants. He had to dive 40 feet into the ice-cold water. It was a really wet birthday party.

Jenkins was on lookout duty when he saw the wake of the torpedo, a silver streak, before it struck the ship. He screamed to the bridge. The captain swung her hard to starboard, but to no avail. Then, making sure that all was being done to save his crew, he was one of the last to leave his ship. He later lost his life while hanging on to some flotsam or debris.

Yet only two lost their lives that morning, with many tales of heroism, courage, frustration and fear. Some had to endure eight hours in the cold late-April waters, hanging on to broken, half-sinking lifeboats, waiting for daylight, calling out in the darkness to see if their mates were still afloat.

We knew that four of the crew and the captain had stayed awhile; salvage was not ruled out entirely. The submarine was staying partly submerged, just out of range. It had been rumoured that the enemy might surface and machine-gun the crew in the boats.

McDonald had more on his mind than a Jap sub; he could not swim. Corson-Crook clutched pieces of wood, an oar and stray dunnage, and helped Mac onto this makeshift raft, but not before he sank twice, spluttering, saying, 'Ye canna knock out a guid Scot.' He could laugh about it later.

But what about Brodie? He had been in Darwin Harbour when his first ship sank, then three weeks before today his second ship had been torpedoed. This was his third disaster in three months.

The *Limerick*, listing 20 degrees, rolled dangerously in the swell, with the conning tower of the sub lurking in the distance, waiting for the rescue ships to answer the SOS the dying *Limerick* was sending out.

There were five in Stewie's half-submerged lifeboat. The increased morning swell was now about three metres high, tipping the lifeboat over several times. At times they sat waist-deep in water in the boat, then the next swell would upend them again. It was only the buoyancy floats in the gunwale of the lifeboat that kept it from sinking.

Dawn could not come quickly enough for these five in the boat, but when it did, they could see nothing but the cold grey ocean — no ships to rescue them — and still they drifted.

HMAS *Colac* had answered the SOS. She was also looking for that sub, and at the first light of dawn she started picking up survivors. It was to be several hours before her crew found Stewie in the half-submerged lifeboat.

Eight hours in that water would make any sailor think twice about going back to sea. We were so cold we could not grasp the nets lowered over the side of the *Colac*. Some sailors clambered down to help us and soon we had dry clothes, a smoke, food — the smoke came first, although I could not keep it in my mouth for my chattering teeth. Some of our mates were already in the mess, relating tales of woe, what they had lost. At least they were alive.

The *Colac* steamed into the Brisbane River, tied up at Hamilton where we should have been that day, and we were taken up to McWhirters [the department store] with 20 pounds from the Seamen's Union office with which to outfit ourselves with new clothes.

Some of us went over to the Salvos, who always helped out. They seemed to know. Maybe it was that look in a sailor's face, an ashen look. 'I have lost everything again: my wife's photo, personal trinkets and almost my life.' My job as a sailor? Well, I could always get another ship — which I did; many, many more ships, for I have been a sailor all my life.

Every Anzac Day, when I stand in solemn silence paying my respects to the fallen, I cannot help remembering Anzac Day 1943, when everything looked fine as we left Sydney Harbour, little knowing that I was about to get a certificate of discharge.

Reveille, January–February 1989

Harold Gordon Mackrell, *born on 17 June 1923, enlisted in the Royal Australian Navy at Williamstown, Victoria, in January 1941, was discharged in April 1946 and died 26 December 2001. The wreck of the* Limerick *was discovered off Ballina, NSW, in 2013.*

Greece and Crete

'"Strewth! Bloody women!" They got a shock.'

— Captain Una Keast,
Australian Army Nursing Service

Scrap Iron
By Petty Officer A.W.C., Ex-Voyager

'Let go aft, let go for'd.' Just one more oil ship finished. The boiler hours were mounting up, and how we counted them; boiler clean meant about 36 hours in harbour and a spell ashore for most of the war-weary crew.

HMAS *Voyager* had left Sydney on Sunday 3 November 1939, on a 24-hour patrol outside the Heads, and here we were, acquaintances of the Mediterranean — April 1941. We were still getting back from that patrol, and with nothing in our future outlook to say we would get back. Getting back wasn't everything, but a spell would have been heavenly.

Forty-six days up the Libyan coast, out with the fleet, out with convoys, up on a stunt with commandos, transporting prisoners, rescuing crews of sinking ships, sinking enemy subs, offensive sweeps, tedious patrols, rushing urgent despatches, carrying troops and wounded: these were just a few of our jobs.

Tonight we had just returned from Alexandria after two days up the coast where — in company with HMAS *Stuart* and a navy auxiliary, and assisted by an HM submarine — we had landed a large party of commandos, who had blown up a lot of important places in Bardia, and then withdrawn and returned to Alexandria. After oiling we had expected to go to sea again as usual, but instead made fast to a buoy in the harbour.

Most of the fleet was at sea the next day, but we stayed in harbour. Cargo and passenger ships began to arrive full of civilians — men, women and children from Salonika, Greece.

The world seemed nice and peaceful to us, all quiet in harbour. A hot, sunny day, and leave until 2245 hours that night. Those who weren't on duty — half the ship's company — went ashore.

That night things started to move. As we neared the ship in the inky darkness, the noise of the engine-room fans meant half an hour's notice of full speed. The buzzes went round quickly: 'We are going to evacuate our troops from Greece.'

At daybreak we left in company with an HM cruiser, HMAS *Stuart*, and two naval auxiliaries, and steamed at 18 knots for Suda Bay, Crete. With very mixed feelings we prepared our ship for any eventuality, especially air raids, and in case we had a chance to get a few rounds in at the Hun troops.

We passed a few empty lifeboats during the trip to Suda, which told tales of our own ships recently lost. We also lost a man overboard during the night, but eventually arrived in Suda at 2300. We could only get 20 tons of oil, the oiler having been sunk in the harbour with HMS *York* by Italian explosive motorboats. We anchored the night.

Early next morning we left — an AA cruiser, three naval auxiliaries, two corvettes, *Stuart* and *Voyager*. We passed subs, a Greek and a Yugoslav, just outside Suda, and proceeded on our way. The action alarms sounded about 1100 — a submarine contact. We steamed clear of the other ships, as, racing across the spot, we dropped pattern after pattern of depth charges. We were certain it was a sub, but we had a job to do escorting the auxiliaries so were forced to leave reluctantly without observing the results.

Early in the afternoon our forces split into two groups, and we proceeded for Nauplia Bay, south of Piraeus, with three auxiliaries, a corvette and *Stuart*.

Late in the afternoon we were discovered by a Jerry reconnaissance, and a little later over came two Junkers 88s. We had been expecting conflict sooner, so were prepared, and opened fire as they came around for the attack.

Shrewdly avoiding the armed ships, they came in on the

auxiliaries: bigger game and easier to kill. Their engines roared as they opened throttle and came down in a shallow dive, all the ships' guns banged, then the four tiny pills came away from the planes and we held our breath. *Splash* — four splashes with the water. Missed astern, but only just.

The second plane was now in position and four more bombs came whistling down. The gun crews on the target were working frantically — *bang! bang!* The old 12-pounder was working overtime, but all to no avail. *Whack!* The first stick scored a direct hit on the forecastle, and the gunners disappeared in smoke and flame.

Both anchors were blown off and hit the water together. She didn't sink but while our men were extinguishing the flames amid exploding ammunition from their guns, four torpedo bombers came in. *Stuart* gave them everything she had, and the result was four misses, so we proceeded on our way.

About 2100 we had slight relaxation from action stations to get a bit of dinner, and a little later nosed our way into Nauplia. The night was inky black, and what appeared to be flares lit the way in for us, but progress was deadly slow. Collisions had to be avoided at all costs. The flares turned out to be several of our ships sunk and sinking, and blazing from stem to stern. An oiler was just a blaze of flame. Even the water around was afire.

The caiques began to come out laden with soldiers, and in the darkness could not find the ships they were detailed to go aboard. The crews were Greek men, and after some jabbering and pointing, we gave them the general direction. The sea had a slight swell, planes could be heard droning overhead, mines had been laid in the vicinity, and burning ships were our only landmarks.

As one caique came alongside, we inquired, 'What ship are you detailed for?' — '*Voyager*,' came the reply, so we made her fast and the troops poured aboard, throwing their gear before them. Caiques clustered alongside, port side, and soon troops were cluttered about our upper deck. The usual shouting was going on: 'Hurry and make that bloody bowline fast — what the hell are you doing up there? Come on, caique, pass your bloody stern line over.' Then she bumped alongside. 'Hey,' said to the black depths of the caique, 'are you bloody coming on board this ship?'

'Too right,' came several female voices. 'Gawd! Women!' someone said. 'Right-o, girls! Jump up! Give us your hand! Mind the guardrail!'

So we got about 149 nurses and about 141 soldiers aboard, and then came the job of stowing them and their belongings. Stowing men was all right, but women — that was different. As many as possible were stowed below, out of the wet and spray and dew. All officers' cabins, wardroom and compartments were filled; petty officers' mess was full. We made them cocoa, tea and sandwiches with our meagre supplies; gave the nurses soap, towels and toothbrushes; roped and screened off a toilet place; and bedded them down for the night. And so we left them and went up on deck to stand around all night.

It was impossible to get all the nurses below decks on the destroyer, so those on deck (some girls did not want to go below — the air was too foul) just huddled on the deck, and we did the best we could with tea and navy cocoa. Some nurses were wounded but had been attended to. With the exception of *Stuart*, our ships had loaded up with troops. *Stuart* was detailed not to take troops, but to stand by in order to pick up survivors in case one of us was sunk; but, nevertheless, one lone soldier found his way aboard, and he was their only passenger.

Everyone had settled down by 0300, and before daylight nearly all of the *Voyager*'s ship's company had shaved and put on clean clothes. There were nurses on board, and the desire to create a good impression was evident. The officers and petty officers were not able to clean up until later, but in true naval style all hands were called about 0800 and breakfast was prepared in buffet style, everyone getting what he could when he could. Our cooks did a marvellous job.

The nurses, after having a clean-up as well as circumstances would allow, found their way on deck, and many very interesting tales were told on either side. About half the nurses were Aussie girls, and the other half New Zealand and English. They all spoke with admiration of their matron and the valour of the nurses who had volunteered to stay behind to nurse the wounded.

Nurse Casey was talking to some of us about those 'so-and-so Germans' when the alarm rattles sounded their vibrant note. Action stations — air raid. Guns were quickly manned and opened fire at one lone plane, a German reconnaissance aircraft, which quickly flew off. We remained at action stations and about two hours later sighted two Junkers 88s coming over. We opened fire as they came round our bow to attack the two auxiliaries.

The nurses and soldiers scattered from under the gun muzzles as we opened fire. Steel-helmeted womenfolk urged on the gun crews: 'A little lower! That nearly got him!' They were as pleased as Punch.

The soldiers, who had mounted two Bren guns on the deck, opened fire as the planes dived in to the attack. Some hits must have been scored, as the planes wobbled and dodged, let go their eight bombs, and sped off. The bombs missed ahead.

Two of our Blenheims appeared and sped after the retreating Huns, but reappeared later and afforded us protection, with the result that we had no more attacks from the air. Hours later, as we neared Crete, the *Vendetta* and *Waterhen* passed us on the way to Greece.

Mufti, December 1956

The author would appear to be **Arthur William Frederick Cooper, DSM,** *who served in the Mediterranean on HMAS* Voyager *during WWII and was discharged as a chief petty officer in December 1948, his last posting having been HMAS Leeuwin. He was born* in Fremantle on 15 February 1909, and enlisted in the RAN on 25 September 1926. He was awarded the Distinguished Service Medal after serving on HMAS Shropshire during operations in Leyte Gulf and during the Battle of the Surgao Straits, the last great sea battle of World War II.

Strewth! The Evacuation of Nurses
By Una Keast

When war broke out I was up in the country. I'd trained at Orange Base Hospital — I went down to Griffith for 12 months, then back to Orange. I decided the thing to do was to come to Sydney and join up, so I did that within the first week or two. I went to Victoria Barracks and was told I was too young. I was told to go away, which I did for a few months. I was then called up on 11 June 1940. I went to the Showgrounds. On 11 October we sailed on the *Queen Mary* for the Middle East. I was with the 2/5th Australian General Hospital and stayed with it from the beginning to the end — although I was sent off to other places if we didn't have enough work going.

We went to Palestine, and then to Greece for about a month. When the Germans came in we left 165 staff men behind — six of whom were doctors — to look after the wounded. The sisters were ordered out by General Blamey. We all volunteered to stay but that was not permissible.

We could hear guns at night in Greece and knew we had to get out. And we did — travelled all night in a big three-ton truck, jammed in there, with legs around the next person in front of us. And we pulled up at daylight for a comfort stop in a barley crop, and the next thing we heard voices. '*Parlez-vous français, mademoiselle?*' Oh God, they were Polish men there!

That was a trip and a half, because on the way down through the Canal to get out, there were dead mules everywhere. And of course if there were dead mules there were dead men, because the muleteers were there. And then we spent a day in a cemetery while they were strafing around it. I don't think they saw us.

That evening we got in the trucks again and off we went, down to a place called Argos, and we were taken out by fishing caiques to the destroyer HMAS *Voyager*, where we boarded. Now these men thought they were getting men on board — they didn't know they were getting women. There were Australians and British — there may have been some Kiwis — and it was all dark except for some burning ships in the harbour which the Germans had set on fire. You had what you could carry. And on the way to the ship we were told things were getting heavy, so you'd open the suitcase and throw out a few clothes. You still had your haversack, respirator, tin hat, water bottle and whatever else you could carry.

So we eventually got to the destroyer, with the boat rocking away, and this sailor said to me, 'Give me your hand, mate', and I said, 'I'm all right, I can manage, thank you.' And he said, 'Strewth! Bloody women!' They got a shock.

The next morning the sailors were all spruced up and the captain said he'd never seen them look so well. They'd had their showers and shaves, because they had women on board.

And that's when we went to Crete for a week. No beds, but we nursed on our hands and knees. We went from Crete across to Alexandria in Egypt. And eight or 10 of us were taken from a ship on one side of the wharf with the walking wounded, and on the other side were British subjects. They were screaming mad because they didn't have any nurses with them, and they wanted nurses. So we were taken over.

They didn't treat us very nicely, actually. Some of them sat up in bed and rang their buzzers, and wanted coffee. We couldn't get to the dining salon — they wouldn't allow us down there. So we sat up with our colonel and some other doctors on the boat deck and ate bully beef and biscuits.

One woman went to the OC troops, and she had a dog with her. She said, 'My dog has not had a bath for two days.' Because water was restricted — men were only allowed half a mug or something for a shave. He just said to her, 'Madam, there is plenty of water over the side.'

Some of these people had come right through Europe and got down as far as Greece, and were getting out. Some of them didn't even speak English but claimed to be British subjects. We slept head to toe and two of us slept on the deck. We were exhausted after being on Crete and working, and sleeping in slit trenches and whatever we could find.

We came home at the beginning of 1942, and were boarded out for some weeks in Adelaide because the trains were crowded and we couldn't get back to NSW. Then when we did, we had a couple of weeks' leave and then went off to Armidale where we spent the winter. At first we lived in the tote house on the racetrack — 10 of us — and we showered in the horse stalls. Then when the rest of the crowd arrived we were moved to the dog track. This was under canvas for the winter and the hospital was on the showgrounds, all under canvas. The patients were mostly soldiers from Tamworth and areas around. We had chip shower heaters, and the water would come down boiling hot or freezing cold.

So we decided we would go to a hotel and book in and have a bath. Four of us went and booked in and we had the bath, and out we were going, and the manager was taking the key and asked why we were going: 'What's wrong?' And we told him we'd needed a bath and he said, 'Oh you can have that any time, except when the clients are using it at this hour of the evening — but bring your own towels.' So we used to go down every second day — we didn't like to make too much of it — and have our hot bath and then sit up in front of the fire and have a little drink, before walking the mile and a half back.

After that we went to New Guinea for 18 months. I came home and went to Goulburn, and I was there when the Japanese broke out of camp at Cowra. So we had some of them in there. And after being there, we reformed and went up to Morotai, and were there for seven months, when the war ended.

A lot of work was pre-penicillin. Penicillin didn't come in until we were in New Guinea, and then it was given in a drip, subcutaneously. Later the injections came in, before tablets.

Over in the Middle East we wore frocks, the usual gear. But in New Guinea we wore khaki and eventually went into grey overalls and boots with gaiters. And worked 12 hours a day.

Looking after the POWs who were released after the war was an absolute nightmare. We'd go off and cry our hearts out when those fellows came back. It was terrible. Those ribs! You don't expect to see kids of 17 and 18 dying, and wanting their mothers. Death is never a comfortable thing to see, no matter how much one sees of it. What amazes me is that so many of them are still alive.

I forgot all about it when I got out of the army. I went and did my obstetrics training and then I took off overseas and I was away for five and a half years, and by that time it was well and truly behind me. I didn't dwell on it.

Reveille, January–February 2004, interview with author

Una Clara Mills *was born at Tottenham, NSW, on 5 August 1915, enlisted on New Year's Day 1940, and was discharged from the Australian Army Nursing Service with the rank of captain in April 1946. In 1972 she married WWII veteran Jack Keast, who died in 1982. Una Mills died, aged 101, on 3 October 2016.*

Escape After the Battle of Crete
By Signaller S.L. Carroll, MM

Arriving at Crete on 26 April 1941, members of our West Australian battalion went ashore in invasion barges. With other members of the AIF we were marched to a reception centre several miles westward. Here a good mug of hot tea, biscuits, oranges and chocolates were served, with cigarettes to follow. These comforts cheered the boys immensely. An atmosphere of security prevailed, a feeling which had come over us immediately when we set foot on the island.

Lack of sleep had left our nerves slightly frayed after 17 whirlwind days in Greece. Silence reigned long before midnight as we huddled together to share what blankets were available until reveille the next morning.

After a fairly substantial breakfast we were again assembled in our respective units and marched off in the direction of Suda Bay. There was a general impression among us that we were to embark for Egypt, but we were soon to learn otherwise. At 3 p.m. we reached a camp site where, except for an occasional enemy aircraft overhead, all was very peaceful. To lie in the grass in the cool shade of olive trees was something we had dreamed of for months. Next day companies took up positions and battle stations, and then followed a pleasant week in which we enjoyed the luxuries of hot meals, cigarette issues and more blankets. It was like old times.

During the ensuing weeks we made another move when our unit was instructed to occupy defensive positions at the western end of the Retimo aerodrome area. About 10 a.m. on 20 May large enemy aircraft were sighted inland, flying in an easterly direction. These machines appeared to be towing gliders and soon afterwards a similar formation was seen out to sea, also travelling in the same direction. Then came a brigade message that 500 enemy parachutists had landed at Georgioupoli and dispersed in the surrounding hills.

Six hours later a large number of enemy fighter planes attacked the Retimo sector. Flying low, they strafed the whole area. Within a few seconds the sky was full of planes and parachutes. The enemy appeared to operate in waves of 20. Each troop carrier dropped an average of 15 parachutists, and, at intervals, they also landed two-inch field pieces, motorcycles, mortars and large containers.

Our 'B' and 'C' Companies took up the attack next morning, our troops covering the two miles separating our forward positions and Perivolia. Through a signaller's telescope in an operation post the enemy could be seen retreating, running from house to house. Artillery had silenced three field pieces, causing the enemy to leave behind machine-guns and rifles which they had used against our advancing companies.

The Greeks managed to cut off the enemy retreat in the direction of Retimo and the whole show would have undoubtedly been over before nightfall but for the appearance of a squadron of fighter-bombers. The enemy signal of one green Very light [coloured flare], meaning 'bring fire to bear', was fired in the direction of our 'B' Company, and a little later repeated in the direction of 'C' Company. Within an hour the whole area was in flames, crops and trees being set alight by tracer and explosive bullets. Bombs were dropped on Sesmes and along the road, and troops were pinned down for the remainder of the day.

Further operations during daylight hours were impossible. Aircraft working in relays continued to bomb and machine-gun our troops from dawn till dusk. Our troops experienced difficulty in obtaining further supplies of rations and ammunition, whilst fresh supplies were dropped to the enemy daily. Troop carriers were making crash landings in the fields, and although our artillery was blowing them up as soon as they came to earth, the enemy managed to get more field pieces and mortars.

It was decided to make a night attack on the German line extending from the beach to the southern end of Perivolia. Moving under cover of darkness to a position well forward, the assault was launched at 3 a.m. Proceedings, however, were suddenly interrupted when a signal came from 'D' Company. It was later learnt that the officer commanding had been badly wounded. 'A', 'C' and 'D' Companies retired. 'B' Company had gone right through and was forced to remain in the village, being caught in a line of machine-gun fire. Activities next day were almost nil, owing to the whereabouts of 'B' Company not being known. At dusk 'A' Company moved forward to cover should 'B' Company attempt to withdraw. Mortars using four-inch German smoke bombs concentrated on the area along the waterfront, whilst artillery shelled visible enemy positions. 'B' Company failed to put in an appearance next morning, but managed to reach Greek lines, arriving in the battalion area at 2 p.m. from the direction of Marulas.

During a battalion withdrawal, movement information was received by wireless of the capitulation of the island. An officers' conference was summoned, and we received instructions to destroy weapons. It was a case of every man for himself.

Hearing whistles blowing on the aerodrome, I went forward on my hands and knees. A number of troop carriers were approaching from the sea; the road was lined with small armoured cars and motorcycles, and Germans were everywhere.

Stripping my webbing I took my water bottle and haversack and bolted for the mountains. Crossing a road I noticed enemy vehicles to both right and left. Bullets whistled round my ears as I plunged into the bush. In crossing the island I overtook a number of personnel from the battalion and by midnight we reached the south coast. Very light pistols and a German signalling torch were used in hopes that naval aircraft might be standing by, but there was no response. On the second night an illuminated plane approached along the coast. There was no mistaking the sound of the engines so I opened my light and called him. He answered with the recognition signal, and circling round several times, dropped six or eight bags of ration chocolate and medical supplies. Opening my light again I sent a message that 500 troops were awaiting rescue. He acknowledged the message, wished us good luck, and headed out to sea.

For eight days we waited, hiding in the hills during the day and returning to the coast at night to mount a lookout, signalling at half-hour intervals. Hundreds of our troops were taken prisoner in the first few days. German patrols occupied all the villages and patrolled the coast. Breaking away from the few of our troops who remained, I made my way back into the mountains and, moving by night, I travelled about 20 miles eastward.

Returning to the coast I met two other chaps. We managed to find a small fishing boat and we set about getting some rigging together. A Greek Red Cross nurse came on the scene and begged us to take her to Alexandria. My companions appeared to think that the more of us there were the merrier it would be, but actually, three would be a risk in a jerry-rigged boat about which we knew nothing. I was saved further argument when they failed to return from a hunt for food and water containers.

Shifting my gear further up the beach at midnight, I borrowed the boat. The rowlocks and oars had been removed by its Greek owner, so I had to use a floorboard to move the boat in order to conceal it among the rocks while I proceeded to rig it. For a mast I used a piece of Oregon, six feet long, which I had picked up among driftwood on the beach. The handle of a fishing spear became a boom, a length of bamboo the peak, and a piece of lightweight canvas from a flour mill the sail.

Escape After the Battle of Crete

The job completed, I shoved off at 3 a.m., intending to make the point before daylight and then pull into a large rock several miles from the mainland to make a general overhaul of the whole outfit. Halfway, the wind dropped, the boat merely drifted, and I was left to await the dawn and the reconnaissance plane which flew round the island three times a day.

Hearing the plane approaching, I put the boat about in hopes that the pilot might mistake me for a fisherman returning to the island. He fired one burst along the water about 20 yards in front of me. I jumped into the water, which I considered the safest place. Meanwhile the plane gained height and continued eastward. Clambering back I found that no hits had been scored, except for a few holes in the sail, which might have been there all the time.

Knowing where several of our officers had been hiding, I cruised along at a safe distance off the coast, but each time I approached a likely looking landing place, enemy patrols opened fire. I was finally forced to turn away and head for Egypt in a 16-foot boat, with two gallons [7.5 litres] of water and six tins of ration chocolate. I estimated the distance I had to cover as 350 miles [560 kilometres] and, allowing for a speed of three knots [5.5 kilometres per hour] in a medium breeze, and sailing 18 hours a day, worked out some idea of what would be my daily ration of food and water.

Each night, using a signalling torch, I swept the entire horizon, using the naval call sign instead of SOS to avoid being picked up by enemy craft. For a compass I used a penknife mounted on a piece of board, so that when the blade cast a fine shadow I knew I was heading due south. At night I used the North Star as a guide.

At dawn on the seventh morning a strong north-wester blew up, which by 10 a.m. had developed into a gale. I was obliged to alter course and run before the wind for more than 24 hours, surfing the waves, which must have been between 20 and 30 feet high. My eyes commenced to give me a lot of trouble, the left becoming badly affected: it caused me to have a blind side and made it difficult for me to judge the waves.

A little after sunrise I saw a haze in the sky away to the south and, taking a chance, I pushed the boat across the waves. It was quite a battle holding her against them. They were striking broadside on. The mast, being a misfit, began to kick from side to side. Twice I took the risk of leaving the tiller to brace the mast with floorboards, only to be nearly swamped.

Keeping on, I sighted land one morning at eight o'clock. I gave the boat every bit of canvas she had, not caring a hang what happened. When the land appeared to be only three miles off, although the distance must have been 10 miles, the boat filled and overturned. The mast smashed a hole in the bottom and my dreams of sailing into Alexandria went with it.

Tying my tunic to the rudder clamps, I fixed the water tin, almost empty by now, across my shoulders and struck out for the shore. It took me seven hours to reach land, swimming, floating and surfing in turns. Nearing the shore I had a terrific struggle to retain my hold on the tin and keep myself from being carried onto rocks on which breakers were pounding and dashing spray high into the air. Fortunately I was able to work myself along to a small patch of sand and came ashore, the breakers spinning me around in all directions. I had to crawl on my hands and knees, feeling too giddy to walk.

I drank most of the water left in the tin and then started inland, heading east along the sand hills. After walking for about an hour, I came across an air force listening post. Two very dark chaps wearing blue peaked caps made me think that I was in enemy territory, but they turned out to be Maltese. A message was sent to 'control' and next morning I was taken to Mersa Matruh.

The Listening Post, Summer 1988

Stanley Lawrence Carroll *was born on 6 January 1915 at Geraldton and enlisted at Southern Cross, WA, in November 1939. He was posted to the 2/11 Infantry Battalion, 6th Division, as a signalman. His award of the Military Medal was gazetted in 1941. He was discharged in May 1943 with the rank of sergeant, and died 15 October 1995.*

Dasher
By SX1543

The late afternoon sunshine was pleasantly warm and I was comfortably stretched out on the fringe of sand along Kalyves Beach, not far from the entrance of Suda Bay, when Dasher introduced himself.

He approached unobserved and intimated his desire to get acquainted by licking my bare feet. I hunched up on an elbow to take stock of my visitor. He took a couple of quick, defensive steps backwards and sat on his haunches, stiffly prepared for instant flight. Except for a white vest centred with a tufty whorl of hair like a duck's tail, he was completely black. His broadly spaced legs were no more than four or five inches long and the measurement from a restless knob of a tail to the top of his neatly erect head was nearly 30 inches. His neck and white chest were definitely bulldoggish, but the triangular ears and pointed head derived from another strain.

I spoke to him. Apparently deciding that I would do no harm, he gravely thrust a damp nose into my outstretched hand. With the introduction thus over, he curled up beside me and promptly went to sleep.

He became my dog from that moment, and in the succeeding days on Crete he rarely left my side. When a cool wind from the sea drove me back to our camp in an olive grove running almost to the water's edge, Dasher followed unbidden. I managed to scrounge an extra tin of bully beef and a few biscuits from the quartermaster's limited supply. He treated the hard meat-flecked biscuits as a new type of bone.

Dasher displayed great interest in the blanket I spread at the foot of a gnarled old olive tree that night. His first reaction, as he gingerly walked on it, was one of stiff-legged suspicion; but finding it softer than most of the odd corners he had hitherto slept in, he signalled his intention of staying for the night by making three or four complete about-turns. Keeping a careful brown eye on me for any sign of disapproval, he tucked his diminutive legs under him and relaxed with a grunt of satisfaction. I couldn't resist the urge to pat him. Reassured, he tucked his nose into his chest and closed his eyes.

Blankets were then at a premium on Crete. One blanket was shared by two or often three men. Their use was purely as a mattress, and we used to put on all the clothes available before turning in for the night, removing only boots for use as a pillow. Before the advent of Dasher, Bombardier John had been my bedmate. He was somewhat dubious about the addition of a dog to the already limited capacity of a single blanket. In the morning, however, Bombardier John enthusiastically agreed with me that the little warm body between us had taken much of the chill from the night air. He even went so far as to suggest that it wouldn't be a bad idea to persuade half a dozen dogs to sleep with us, if one could make such a difference to our comfort.

Dasher enjoyed himself as only a happy dog can, and I lavished on him all the care and attention Crete and circumstances permitted. I made arrangements for a Greek to deliver a pint of goat's milk each morning. This was always waiting in a treacle tin when Dasher woke. At meals he had his share of whatever was going and developed a passion for bully beef. On one occasion our milkman brought a few eggs which I fried in olive oil in my mess tin. Dasher devoured four with great gusto before he was satisfied. After that, whenever I visited one of the dozens of egg-and-chip stalls which enterprising Greeks had established among the olive groves within a day or two of the arrival of the ever-hungry Anzacs, Dasher always expected and received at least one egg.

In response to Major General Freyberg's [Lieutenant General Sir Bernard Freyberg, VC, DSO] appeal to keep fit and tough, because the Germans were expected any day, our battery went for strenuous route marches along the dusty roads winding through Crete's innumerable olive groves and colourless, scattered villages. Dasher always marched with us. Sometimes he would bound ahead to rest, panting, in the shade of a tree or bush until the column caught up with him.

Dasher had two intense dislikes — air raids and a bath. Whenever the Stukas and Dorniers came over and our defiant anti-aircraft guns filled the sky with a fleecy confusion of white and grey, he would creep between my legs and sit there dejectedly trembling until the cacophony of guns and bombs had ceased. Often he watched the diving, twisting planes as though he understood their portent and the menace they carried.

We withdrew from our position on the hillside one morning. During a day of ceaseless dive-bombing and machine-gunning by the Luftwaffe, we traversed the two or three miles to the valley below. At nightfall we were told that the Hun was to be held by a rear-guard, and that all troops in the valley were to make for the coast on the other side of Crete. So Dasher and I joined the throng — military detachments and Greek civilian refugees — on the one road over the rocky mountain divide between the north and south coasts of the island.

I had become so accustomed to Dasher trotting along behind me that I did not notice his disappearance until I stopped for a rest after a couple of hours' steady plodding. When five minutes had passed I realised something was amiss. I gave a low whistle — a signal which he had learned to recognise — and called his name, but there was no response. I walked back for nearly a mile, stopping every few minutes to whistle. But my search, hampered as it was by the darkness and continual movement along the road, was in vain. With a sense of very deep loss I decided to continue the southward march without him.

As the night wore on, walking became a mechanical motion of placing one foot in front of the other. With the ever-increasing number of stragglers dropping behind, the column, which had begun as a nearly solid mass, thinned out to a long line of weary men whose spirits drove them even when their bodies seemed incapable of continued effort.

At dawn I was halfway through the pass. For two or three hours I slept on a heap of rubble by the roadside. As a result I gained new energy and decided to keep walking until planes drove me to cover. I was resting in the cool shade of a little village chapel, about 10 miles from Sfakia, when the first planes — Dorniers — came over to drop their bombs wherever they thought troops were concealed. Shortly after midnight I arrived in a steep-sided, tree-covered gully within sight of the sea. There the rest of our regiment were assembled for the final march to the beach.

At dusk we were organised into groups of 50. We knew that the thought of escape so near gave us a reckless disregard for the difficulties and dangers of the boulder-strewn, cliff-side track we chose as the shortest route to the beach. But the short cut proved to be the long way, and we eventually reached our destination too late to embark that night. We turned back to shelter in the hills.

A few of us found a cave inhabited by some Greeks, and here we stretched out among the debris on the dusty floor and slept. I awoke conscious of a terrific itchiness, which investigation proved to be caused by a score of prodigious fleas.

The rest of the day passed uneventfully enough. Towards evening I went down to the beach to discover what I could about future movements. While I was there Bombardier John, whom I had not seen since Suda Bay, walked up.

'I thought you must be about somewhere when I saw your dog,' he said.

I told him that Dasher was 40 miles away, so far as I knew. And then, bounding over the litter of the beach, came Dasher — an elongated black streak that appeared to skim over the ground, so fast did his twinkling legs carry him towards me. The speed of his arrival launched him right into my arms as I stooped to receive him. Wriggling from my grasp he leapt about in an ecstasy of delight and wagged his tail with nearly enough violence to break his back, it seemed. He was a very lean Dasher, it's true, with ribs showing out as ridges along a now bedraggled coat.

Midnight found us on the crest of a steep hill waiting for the signal to descend to the barges drawn up along the beachfront below. A muttered word from the leading officer, and the silent line moved forward. Fearing that Dasher would be unable to negotiate some of the steeper drops, I tucked him under my arm before I began the descent.

Safety was discarded in favour of speed. A careless jump threw me off balance, and before I could save myself I was rolling over and over. I hit the beach with a terrific jolt. A sailor urged me to my feet and bundled me into a crowded barge on the point of pulling out from the water's edge.

When I fell, Dasher had slipped from me and had gone tumbling off into the darkness. My scattered wits returned as the barge slid towards the shadowy outline of a destroyer out to sea. This time I knew I would not see him again.

Crete is now a distant memory, but I often think of my dog and the simple, companionable part he played in my life at a time when lives were little more than desperate things for the giving and the taking.

The Queensland Digger, 1 April 1942

SX1543 was the service number of **Dudley Mark Coleman**, *was born 19 January 1917, at Blyth in the Mid North of South Australia. He enlisted at Blyth in December 1939, was assigned to the artillery, AIF, and was discharged in September 1945 with the rank of lieutenant. He died 28 June 1975.*

Prisoners of the Nazis

'We had been captured nearly two months, were all rotten with dysentery and had been forced to work hard by our captors, on starvation rations.'

— Private Norton Foster

Escape from a Prison Train in Greece
By Norton Foster

Here we were, four Australian soldiers, trudging along the edge of a railway track in the middle of the night, somewhere in the centre of northern Greece. We were all in high spirits for we had just escaped off a German prisoner-of-war train which had left Salonika some two hours earlier bound for Germany. Our escape from the train had been unpremeditated. However, from the time some 56 of us had found ourselves packed jam-tight into a cattle truck, we were sure there would be no way we would be willing to see out the expected eight-day journey to Germany in those conditions.

There was absolutely no comfort in our situation, no seats to sit on, or even room where one could lie out flat. We either had to stand up or sit with our knees up under our chins, and as there was insufficient room for everyone to do the latter at the same time, everyone had to take turns at standing up. To make matters worse we were rotten with dysentery, which had plagued most of us from the first couple of weeks after we were taken prisoner on Crete some two months earlier — 31 May 1941, to be exact. We were also emaciated, lousy and unwashed, and altogether not a pretty sight.

The cattle truck is a pretty common sight around Europe even today but during the war it was the sole means used by the Nazis for transporting millions of people to places they didn't want to go. It is a rail box wagon about six metres long, three wide and two high. It has a sliding door on each side about 1.5 metres wide reaching from floor to ceiling. With the door closed the only ventilation inside was through two small openings about 50 centimetres wide and 35 centimetres high, placed high up under the roof at one end of each side wall and open to the elements. In our wagons these were crisscrossed with strands of barbed wire stapled to the outside of the wagon at about 10-centimetre intervals.

In true German fashion it was planned to stop the train every hour and unload the prisoners a wagon at a time for us to attend to the calls of nature on the side of the track. But dysentery waits for no man, so, not long out of Salonika, one of the corners of the wagon was cleared for use as a toilet. In spite of this, and hampered by the darkness and the crush of bodies, people at the far end were often unable to make it in time. It is not hard to imagine the results.

On the way back to the train after the first stop, and eyeing the window from the outside, someone said, 'You know it would be pretty easy to escape from this bloody death-trap if we could only get out that window. Once out we could swing around the corner of the wagon onto the buffers and jump off from there.' We all looked at each other but had our doubts.

We got back into the wagon and started to discuss the possibilities. After a while we came to the conclusion that it was worth a try. If we got onto the buffers and waited for the train to slow down going up an incline before we jumped off, we could roll away in the darkness.

First up we tried putting our hands through the wire while standing on the back of one of our mates, who was kneeling on the floor, and trying to lever the wire off the outside with our mess knives. However, neither our backs nor our equipment were up to the task and we soon had to abandon it. Then someone got the bright idea of lifting up one of our lightweights horizontally and getting him to kick the wire off with his army boots. We soon gave this a try and when it seemed to be a goer, decided to attack it in earnest after the next train stop which would be soon due. There were no guards on the outside of the train while travelling (these were to come later). Our guards travelled in a passenger coach at the end of the train, the prevailing blackout conditions preventing them from looking out.

Soon after the train was nicely on its way again we attacked the barbed wire with a vengeance. At first it seemed hopeless but slowly, gradually, it started to budge. After about 20 minutes and many changed shifts, one end of each wire had been freed and bent back out of the way. We were ready to go.

It was obvious we would have to get through this small window feet first if we were to avoid doing ourselves an injury if we slipped. We soon worked out that the best way to do this was to stand with our back to the window and, while clinging to the shoulders of a couple of mates in front, have two others lift up our legs and feet from behind and feed them through the opening.

Little Leo Barnden, who had had first go at kicking at the wire, was first to leave and was soon out of sight. I was about sixth in line, being preceded by Joe Plant, 'Aussie' Osborne, Noel Lumby and Reg Clarkson, all members of the same army platoon. Reg had agreed to wait for me on the buffers so we could get off together, in case we got separated from the others. Once outside, it was relatively easy for us to swing around the end of the wagon onto the buffers although it was pretty hairy making the leap as the train slowed down. Nevertheless we both got off safely — triumphant, if somewhat shaken.

The arrangements were that once we were off the train we could walk back along the track until we met up with Leo, who would be waiting for us where he got off. We would then all head off east, moving by night and hiding by day, and eventually make our way into Turkey, which was a neutral country at that time. None of us had much of an idea of what was involved in this but, fired with the enthusiasm of escaping, we did not much care.

Thus we found ourselves — Clarkson, Osborne, Lumby and Foster — picking our way along the track hoping to meet

Barnden and Plant further ahead. It was incredibly dark and the going was difficult. As far as we could make out, it was open country with not a glimmer of light to be seen anywhere. We had been walking for 10 to 15 minutes and I figured we must be getting close to where Leo had got off the train, when 'Aussie' kicked something soft and heavy with his boot. He stopped, bent down, peered at it for some seconds in the darkness and finally picked it up.

'Bloody hell! It's an Aussie army boot!' he said, somewhat surprised. 'A small one.' And with a cry of anguish, 'Gawd, it's got a bloody foot in it. Leo must have slipped when he jumped and fallen between the rails and the wheels cut his foot off.'

We stood still, straining to hear cries or moaning of any kind — stunned that our little mate could have come to such a tragic end — but all was quiet.

Before we had a chance to organise there was a loud pained exclamation from 'Aussie'. 'Aw shit!' he cried, and then started to laugh. 'The bloody boot's full of shit!' and he proceeded to throw it away from him as hard as he could and rub his hands in the dirt as though to erase forever the thought of that horrible thing.

It is easy to guess what had happened: someone on the train, caught in the grip of dysentery, had used his boot as a toilet and pushed it out the window. Four frightened soldiers breathed a great sigh of relief, collected their wits, and proceeded on their way. We never did find Leo or Joe that night. After walking another 20 minutes along the track we concluded they must have set off together eastwards on their own.

Unfortunately none of us had any idea how far it was to Turkey or what type of country we would have to traverse before we got there. Of course we had no maps or compass. We set off in silence at a cracking pace, thinking that if we could put 15 to 20 miles between us and the railway before dawn, we would place ourselves out of harm's way. We could then find some place to lie up during the day and continue our journey, moving by night. Food was going to be the problem, for we had only the meagre rations the Jerry had given us for the train journey, but we were confident we should be able to live off the land.

This was all very well in theory, but unfortunately didn't work out in practice. We had been captured nearly two months, were all rotten with dysentery and had been forced to work hard by our captors, on starvation rations, clearing the wrecked German transport planes and troop gliders which had crashed or been shot down on the Maleme aerodrome in Crete.

After a couple of hours' marching we began to tire. We must have been a good 10 miles from the railway. What initially had appeared to be flat country turned out to be quite undulating and crisscrossed with wadies or dried water courses. This had held up our progress so we were glad to call a halt and camp for the rest of the night.

We slept fitfully and, cold and stiff, were relieved to see the arrival of dawn. As soon as it became light enough we began to look around and saw a group of houses, a village, a couple of miles away. 'Let's get closer,' said Reg. 'We might be able to scrounge something to eat before anyone gets about.' We made our way closer to the village, keeping out of sight as best we could, until we were about 100 yards from the nearest house.

We kept watch on the house and after a while a young man came out and hesitantly started to move in our direction. He stopped a short way off. We thought the game must have been up and decided to send someone out to meet him. Lumby agreed to do this, showed himself and went out. None of us could speak Greek, nor could the fellow speak English, so things were a bit difficult for a while. He could see from our uniforms that we were British (if not Australian) soldiers, and it was soon evident that his sympathies were with us. He motioned Lumby to go back and lay low, and he would bring us out some food and water. True to his word he appeared shortly with some farm bread, cheese, tomatoes and an array of vegies from their garden, the like of which we had not seen for months.

Towards evening the young fellow came over with an older man, obviously his father, bringing us more food. The father seemed pleased enough to meet us, but showed his concern that we should not stay where we were, so close to the house, as they were afraid of reprisals from the Germans if they found us there. By gestures, they told us that they would take us, after dark, and hide us up in the hills, about a mile away. We would be able to stay there in a safe place until we recovered our strength and they would bring us food each night. As soon as it got dark they led us around the village and into the hills.

We ended up at what looked to be just like a typical biblical sheepfold: a sheep yard fenced with a dry-stack rock wall, with a gate at one end and a little roofed shack for the shepherd at the other. It was an ideal hiding place for us, for we were well out of sight and had a good long-distance view if anyone tried to approach.

The village people were peasant-type farmers and the kindest people one could ever wish to meet. Word gradually spread of our presence and before long they had organised themselves to take turns to deliver food to us on a nightly basis.

One of the first things they wanted us to do was to shed our army uniforms and don civilian clothes and thus make ourselves less conspicuous if Germans happened to come our way. We kept our army pay books and identification discs. After we had been in the hut a few days, one evening at dusk we saw three men approaching up the track. We recognised Viachios but not the other two. Then we realised it was Joe Plant and Leo Barnden — they too were decked out in old civvy gear and had their hair dyed a dull jet black as they were both naturally blond-headed. Joe and Leo had been taken in hand by Greeks in another village. The local grapevine must have told their benefactors of our presence, so they'd brought them to join us.

There were now six of us in the little hut: Leo Barnden, Reg Clarkson, Noel Lumby, 'Aussie' Osborne, Joe Plant and Norton Foster, all members of the same platoon of 'B' Company, 2nd/11th Battalion AIF.

The group of six stayed in the area for some two months, assisting the villagers in raking up grain stubble and baling it. They were then taken to Salonika and escorted to a remote coastal area where British submarines made occasional visits to rescue escaped prisoners and stragglers from the Greek campaign. All six, who had enlisted at Northam, WA, in November 1939, were thus repatriated eventually to Australia.

The Listening Post, Winter 1996 — Autumn 1997

Norton Henry Foster *was born in Melbourne on 7 August 1919, enlisted at Northam, WA, on 10 November 1939, was discharged with the rank of private in November 1945 and died 16 February 2004.*

Noel Percival Lumby *was born in West Maitland, NSW, on 20 April 1916, was discharged as a corporal in December 1945 and died 7 February 2010.*

Reginald Thomas Clarkson *was born in Dongara, WA, on 28 October 1917, was discharged as a private in September 1945 and died 17 January 1970.*

Henry John Osborne, nicknamed 'Aussie', was born in Birmingham, England, on 30 September 1911, and was discharged as a corporal in September 1945.

Joseph Vernon Plant was born 7 May 1916 in Merredin, WA, was discharged as a lance corporal in September 1945 and died 4 September 1998.

Leo Edward Barnden was born 19 January 1918 in Geraldton, WA, was discharged as a private in August 1945 and died 17 October 2012.

A 'Lousy' Trick
By U.G. Ryan

Early in 1942 at a POW working camp at Lockhausen, Bavaria, our camp commandant (known as the Bull-Frog) insisted on one man being detailed from the sick parade to clean his quarters.

One of our men, Sam, a WX, who had been on the sick list for some time, was detailed for the job. We still suffered the discomforts of vermin, originally acquired in Salonika where we had been quartered for some weeks in old Turkish barracks, and a nightly ritual among the men was the removal of all vermin within sight from their underclothing.

Each Sunday morning the Bull-Frog, who spoke a few words of English, would make an inspection of our barracks. Invariably his question would be, 'Have you any lice?' Equally invariably our reply would be, 'No.' Then would come, 'Now do not be ashamed, because I have them too.'

Of course he had them, for each night Sam called for a tarpaulin muster into a tobacco tin and each morning sprinkled them through the Bull-Frog's blankets.

The Listening Post, September 1949

Urban Gerard Ryan *was born 28 May 1907 in Perth, and gave his residence as Kalgoorlie when he enlisted at Subiaco in January 1940. He was discharged in September 1945, having served with the 2/11th Battalion as a corporal, and died 18 November 1968.*

Stalag 383's £5000 Spitfire
By Keith H. Hooper

We who were prisoners of war in Stalag 383, Hohenfels, between Nuremberg and Regensburg, Germany, bought a Spitfire, which flew and fought over Germany — and the Nazis helped us, without knowing it.

Letters in code, which completely fooled our hosts (they always claimed that they had a foolproof censorship system), passed in and out of our camp, telling us that the sum of £5000 sterling, sent through our pay-book credits, had been paid to the British 'Wings for Victory Fund'. A Spitfire had been bought with the money and the machine had been in action over Germany.

And the kite bore the name we chose for it: *Unshackled Spirit*.

It typified our spiritual resistance to our enforced environment, although the name was suggested by one of the camp bootleggers.

The idea originated from a British anti-aircraft battery man, captured on Crete, Sergeant Doug Miles-Osborne, who organised the whole business. His idea was adopted instantly, because we incarcerates were as sore as hell at not being able to take part in the climax of the war.

Doug knew personally the then British parliamentary secretary to the Ministry of Supply, Duncan Sandys, Prime Minister Churchill's son-in-law, who had been Doug's battery commander at one stage. Doug wrote that we were sending 5000 smackers for the Duncan Sandys Welfare Fund.

We'd been permitted to establish in the camp a pay office through which we frequently transmitted money to our folks at home. Whenever a prisoner died a welfare fund would be got up by his cobbers to send a monetary tribute to his relatives. We hoped that the German censors would think the Duncan Sandys Welfare Fund was another of these. They did!

A committee was formed. Two men went from hut to hut canvassing subscriptions. A third kept nit outside for 'snoops': nasty Huns whose special job was to prowl round listening at doors, peeking through windows, and crawling under floors to locate our secret radios and detect any other illegal activities. But the collection obviated this and other hazards. The money poured in quickly.

Hundreds of blokes (there were 4529 in the camp at that stage) who didn't hear about the collection until after the fund closed complained bitterly for not being given a chance to subscribe. The organising committee was even accused of being cliquey. We do believe that we might have been able to rake up enough for a bomber squadron. But the Huns might have taken a tumble to that.

Duncan Sandys told Doug, when they met in London after the defeat of Germany, that the money started turning up before he got the code letters explaining what the idea was.

Unshackled Spirit was battle-borne early in 1945. Copies of the letter telling us of that event were plastered all over the camp — in huts, washhouses and latrines. And the letter carried the Nazi Geprüft [censorship] stamp. As it came at a time when conditions for us were decidedly unpleasant — no fuel, little food, bitter cold, and news that the Huns were bursting out of the Bulge — the letter bucked the mob up.

Every time an Allied squadron passed overhead we imagined that among the scurrying fighter escort was our Spitfire.

Mufti, September–October 1956

Great Australian World War II Stories

Keith Horton Hooper, *born 27 August 1918, was a sergeant in the 2/6th Infantry Battalion, wounded on Crete and captured by the Germans in 1941. He had enlisted at Prahran, Melbourne, in November 1939 and was discharged in January 1946. He died 11 March 2010.*

Escape from Marburg
By an ex-member of the 2/1 Battalion

I had been three years behind barbed wire when I was sent to the prison camp at Marburg, Austria [now Maribor, Slovenia]. There, with 18 other Australians captured at Benghazi in 1941, I was set to work on the main Klagenfurt–Vienna railway line. Eighty British prisoners were included also in the maintenance gang. Although we were treated well, our desire for freedom was very strong and plans to escape were soon formulated.

Across the border, in Yugoslavia, Marshal Tito's partisans had become very active, harassing German patrols and upsetting their communications. We were able to contact them through a young Austrian girl who posed as a friend of the German guards but was actually a member of the partisan forces. An escape plan was drawn up.

At this time we were working in the Drau Valley, about 20 miles from Marburg. Each morning at seven we left camp in a special two-car train and were taken to the job. The same train returned us to the camp at 7 p.m. Methodical German procedure was to provide the key to our escape.

Just before 8 a.m. on 30 August our train stopped at a lonely spot on the bank of the Drau River, where we had been working the previous day. We got out, followed by 17 German guards armed with rifles.

Immediately, from the dense spruce forest on the hillside above us, a party of 70 Yugoslav partisans appeared, armed with machine-guns and grenades. They covered our guards, calling on them to throw up their hands. With remarkable promptitude the Huns obeyed the command, and in less than a minute we were away, our destination Italy. Not a shot was fired, and the whole operation was quietly and speedily carried out.

The partisans covered our getaway from machine-gun posts they had prepared during the night overlooking the railway line and road along which a pursuit party would be expected to travel should word of our escape reach the strong German post at Lorenzen [now Lovrenc], a half-mile away.

The weather was perfect, and we were in great spirits as we headed south. Good progress was made that first day. At 5 p.m. we contacted a second partisan patrol who fed us. The Jerry guards with three German civilian engineers from the job were brought in at dusk. Partisans took their boots and clothing and then turned machine-guns on them. We realised that we could expect little mercy if recaptured.

On the evening of the second day, with eight well-armed guerrillas at the head of the party, we proceeded south through dense fir forests. The need for extreme caution was emphasised when partisan scouts brought word that several German parties, of battalion strength, were reported moving across our route.

Every Man for Himself
At midnight it was necessary to cross an open field to reach the cover of a mountain range running south. When the first file emerged from the cover of the forest into the moonlit field, about a dozen machine-guns opened up on us from a point straight ahead and at a range of about 600 yards.

Four Tommies were killed in the opening bursts. The remainder of the party dived for cover in the forest. I could hear German officers barking commands and knew enough German to understand the order to surround the wood in which we had taken cover.

It was now a case of every man for himself. I found myself alone and decided to lie quietly under cover, in the hope the Germans would overrun me in pursuit of the main party, which could be heard crashing through the trees. A platoon of machine-gunners from the ambush passed about 12 yards from my hideout. When they had passed I quietly picked my way out of the wood and continued walking west throughout the night.

For the next seven days I made good progress, without mishap. After four days on an unvaried diet of fruit, I decided to risk a visit to a farmhouse in search of something more substantial. That night I went to a large farmhouse and knocked up the Yugoslav farmer. He was able to understand my poor German and received me hospitably enough, giving me an excellent meal of black bread and sour milk with a large jug of *most*, the national drink, which resembles cider but is much more potent. The farmer obviously was uneasy at the possibility of a German patrol arriving and finding on his farm a man in British uniform, so I pushed on as soon as I had eaten.

I Meet the Partisans
Early on the morning of my eighth day of freedom I met a partisan patrol of four men and two girls, who invited me to rest with them for a day. They told me a neighbouring party had contacted a British escapee, and at midnight he was brought to me. His name was Maltby, and he had been in the main party when we ran into the first ambush. He had spent most of the time since then with partisan bands.

On the following evening, accompanied by three young partisans, Maltby and I headed south. During the night we were going along a spur of the main range when heavy firing broke out immediately below us. Tracers were flying about our position and we were not sure whether a German patrol was firing at us or another partisan patrol. However, grenade and mortar action convinced us that it was the latter, so we hurried on.

The Second Ambush
In the early dawn we were passing a deserted farmhouse when we

ran into an ambush. One machine-gun post opened on us from the front at a range of less than 200 yards, and another on our left flank about 400 yards away. Two of our partisan friends were caught in the crossfire and literally cut to pieces. Maltby ran for about 60 yards in a heavy stream of fire and reached the cover of the timber uninjured. I darted around the corner of a barn.

The Germans were running down the hill on the other side of the barn, firing bursts into the hayloft above me. I dived into a narrow concrete stall and covered myself with the little straw and dung lying about and had just settled in when two Germans passed and fired a burst into the corner opposite where I lay hidden. When they had gone I examined the two partisans who had been shot. Nothing could be done for them, so I made my way alone up the hill.

A mile from the site of the ambush I was challenged by partisan troops who had heard the shooting and were stalking the German ambush party. I stayed with them until dark and then set out again, considerably worried about Maltby.

For two days I followed a high and narrow mountain running south, and towards evening of the second day looked down on the township of Ljubno, the most beautiful spot I had ever seen. After carefully observing the place for an hour I felt sure that the troops moving about the town area were partisans, so I went forward to enter the town.

About a mile from the outskirts I was harshly challenged by a partisan sentry, who flatly refused to believe my story and forced me to remain with him for two hours until his relief appeared. Then I was marched to the Yugoslav commandant of the local troops. He accepted my story and directed me to an English-speaking Yugoslav who lived in Ljubno. He and his wife fed me well and gave me a bed for the night. At dawn on the following day I went on with a partisan courier going south.

From Ljubno south, Marshal Tito's forces had made a distinct impression on the German forces. The going here was better, although we were again travelling only at night. In five nights I covered well over 100 miles, and although food now was quite plentiful, I was feeling the strain. On 31 September I reached a large village on the Croatian border, and was overjoyed to find the main party camped in the village, Maltby among them. He had arrived an hour ahead of me.

Rescue from the Air

The partisans here were in radio communication with the British forces in Italy and had notified them of our escape. Instructions were given to prepare an airstrip on the riverbank so that British planes could attempt to rescue us by air. In three nights a tiny dirt strip was completed and we gathered there to await the arrival of the planes. It seemed impossible that large transports would be able to land in darkness on such an ill-prepared strip. Three smudge flares marked the field. Soon after midnight we heard the drone of the planes. The first, a DC-3, cruised over the strip at about 500 feet, and after circling in a wide arc, again passed over us.

One of the crew from the Douglas parachuted to the field, and by means of a small radio he wore strapped to his body, directed the planes onto the strip. At the third attempt the first plane came in steeply to land, switching on landing lights when no more than 100 feet above the ground. Four more followed. They took off again at 10-minute intervals, each carrying a full load of escaped prisoners and many badly wounded partisans, including several girls.

At 4.30 a.m. we landed at Bari, on the Adriatic coast of Italy. Our adventure was over. We had travelled 286 miles on foot through German lines, dressed in full British battle dress, and had lost only four men on the trip.

Reveille, 1 April 1946

The Long March:
Dombrova, Poland to Regensburg, Bavaria
By Pte G.C. Anderson, HQ Company, 2/11th Bn AIF

During the last week of December 1944, our work party of 100 POWs was suddenly transferred from a punishment camp coalmine near Katowice in Poland where we had worked for two and a half years to another coalmine at Dombrova [now Dabrowa Górnicza] — a standard POW camp close to Kraków where 500 British and Allied POWs worked.

During the next few weeks we learned that the Russians had taken Warsaw approximately 250 kilometres away and the talk was of the camp moving out.

It was now winter with heavy snow and temperatures around minus 30 degrees Celsius. On 20 January 1945 we moved out to join a column already on the march as the Russians were developing a pincer movement in their drive to Germany.

We were issued with one two-kilogram loaf and a half-pound tin of meat between two men, and one Red Cross parcel each, to last six days, when we were told that we were to entrain for the rest of the journey. However, late on the third day (after marching 12 hours a day) we stumbled into Gnadenfeld [Pawłowiczki]; it lay almost in the jaws of the pincer which were only 18 miles apart. We were billeted in a large barn on the outskirts of the town which already contained many men who had been on the road ahead of us. Our column had increased from 600 to about 1400.

No one could sleep: the rumble of guns which we had heard in the distance now seemed to be drawing closer — even the sound of machine-guns was quite plain. At around midnight the German guards came screaming to get us on the move again — the

The Long March: Dombrova, Poland to Regensburg, Bavaria

Russians had almost closed the gap and the Germans were falling back. Most of the POWs now found great difficulty in getting their boots on (having taken them off to relieve aching feet) as the sweat had turned to ice and the leather was now like iron. Further, the big toe on my right foot was frostbitten and both my heels were red raw. Struggling through the straw on my way to the door, I came upon a group of about 15 men who were too tired or sick to carry on and were being left behind for the Russians to pick up. So, taking a chance on being shot, as this was often the way of leaving men for the Russians to pick up, I joined the group.

The main column had departed. I began to think that perhaps it was not a good idea; that it may have been better to stick with the main column.

After about an hour our attention was attracted by the sound of a heavy vehicle coming up the drive towards the barn. Every man rose to his feet thinking, *Russians*. A voice speaking German ordered us to climb aboard. The lorry then quickly drove after the column with stray bullets striking the road and the lorry. We finally drew up in the town of Wehen. A new German front was now holding.

The column was drawn up on one side of the main street while in the centre carts of all shapes and sizes — some drawn by horses, others by ordinary dairy cows — were battling to get out of town as quickly as possible.

On 26 January we reached Auschwitz where we stayed for two days. Inmates from the concentration camp joined us and we linked up with other groups of POWs including many Russians. It was said that the column was now 20,000, a large portion being German troops and equipment using the column for security against air attack. We were on the end of the column and were a group of about 1500 POWs together with a large number of guards and wagons — we saw little of anyone else.

On leaving Auschwitz we were warned that any person falling out of the column would be shot. We were soon to see evidence of this as bodies partly covered by snow were seen along the roadside — political prisoners, men in khaki and in brown [Russians].

Prior to reaching the town of Unter Jellen [Horní Jelení] on 14 February, we passed through the town of Wildenshwert [Ústí nad Orlicí] where the Czechs handed out some food. This was a lifesaver as many were suffering from frost bite and a shortage of food, and were chewing snow for liquid and food. We were now 370 kilometres from the start.

During the next 15 days we passed through the outskirts of Prague and Lidice, heading north to Lipa then across to Tuhein, arriving on 27 February having covered 580 kilometres.

The march now became even more gruelling as food was non-existent, but then on 8 March the column reached the town of Krippau (629 kilometres) to see a long line of International Red Cross trucks loaded with parcels. The column stayed in Krippau until 10 March. At this stage large numbers of American Superfortresses were seen flying overhead on their mass bombing raids.

The route now lay over the Moosbach Pass, and after many days of heavy climbing and slippery descents, the column reached the town of Letzen just inside the Bavarian border and about 870 kilometres from Poland.

The column then travelled from Letzen to Weiden where, during the night of 26 March, the POWs were loaded into cattle trucks to travel via Nuremburg to arrive at Regensburg on 27/28 March.

The POWs were in Regensburg for about two weeks, during which time there were many air raids. The POWs were then moved again, this time on the road to Munich. The writer and 15 other POWs who were injured or wounded were left behind as they were unable to face the march. Instead of guards they were left with a German doctor and nurse.

The Long March: Dombrova, Poland to Regensburg, Bavaria

For two days the party remained in a large foxhole while the battle rolled on. Then the rumble of heavy tanks was heard as Patton's Army arrived — the date was 27 April 1945.

The Listening Post, Winter 1995

George Charles Anderson *was born on 11 April 1919, and enlisted at Northam, WA, giving his residence as Kalgoorlie, in November 1939. He was discharged on 25 August 1945 and died 24 July 2004.*

The War in the Air

'169 airmen did not return that night. Of the 140 killed or captured, 27 were Australians.'

— Flying Officer John Clulow

The Spy
By Slim Johnson

When the Empire Air Training Scheme had been completely established in Canada, Fritz had his spy system in full swing. Rookies were continually warned to be on their guard for suspicious characters: 'Don't tell 'em anything.'

This piece of wisdom almost landed us in the blue.

During one of those usual unexplained train hold-ups we were approached by a man about 34. His blond hair and too-English accent, his baggy civvy trousers and his wandering eye made us remember the warnings, and the fact that he was so young, and not in uniform, confirmed it.

'You chaps are Aussies, aren't you? New chums?'

Our Australias were on, so what the hell! 'Yes,' we chorused.

'Going to get your first taste of the air, eh?'

It was the truth, but if he was a spy ...

Bill K. took over, giving us a broad wink first. 'No, we are on the last leg. Conversion course on to fighters; we'll be flying in ops.'

The blond man seemed interested and surprised. 'Really?'

'Yes,' said Bill. 'Won't be long now.'

'What fighters are you going to fly?'

Bill paused. 'Tiger Moth fighters.'

Baggy Britches seemed puzzled. 'They must be new.'

'Not exactly, sport.' Bill still had his tongue in his cheek. 'But they're still on the secret list.'

'They must be something extra special, then,' he smiled, smugly.

'Special? They're the greatest things with wings! They cruise at 400, two-seaters, range 4000 miles and carry eight Brownings and one cannon in the nose. They're honeys to fly, too.'

'Well, I'll be ... And ...'

But a whistle had gone, and we had to fall in and entrain.

Bill kept us laughing almost the entire four-hour trip to Edmonton. It brightened up the trip, but we were glad when the journey was over.

When the CO had given the customary pep talk, we were introduced to our chief flying instructor. He gave us a short talk on the luxury we were getting for nothing — and then told the whole crowd of the very interesting talk he'd had with some Aussies that afternoon about a new fighter called the Tiger Moth.

Were our faces red!

The Listening Post, March 1949

Raid on Berlin: I Learned from This
By Flight Lieutenant Bob Nielsen, DFM

The date was 1 March 1943. We had been briefed for our night's operation and the target was Berlin. It was to be our first trip to the city and the whole of 460 Squadron was thrilled at the prospect of pranging the big city.

With the assistance of the bomb-aimer I prepared charts, collected navigational flimsies and drew signal cartridges, and eventually the hour of departure came. Take-off was normal and soon we were climbing steadily out over the North Sea, checking track with loop bearings and computing new air speeds as the temperature decreased with height.

I wasn't worried as to the navigational difficulties — hadn't I done 37 operational flights with the same pilot? Hadn't we always got back without much trouble, apart from a couple of radio bearings? Before the night was over I was to be shaken from my complacent state, my self-confidence badly undermined, but firmly determined to brush up again all the finer points of air navigation.

We found Berlin easily enough. The Germans had tried hard to camouflage their capital, but two things they couldn't hide were the River Spree and the Unter den Linden — both visible for miles. Alan gave his usual steady bombing run — 'bombs gone' — and just as we started to dive away, something hit us with a terrible *whack* and we were thrown into a vertical dive, out of control. We thought it was a direct hit from flak — later we found that an aircraft above us had dropped his incendiaries on our machine.

We fell from 18,000 feet to 4000 feet in a matter of seconds. By a superhuman effort, Peter (Isaacson) brought 'Queenie' back to normal. The Lancaster was badly damaged; our mid-upper gunner was wounded and we were 850 miles from England.

From here started an inglorious chapter in the life of one experienced Bomber Command navigator.

The flight plan had provided that we fly for two minutes due south of Berlin (at a speed of 200 knots) and then set a course for the coast. I allowed four minutes, overlooking the fact that we had dived out at a speed of something like 400 knots. Consequently, when we turned we were already 25 miles south of track. Over Germany that can be very dangerous; in a damaged bomber it is virtually suicide.

The next mistake came when Peter reported two big cones of searchlights 20 and 30 miles north of our track. 'Okay, don't worry,' I said, 'that's Hamburg and Bremen. We're probably a bit north of track. Weave a bit more to the south.'

Take a look at the map of Germany — note the positions of Bremen and Hamburg, note also Hanover and Brunswick. We were seeing the fireworks of the latter towns, and getting further and further south of our track. Note too that I hadn't checked this fact; I was happy to assume that Bremen and Hamburg were on our starboard.

The sky was ablaze with stars, but my sextant was under the table — untouched. We flew on and more searchlights appeared ahead. 'Okay, Peter, go south. Groningen ahead.' He did so. A hundred more appeared ahead of us. 'Go south, Peter.' Once again he did so. As if to mock us, a hundred more were exposed right in our path. 'I'm going through them, Bob.'

The nose dropped, 'Queenie' gathered speed and in a few seconds we were viciously coned. The flak was continuous; we could hear it exploding above the roar of the engines. Peter flew on his instruments alone. We eventually descended to 900 feet — too low for the gunners to depress the guns to hit us, and after 15 minutes of sweating and praying we were through.

Once again I was wrong: the searchlights were not at Groningen but Münster and Hamm.

Fifteen minutes' flying and we were across the coast and back to base an hour later. The CO had marked us down as missing.

From this trip I learnt plenty. I found that no matter how much experience a navigator had, he can never have navigation sewn up. Never again would I doubt my DR, never again would I ignore the flight plan, and I had blindly broken the cardinal rule — 'Never pinpoint on searchlights or flak.' And never would I kid myself that I could navigate on instinct alone, with a sextant under the table and ANTs in my bag.

Next day my crew presented me with a leather medal on which was inscribed, 'Check, check and check again'. And the CO lent me D.C.T. Bennett's book *The Complete Air Navigator*.

Rising Sun (South Australia), October 1943

Robert Stanley McFarlane Nielsen, *DFM, born on 16 February 1921, was a navigator with Bomber Command, initially as a sergeant, later as a flight lieutenant. He died in California in November 2001.*

In May 1943, the brand-new Lancaster 'Q' for Queenie, ED 930, took off from Scotland headed for Australia, finally arriving at Amberley airfield, west of Brisbane, on 4 June. The crew included Flight Lieutenant Peter Isaacson, DFC, AFC, DFM (captain) and Flight Lieutenant Robert Nielsen, DFM (navigator). In October they flew the aircraft on the 4th Liberty Loan Tour of Tasmania, Victoria and NSW, achieving fame by flying under the Sydney Harbour Bridge on 22 October to raise funds for the war loan.

Bombers, Fighters — and the Occasional Church Spire
By Squadron Leader Keith Thiele, DSO, DFC and 2 Bars

I was in Christchurch when the war started, and I joined up immediately in the air force. That was 1939 but it took me nearly a year to get in and get trained, so I finished up going to England just at the beginning of 1941. I was hoping to fly Spitfires and Hurricanes of course, as we all were, but unfortunately I got posted to Bomber Command. So I was trained on Wellingtons, and I did a tour on them, and then we converted to Halifaxes and did a tour on them. Then I transferred to an Australian squadron, 467. It was a new squadron, just being equipped with Lancasters, at a place called Bottesford in Nottinghamshire. So I did a tour on Lancs — I did about 62 trips on bombers before I transferred to fighters in '43.

Nearly all my bombing trips were over Germany. I did the Thousand Bomber Raids: the first three of them, Berlin, the Ruhr, Essen — all those sorts of places. And I had a go at the German pocket battleships, including the *Scharnhorst*, that went through the Channel in February 1942 — that was in an old Wellington. That was a good one because I was one of the few who found them. The weather was crook and I popped out of cloud right over them, which was a bit disastrous. I didn't have time to open the bomb doors and drop my bombs, but I got about 42 holes in my aeroplane. I think about 17 poor old Swordfish went out to have a go at them and not one survived. They shouldn't have got through. We knew they were coming because we were on stand-by over the Christmas period, but it was a disaster for England to have the Germans get through their Channel. The weather was bad — low cloud. The Germans timed it very nicely. They waited till they had the right conditions.

The most successful mission we did was on Cologne, the first of the Thousand Bomber Raids. We really hammered that place. It was the first trip on a Halifax and I couldn't get the bombs off. They hung up on me, and I was going round and round in circles over Cologne with a thousand aircraft going past me. I don't know how many collisions there were but it's amazing there weren't a lot, because we weren't allocated a height or a track, or anything organised like that — we just went. It was a beautiful moonlit night and Cologne was easy to find because of the River Rhine.

Prior to that we had very great difficulty finding our targets. I think we killed more cows than we did damage to the German cities! Once we got the Pathfinders [aircraft used to mark targets with flares] it was a different story, but before that we used to wander around lost most of the time.

The Germans were very appreciative that we didn't clobber the famous cathedral in Cologne, but that was probably because it was our aiming point. I met some Germans recently who came from Cologne, and they said, 'Thank you very much — we've got a nice modern city now.' We just bombed the whole city. The only real aiming point we had was the Krupp's factory at Essen, and the most successful was the Renault works in Paris — it was a beautiful moonlit night and we clobbered that pretty well.

Berlin was always well identified by the mount of flak and searchlights. But it was a matter of hit-and-miss in the early days. In fact we seldom got home to base — I think I saw most of England heading back because we could never find our own aerodrome half the time. We had a good system — the aircraft were equipped with a little CB radio to communicate with the tower. They had about a 10-mile range and scattered all over England were these Observer Corps things, and if they heard you calling on the radio they knew you were within about 10 miles of them. So then all the searchlights in the area would come up vertically and wave towards the nearest aerodrome, so that's how we found it. The call sign for the Observer Corps at that stage was 'Darky', so we used to wander around over England calling, 'Hello Darky, Darky — you little bastard, where are we?'

I flew more than 80 missions over Germany. The squadron I was on first was a Canadian squadron and we had the old Halifaxes — we'd changed from Wellingtons to Halifaxes. It had been running for 12 months and I think I was the first pilot who ever finished a tour of operations at that stage. I was very lucky. I had a system, which I'd thought up. Most of the pilots tried to get up as high as they could, especially on Lancs — they'd try to get up to 20,000 feet. I decided that the light flak was only good up to 6000 or 7000 feet, and the heavy flak was no good above 12,000 feet — it couldn't be accurate. So I used to bomb from around 8000 feet. It worked out all right, so after I'd dropped my bombs I'd immediately whiz down to the deck because I figured in the dark there'd be no fighters at low levels.

The only hazard, of course, was the odd church spire, and I managed to survive most of those, except on one occasion. This was in a Lancaster. I came out over the French coast at nought feet, and just as I crossed the coast — *bang* — I lost two engines on one side. I managed to get back to England on the other two. One just throttled back and I couldn't get any power out of it, and the other was overheating and on fire.

So I headed straight for a little fighter aerodrome on the south coast of England called Ford, and when I went to put the gear down, I found my hydraulics had also been knocked out, so I had no gear. The Lancaster had an emergency air system so you could put the gear down — it was compressed air — so I used that, but unfortunately one side of that had been knocked out so it only put one leg down and not the other. What I didn't know was that once it's down, with no hydraulics you can't retract it, so I'm floating round a little fighter aerodrome with two engines out and one wheel! So I couldn't use flaps or anything. I thought

Bombers, Fighters — and the Occasional Church Spire

I'd just put the landing lever up, and when I touched down it'd just fold up and I'd belly land. Of course it didn't fold up and I landed on one wheel. It was quite smooth, actually, and I ran the whole length of the strip, and finally the wing dropped and there wasn't much damage to the aeroplane. I'd have probably stuffed it up if I'd known I was landing on one wheel!

It was unfortunate that on each tour there were only 20 trips, so on my second tour I was with a new crew. We got to the end of my tour and I was taken off, and unfortunately my crew still had 10 trips to do, because it was 30 trips for them. I thought that was most unfair: I applied to Group so I could do another 10 trips with them. They knocked that back. Then I applied to have the crew taken off operations. They wouldn't do that either. So all my crew finished up perishing with other skippers. It was a shame. I thought that was pretty cruel, really.

When I was on the Aussie squadron, there was a mate of mine, young Mant, who thought that because I'd done so many trips and survived, I had some technique. I tried to convince him that it was only luck, but he tried to adopt my technique of bombing low. The main risk you took with that, of course, was copping some bombs from the blokes up top. He didn't come back one night. He went missing, and I knew he had. We used to break the rules by having a little chat over the target area — we used to sing a little song and hope the Huns were listening — something like 'I don't want to set the world on fire, I just want to start a flame in your heart'. This night he didn't come up on the radio.

Strangely enough I was in Queensland on Anzac Day a few years ago, and to my surprise I met his navigator and I found out that's exactly what happened to Mant. The navigator wasn't sure at that stage whether it was an anti-aircraft shell that came up through the wing or a bomb, but anyway something went right through the wing and set the aircraft on fire, and it blew up. The navigator was lucky to get out because he was right near the escape hatch. [467 Squadron records show that

Pilot Officer Graeme Smyth Mant, RAAF, was killed on 11 March 1943, aged 26. The target was Stuttgart.]

I started off with bombers in 405 Squadron, which was a Canadian squadron, and when I finished my tour with them I was posted to a training unit on old Whitleys, and I hated that. I was a squadron leader at the time and I applied to go back onto operations, and I had to drop rank to do it, to flight lieutenant. I was posted to the Australian squadron, 467, and did my second tour with them.

After that I had a mate in the Air Ministry and I teed up to go on Spitfires, but I think Harris [Air Marshal Sir Arthur Harris] was a bit upset with me. I got a message one day to go across and see Guy Gibson [Wing Commander Guy Penrose Gibson] at Scampton and he was in his room, with a heap of mail, surrounded by WAAFs, and he was dictating letters — he'd just got his VC for the dams raid. He said to me, 'When are you coming over?' I said, 'What do you mean?' He said, 'Don't you know anything about it? You're coming over, aren't you?' I didn't know but I was supposed to be coming over to take his place. He said, 'Don't you want to?' I said, 'No, not really, I've teed up to go to Spitfires.' And he said, 'You lucky bugger — I wish I could.' So I knocked it back — if I'd accepted that I'd have been wing commander on 617 Squadron, the Dambusters. I'm glad I knocked it back because their next raid was on the Dortmund–Ems Canal and they lost the lot — 17 aircraft.

So Harris, when I did that, said, 'You're not going to bloody go to Spitfires', and they posted me instead to 24 Squadron, which was a transport squadron at Hendon. Then I managed to get posted to Transatlantic Ferry Command in Canada — I took three crews over to ferry the Canadian Lancasters. I delivered the first Canadian-built Lanc back to England, and while I was there I went and saw my mate in the Air Ministry and wangled a transfer to Fighter Command.

I got onto Spitfires for a tour and joined 41 Squadron at

Tangmere. I had to drop to flight lieutenant again: I hold the record, I think — I was five times a flight lieutenant! When I got onto Spitfires they were all full of awe because I arrived as a flight lieutenant and at that stage I had a DSO, DFC and bar, and no experience! I was 21 or 22 then. I'd spent my 21st birthday over Hamburg.

In 24 Squadron we did patrols, a lot of recces, and convoy escort up and down the Channel — we spent a lot of time escorting a bloody tub towing a great big concrete box, and we thought, *What a waste of bloody time!* but I think it was Mulberry Harbour they were getting ready for D-day. I was over the beachhead at Normandy on D-day but that was quite uneventful — didn't see a Hun or anything, just a big convoy of ships.

We were taken off our normal operations when the German V-bombs started. So we were chasing doodlebugs. I was flying a Spitfire Mark 12, which was the first one with the Griffon engine — it was the fastest aircraft then, until the Tempest came along. We couldn't catch them straight and level, so we used to patrol at about 8000 feet and then dive on them. I got a couple but they were very difficult to catch. The Tempests got most.

I was posted to a New Zealand Squadron, 486, on Tempests. I went as a flight commander there and when the CO was lost I took over the squadron. We had heavy losses at that stage, strangely enough. January was a satisfactory month because we shot down something like 84 enemy aircraft, and destroyed a couple of hundred trains, trucks and transports, and only lost eight aircraft. The squadron history goes on to say February was less satisfactory because we lost 31 aircraft.

Then I went as CO of 3 Squadron on Tempests. It was in February 1945 that I was shot down, and that was the end of my war, really. I was hit by flak while attacking a train. The engine immediately stopped and I had little yellow flames licking up around my boots, so I thought I'd better get out, and like a fool I jettisoned the canopy before I undid all my harness and everything, and the little yellow flames became a blast furnace and I had to undo my straps and everything, and roll the aircraft upside down and drop out. I got second-degree burns to the face and the arms.

When I bailed out I landed right next to the railway station. There was a flat train in the siding and there were about 200 Huns who'd been waiting about two bloody months for this train. It had just come into sight and it was pissing steam down the track where I'd just clobbered it. They weren't too pleased to see me. They were all shouting, 'Women, children, churches, hospitals', and the little stationmaster was trying to kick me in the balls. The crowd was very obviously in the mood to lynch me — and a goods train came through the station at this stage. Then I was taken over by the police and shoved into a cell at the police station. It was the middle of winter and pretty miserable, and I had no blankets, just bare boards with a bench to sleep on. Finally two old German guards took me to an interrogation centre at Frankfurt and from there I went to a transit camp.

The old guards were like Laurel and Hardy. They left me sitting on the platform at the railway station looking after their guns and they went to sleep. I was able to go down to the toilet and I had all my flight plans inside my boot with all my courses — they'd have been able to track that back to the aerodrome — and I was able to flush those down the toilet while they were sound asleep.

I was in the transit camp for a couple of months. The Allies were approaching the Rhine so the Huns evacuated the camp, and marched the poor buggers north into Silesia or Austria or somewhere. Fortunately there were 16 of us who were unfit to travel and they left us with just a couple of old home guards, and we just gradually took over the camp. There was no security. Terry Spencer [Squadron Leader Terence Spencer DFC] — an old Spitfire mate from 41 Squadron — spoke excellent French, fortunately. He and I virtually just walked out to the local village, which was full of displaced persons, a lot of them French troops who'd been captured and had been farming around the area. Terry asked if there was a car in the village, and they pointed to a big house and said he had a car. So we knocked on the door and the old Hun denied he had a car, but we made him open his garage and there was a little two-stroke motorbike, so we pinched that. And using my escape compass we steered west because we thought we had to hit the Rhine and Cologne. We saw German troops doubling across behind hedges, and heard gunfire, and found a dead Yank on the side of the road at one stage, and finally we hooked up with the Yanks at the Remagen Bridge, and they took us across, and we rode the motorbike home to our squadron in Holland.

I didn't get to fly again because they wouldn't let escaped POWs fly. I got sent back to New Zealand and they gave me a job as CO of Air Training Corps. I had my own Harvard aircraft, based in Auckland, and would fly around the country inspecting the boys, and then go to the pub with their COs. Then I got a job back in England with the Air Historical Section — they gave me the job of doing the narrative for the New Zealand Fighter Command history of the war, so I was out at Stanmore at Fighter Command headquarters. I didn't do any work at all, fell out with the bloke who was in charge, applied for a discharge, and got discharged in London.

Reveille, 2002, interview with author

Keith Frederick (Jimmy) Thiele, *DSO, DFC and 2 Bars, was born in Christchurch, NZ, on 25 February 1921 and educated at Christchurch Boys High School. He joined the RNZAF in December 1940. After the war, he moved to Sydney, where he became a senior captain for Qantas. Thiele later built and operated a marina in Sydney and, when he was 80, sailed his own yacht across the Tasman Sea to see New Zealand's first America's Cup defence. He died in Sydney on 5 January 2016.*

Old Pilots Never Die
By Ted Kirk

On returning to England, I was posted to a Tiger Moth unit at Worcester to keep my hand in, and I was able to indulge my passion for aerobatics. In due course, an air officer commanding (AOC) inspection came up. The commanding officer of the unit told me that the high-ranking officer who was to conduct the inspection was very keen to do aerobatics, and asked me to take him playing for the day to get him out of their hair.

No sooner said than done and a good time was had by both of us, leaving the unit in peace. Following the aerobatics session, the AOC told me how much he had enjoyed the day and asked if there was anything he could do for me.

Before going to Worcester I had been billeted in a hotel in Brighton where I had often watched Typhoons returning low level from sorties in France. I decided there and then that I really wanted to fly the Typhoon, so I asked the AOC if he could get me posted to a Typhoon squadron. Shortly after that I was posted to a Typhoon Operational Training Unit at Charmy Down [near Bath, in Somerset].

When I arrived it was a cold day and all the instructors were huddled around the coke stove in the dispersal hut, which they were disinclined to leave. I was told to 'have a look around the Typhoon at the end of the line. If you want to know anything else about it, come and see me. If you are happy with it, just take it for a spin.'

I was initially rather overawed by the size of the aircraft in comparison to the Spitfire, but I taxied out and took off. The sheer power of the Typhoon was really something, and I was at

1000 feet before I thought about retracting the undercarriage, but the more I flew it, the more I got to like it.

The Typhoon was a formidable ground-attack aircraft. I flew the version armed with 60-pound rockets. The standard load was eight rockets but they could carry 12, plus four 20-millimetre Hispano cannons. The warhead on a 60-pound rocket is, in effect, a six-inch shell, so an attack by just one Typhoon was devastating. I was an AA shot with rockets and could put all of them in a 25-yard circle.

The Typhoon was underrated. It did a lot of useful work over Europe, but the glamour aircraft was the Spitfire. I heard that the casualty rate was higher on Typhoons than any other single-engine aircraft.

Following OTU, I was posted to 198 Squadron, which was then in Gilze-Rijen, Holland. The squadron had done great service against German armour in Normandy and had lost more aircraft in the process than any other Typhoon squadron. They were now tasked with attacking ground targets and also anti-shipping strikes. The shipping strikes were the most daunting. When you fire your rockets and you see them all streaking away from you, that's fine, but when a ship fires a whole salvo of 20 or so rockets at you, that's a different story!

Of course you have to hold the aircraft dead steady until you release your rockets, but then you fly exactly how you were taught not to: you put the rudder in one corner and swing the stick to the opposite corner of the cockpit. The aircraft is now facing in one direction but going in another. Hopefully the gunners place their rounds in the direction in which the aircraft is pointing!

While we were in Gilze-Rijen, living in a two-storey brick building, every morning on the dot of eight o'clock, doodlebugs came puttering over just above the roof, heading for London. A little further on there was a zone called the 'Diver Belt' where girls operated their anti-aircraft guns. You would hear the *bang, bang, bang* and then *boom!* Very few of them got past.

One afternoon a V2 rocket apparently went astray and landed just off the corner of our billet. The ceiling fell in on my head and there was dust everywhere. It virtually wrecked the building, but nobody got seriously hurt; some got a bit of flying glass. We would sometimes see box formations of American Flying Fortresses heading into Germany and, a few hours later, the same formations coming back with many empty gaps in the boxes. Each Fortress had a crew of 10 men.

From the Operations Record Book:
On March 20 [1944] the squadron was expecting to move to their new location at B.91 [at Kluis, near Nijmegen on the Dutch–German border]. This was deferred to March 21 to enable the squadron to carry out an attack as part of the Wing on the German Headquarters at Hilversum. This was a joint operation with 183 Squadron of dive-bombing Typhoons. At 1335hrs, 12 aircraft of 198 Squadron and 12 aircraft of 183 Squadron took off, led by Wing Commander J.C. Button DFC to attack the target. At least four salvos of rockets, including Ted Kirk's, were seen to be direct hits, and after being bombed by 183 Squadron, the target was seen to be completely destroyed.

Another congratulatory message was received from the AOC, 84 Group, on the result of this show. Ted's logbook entry states: 'Scored direct hit, moderate flack, 12 R/p salvo. Later confirmed building destroyed. Casualties included 1 Colonel, 200 Huns and the Officers' Mess destroyed.'

This operation was on the third day I was on the squadron and was my first operation. I flew as number 4 to Wing Commander Button, and we carried a double deck of 12 rockets. For somebody not having flown Typhoons for very long, that was a heavy load and you could feel it in the flight.

We attacked the headquarters and peeled off one after the other. Seeing as it was my first operation, I wanted to make a good impression, so I ignored the flak and stayed steady on the sight and let go of my salvo. I managed to get a direct hit.

Out of the 24 aircraft there were only four direct hits recorded. The others were near misses but they did a lot of damage too. So that was my introduction to flying Typhoons on active service.

Then there was the headquarters near Doesberg. We attacked that and I was unsuccessful that day; my rockets fell short of the target but we did a lot of cannon strafing. Being a headquarters it was well protected, so we had a lot of flak and I got quite a few holes in my aircraft, including one in the leading edge of the main plane, which is where the tank is located.

As I flew it on the way back, the fuel was coming out of the tank and flowing like a spray over the top of the wing. It was only a matter of two metres from the manifold, which was spitting fire. I decided it was too risky so I pulled up to get a little bit of height to get out. When I went to jettison my canopy, it had been hit and it wouldn't jettison. I tried to open it manually, but I couldn't. I was getting a bit frantic by then, so I decided to take it as far as it would go before it blew up! I flew it, but it never did anything. When I got back to the strip, I didn't do the usual thing: a beat-up, a chandelle [an abrupt climbing turn], and come in and land. I went straight in and put it on the ground and yelled for the fellows to knock the top off so I could get out. That was rather shaky, but anyway, I survived it.

End of the War
If we weren't on duty we used to go out and have a look around. We had a truck at our disposal with a big canopy over the back, and quite a few of us got in and the driver took off. We'd gone quite a distance when, looking out through the back, I saw German soldiers beside the road, lying on their packs, still with their rifles. They were armed and they were all just lying around as though they couldn't care less about anything. We

tried to tell the driver, we tried to knock on the cab, but he didn't take any notice, just kept going.

Germans had been given orders to surrender. In that town there was a Polish prisoner-of-war camp. The Germans released them and they took charge of the surrender. They had all the Germans filing in and dropping their weapons in a shed. So we looked at the weapons and managed to get a souvenir or two: swords and things like that.

We went to another shed that was full of motorbikes — dispatch riders' bikes — but among all those BMWs, or whatever they were, was one BSA [Birmingham Small Arms], a 500cc English bike painted in camouflage colours. We decided that this would be good property, so we put it in the truck and took it back to the camp.

When we got back there were great celebrations: the war had been declared over. There were fellows running around shooting Very pistols into the air and lighting bonfires. That night there was a big celebration.

RSL Queensland, 2014, as told to Peter Raffels

Edward Gladstone Gilchrist Kirk, *OAM, AFSM was born at Gayndah, Queensland, on 6 February 1924 and enlisted in July 1942. His basic training was on Tiger Moths and Wirraways, before he was posted to England and then to the Middle East, where he flew the Spitfire MK V. He then returned to England and saw out WWII with the RAAF in Berlin. He was discharged with the rank of pilot officer in June 1946. Ted Kirk became a successful grazier, and in 2016 the upgraded Gayndah Airport was renamed the Ted Kirk Field. He died on 10 March 2016.*

Rendezvous Over Essen
By Pilot Officer, Bomber Command

This plain but gripping and authentic narrative was perhaps not intended for publication. It was written by a young pilot officer, of Bomber Command, who originally came from Alderley, Brisbane. He had recently been listed as killed over enemy territory. This story is his account of his first operational flight; it is that rather rare thing — an airman's own personal, unadorned tale.

We are a crew of a Wellington aircraft — G for George — on a squadron of Bomber Command. The day is 25 July — and a beautiful summer day, too.

We have been told that ops are on tonight so, during the morning, each member of the crew gives his particular work in the kite a good inspection, making thoroughly sure that everything is okay. The skipper runs up his engines and watches intently each dial and light on his vast panel of instruments, checks the rudder and control mechanisms, and makes sure that everything is to his satisfaction. Wild horses could not drag him away at a time like this.

Then the navigator checks all his instruments and, in his little compartment, with the shaded light on his face, he seems somehow to ease, poring over maps and charts, and now and then referring to tables and books. Yes, he is the man in whom we place our utmost confidence, and we have yet to see the results of his work when we cross the enemy coastline.

Seated near him is the wireless operator with his rows of dials and switches and coloured lights. He calls up each member of the crew on the inter-communication system and in turn they all reply. His inspection done, he calls up the skipper and tells him that everything so far is okay.

Day of Quiet

The rest of the day is ours for rest, or whatever we wish to do. Camp is closed and no one is allowed out without special permission. In the sunny quiet spots the crews gather in armchairs and doze for a few hours or perhaps idle the time in their rooms.

Briefing time comes and everyone gathers in the operations room, on whose walls are hung huge maps of enemy territory, studded with discs and crossed by ribbons indicating routes to be taken. Weather reports are given, along with everything pertaining to operations that night. There is no solemn air about the place; everyone is talking and joking — perhaps some to hide their true feelings, for the target tonight is Essen — in the heart of the Ruhr. We look at each other for a second or two, but nobody says anything — there is nothing much to say.

We file out and prepare for the time of take-off. This is our first trip and our thoughts are kept to ourselves for fear of betraying what we really do feel.

Down at the 'Flights' warm clothing is donned, together with Mae Wests [life vests] and parachute harnesses. Outside the crews have gathered and are waiting for transport to the various dispersal points. We collect all our gear and stack it near the plane.

We have 45 minutes to take-off, so we lie around on the grass, smoking and chatting with the ground crew. The last traces of day begin to wane on the horizon.

We take our places in the aircraft and roll off the dispersal pan, with a thumbs-up from the grimy but cheerful ground crew. Their farewell and sign of good luck is returned by a wave from the rear-gunner, and we are off to a point where a chequered box stands, signalling the lines of aircraft, moving along the taxi-tracks to the take-off point.

Behind us are other aircraft moving up. They can be seen only faintly in outline through the dusk, but their navigation lights tell us of their presence.

We are given a 'green' and roar down the runway past the chequered box. Climbing to our given height we set course dead over the centre of the 'drome and settle down.

Mysterious Enemy

For about 50 minutes we have been flying over the sea, gaining height all the time and leaving thick layers of cumulus cloud below. The sky, dark to starboard and light on the port side, blends in a haze towards the rear and visibility is rather poor.

The silence, maintained for about 15 minutes, is suddenly broken by a crisp note of attention to all from the bomb-aimer flying 'Second Dickie': 'Aircraft starboard bow, unidentified, about 700 yards .' Suddenly, it passes into my zone and I see it flying a parallel course, though in the opposite direction. Peering hard, I define some similarity in outline to a Junkers 88 — a night fighter-bomber. Everyone is tense and I feel a terrible strain on my muscles. Will it turn to attack?

No, probably it has something else to do, and it passes well to the rear and into the light part of the sky and can be seen only as a speck in the distance.

The wireless operator in the astrodome is asked to keep a sharp lookout. I probe the opposite side. Who knows if that aircraft may have been a decoy for another waiting around?

Twenty minutes pass, and then a report comes from the skipper concerning searchlights and light flak ahead. (He had been second pilot on two previous trips and knows what to expect.) This information tells us we are approaching the French coast, so now we are really approaching and expecting anything.

I see the searchlights now — long pencils of light searching the sky for marauders. I watch them closely and report their movements to the skipper. If they close in, we evade them.

Deeper and deeper we cross into enemy territory, occasionally reporting flak and the position of gun flashes.

Over the Target
The glow of fires can be seen in the distance and now Jerry has predicted ack-ack fire on to us, some bursting rather close with a *wham, wham.* Each time the old Wimpy shakes and then settles down again.

We climb higher still, till we are closing in on the target. I feel cold now and something has gone wrong with my heated gloves and my hands begin to lose their feeling. We pass between two huge cones of searchlights, about 30 in each, and in one cone I see a dark shape flitting about like a moth around a light bulb.

Then up comes the heavy stuff pouring into the cone. I cannot look too long. We have ourselves to look after. Peering down, I see that we are right over the target area and flares burn brightly.

The bomb-aimer is in position and with a few curt orders to the skipper he presses the 'tit' and away they go. 'Bombs gone!' is heard, and the aircraft lifts and creaks as if sighing. The kite turns tightly starboard and we set course for home.

We are not out of it yet by a long way, for more searchlights probe us and suddenly we are caught by two. For a few seconds I am partially blinded by the glare. I shout into my mask, giving evasive action.

The skipper knows what's to be done, and each man holds tight as the kite is flung about.

Suddenly a big black puff of smoke appears beneath the starboard wing and the kite lurches dangerously. Another *wham* and yet another, and we know that we have been hit somewhere. Grimly the skipper fights the controls and once more we are somewhere back to normal.

'Everyone okay?' he calls immediately.

This has lost us some 3000 feet and once more we begin to climb. From all sides we see searchlights and flak. After about 20 more hectic minutes it is all behind us.

Yes, it is behind us and I can still see the fires of the target glowing dull red and orange, with high banks of black smoke above. It was another 'prang' at the famous Krupp's Works, and yet a further episode in 'The Battle of the Ruhr'.

Homeward Bound!

The boys are all chatting now and drinking coffee from their flasks or eating chocolate, and at the same time chatting about the 'run'.

I put my hand to my forehead and find it is damp with perspiration. The English coast drifts by, far below.

Once on the ground we just look at each other for a while, red-eyed and weary, till the skipper grins and says, 'Well, boys — our first ops.'

The Queensland Digger, April 1944

Air Raid on Revigny:
A Long Hard Day at the Office
By John Clulow

Seven weeks after the Normandy landings on 6 June 1944, the British and Canadian divisions of the Second Army had secured the ancient but totally devastated city of Caen. Their further progress was now being held up by fanatical resistance from Germany's crack 5th Panzer Army, holding favourable ground to the south and south-east of the city. The time had arrived for Operation Goodwood.

At 5.30 a.m. on 18 July 1944 the obliteration of the German defences began with a concentrated air assault by 927 aircraft of RAF Bomber Command, followed by 570 American bombers. The break-out was underway.

Included in the RAF's contribution was the usual percentage of Lancaster bombers from No. 5 group, based at various airfields in Lincolnshire. On returning to their bases later that morning the crews could have been excused for thinking they had finished for the day, but some of them from each squadron were in for a surprise — Revigny had not yet been put out of action.

Revigny-sur-Ornain (to give it its full name) is a small French provincial town some 240 kilometres due east of Paris, with a population, during the war, of about 2500. It had no industry to speak of, except for a nut-and-bolt factory and maintenance sheds. It was, however, a very important railway junction and marshalling yards, with two main lines feeding in from Germany's industrial Ruhr Valley and also from the cities and towns of southern Germany. Along these tracks flowed the vital

Air Raid on Revigny: A Long Hard Day at the Office

war supplies and reinforcements for the German armies starting the retreat from the Normandy battle fronts.

The Allied Air Forces' attacks on the lines of communication throughout France and the Low Countries had commenced in earnest in March, when the bomber force had been switched from German industrial targets mainly in the north of France. Naturally the German Luftwaffe redeployed their fighters and night fighters to the same area, and RAF losses continued to mount (27 lost in March, 66 in April, 108 in May and 173 in June). However, the percentage loss for Bomber Command remained at a very acceptable 2.5 per cent.

This then was the situation over France on 8 July 1944 when the decision was handed down from Allied air chiefs HQ to attack Revigny.

The task of taking out this target fell to No. 1 Group and, after three cancellations through bad weather, the raid was finally made on the night of 12/13 July. A total force of 109 aircraft from seven squadrons were airborne from 2100 hours plus and were routed around the Channel Islands, across France (south of Paris), then north-east to the target. The railway junction and yards were not visible because of unexpected light cloud and haze in the Revigny area, and only a few aircraft dropped their bombs before the force was ordered back to base. (It was then policy not to jettison bombs, which could result in casualties to the French population.) Night fighters and flak had been active, and 10 Lancasters were lost. The railway junction and yards remained operational.

The second attempt was made on the night of 14/15 July, with all aircraft again being supplied by No. 1 Group. Bad weather once more caused the cancellation of this raid after only a few planes were able to bomb, and the target once again escaped substantial damage. An almost identical route had been flown that night (1550 track miles) and planes were in the air for over nine and a half hours. Seven Lancasters were shot down.

And so, on the morning of 18 July, the No. 5 Group Lancasters were returning to their Lincolnshire bases from the successful Normandy operation, confident of being stood down for at least 24 hours (into Lincoln for a few beers in the White Hart). But no such luck for a number of these crews: they were 'on again for tonight'. Revigny again.

The lead-in procedures and briefings etc. took up all the afternoon hours, and in spite of their all-consuming tiredness they took off from 2336 hours for north-eastern France. This time the forces consisted of 106 aircraft and the route showed a crossing of the French coast at Le Tréport (near Dieppe), then a straight run for 170 miles to the twisting River Aube, then a turn north-east to Revigny. This direct route took the bomber stream over many of the night-fighter bases, some renowned flak areas, and searchlights across the whole track.

That afternoon the BBC had broadcast a message directed to the citizens of Revigny to the effect that they should stay away from the railway that night, the RAF was coming again. (This was a condition given to the French by the War Cabinet to warn the population of railway towns of any impending raid.) However, the Germans also worked it out and were ready for the fray.

From the time the first Lancaster crossed the coast at 0400 hours, engagements with the Luftwaffe commenced. Our bomber, from 49 Squadron, escaped from an attack by a JU88 [fast, versatile, Junkers 88 twin-engine aircraft] and six minutes later was in action again against another JU88. Later, over the target, we were attacked by an FW190 [Focke-Wulf 190 single-engine fighter]. Flares were being dropped all along the track, and the route ahead was lit up like day. We still had over an hour's flying time to reach Revigny.

By the time the force reached the target, no fewer than 17 Lancasters had been shot from the sky. Of the 109 crew members, 105 were dead — all in 45 minutes.

At the target the pathfinders were experiencing difficulty in marking the aiming point, and the main force was ordered into orbit for up to 15 minutes. Confusion seemed to be mounting, and during this period a further four planes went down.

In due course the target was successfully bombed. Twenty-one bombers had now been lost, 121 dead. On the way out, three more fell to fighters and flak.

The success for the night fighters has been put down to the skill of their experienced pilots and the credit they gave to the recently developed upward firing cannon known as *Schräge Musik* — it created havoc.

The dreadful toll for this one raid finally stood at 24 Lancasters destroyed (a loss of 22.6 per cent). One hundred and sixty-nine airmen did not return that night; 129 of these were dead, 11 became POWs and 29 successfully evaded capture, heroically assisted by the French Underground.

Of the 140 killed or captured, 27 were Australians.

The target was at last out of action and through traffic stopped. It certainly had been a 'long hard day at the office', but did the results eventually achieved that night justify the deaths of 129 fine young men?

After 57 years to ponder this question — I don't think so.

Reveille, September–October 2001

Flying Officer John Cecil George Clulow *was born in West Maitland, NSW, on 16 January 1923 and enlisted at Sydney in August 1942. He completed 24 operations in Lancaster bombers with RAF 49 Squadron, serving as a wireless operator. He was discharged from the RAAF in January 1946, his last posting being with 9 Aircrew Holding Unit. He died on 29 October 2008.*

On the Russian Front, 1942
By Wing Commander Robert Holmes

The following is a speech made in 1946 by Wing Commander Robert Holmes, CO of No. 455 Squadron, RAAF, about the squadron's experiences on the Russian Front in 1942.

In August 1942 an Australian long-range torpedo bomber squadron was operating from the east coast of Scotland at Leuchars in Fife. It was beautiful spring weather and, when not operating, we played quite a lot of golf with our colleagues in the RAF, which also had a squadron engaged on the same work.

Early in the month, the CO of the station summoned both squadrons and told us to prepare to go overseas.

It appeared the whole German battle fleet was situated in the northern fjords of Norway and presented a serious menace to our convoys to Russia. This was when Stalingrad desperately wanted material from America and England. The July convoy had been attacked by this battle fleet, with 30 of 35 ships sunk. Our two squadrons received orders to proceed to North Russia.

At dusk on 3 September, 34 aircraft and crews left the Shetland Islands bound for Kandalaksha on the north shore of the White Sea. The weather forecast was bad, and we were without any wireless assistance from Russia. It was a bad night and we lost 10 aircraft in all, due to ack-ack and the weather, but 24 crews arrived at Kandalaksha, most of whom had been shot at by the Russians as their system of communication had broken down and they had not been informed we were coming.

On the Russian Front, 1942

We were informed that the German lines were seven miles away and we could sleep for three hours, but we had to get away by one o'clock as the Germans might come over in their tanks and crush our aircraft into the ground. We took off right on one o'clock and proceeded to Vianga [now Severomorsk], 150 miles north, escorted by a Russian bomber.

During the next two weeks we were subjected to three air raids per day, whenever it was fine, regularly at 11 o'clock in the morning, four in the afternoon and 10 o'clock at night, but without any serious mishaps.

Some PRU [Photo-Reconnaissance Unit] Mosquitoes had also arrived at this aerodrome and they acted as reconnaissance planes for us whilst we were waiting for the German fleet to come. During this time we were on two hours' standby so we did not see much of the life that went on in the village. However, our operation was successful, and the convoy got to Archangel without loss and the supplies arrived at Stalingrad on time.

Because of adverse headwinds which would prevail all the winter, we had not the range to fly home, so the Air Ministry told us to hand our aircraft over to the Russians and teach them to fly them.

During the ensuing weeks, whilst we were waiting for a ship, we were able to observe the people and their customs. We invited the general and his staff over to a dinner when the Russian ordinance supplemented our tinned food with smoked salmon and vodka.

Apparently when drinking vodka (which we had not tasted before), it is custom to drink the health of someone in one gulp. If any is left in the glass it means bad health to the person to whom you are drinking. Vodka has a terrifically high alcoholic content; by the time we toasted one another, most people were slurring their speech. However, a terrific feast ensued and, except for a few casualties, it was a very pleasant evening.

Next the Russians invited us to use their baths, visit the theatre and look over their town; from then on we had one bath and two visits to the theatre each week.

The people all lived in community barracks, ate in community kitchens, and had their clothing and cigarettes issued to them. In fact, everything was issued to them by the government. Everyone was employed by the government and money was no good except in Moscow and a few other big cities.

We saw a couple of English films, and although they loaned us their theatre for the evening, no Russian was permitted to join us because this would have shown him how the other half of the world lived and it was a principle of the Soviet Union to keep this information from most of the people.

I often saw companies of women in uniform, fully equipped, marching off (with rifles) to take their turn in the frontline, and they were all singing.

All this time the air raids went on and the days got shorter and colder whilst we waited for our ship. Eventually we had daylight from 11.30 a.m. to 2.30 p.m. The sun just appeared over the horizon but it was too cold to venture out except for meals.

On 30 October our ship arrived — the latest Dido Class cruiser *Argonaut* on her maiden voyage — escorted by two destroyers. We went home via Iceland, which took us six days.

The Listening Post, Autumn 1993

Wing Commander Robert Holmes *was born in Fremantle on 30 October 1915 and enlisted in Perth on 11 November 1940. He served with the RAF in both Bomber and Coastal Command, and took charge of the squadron of Handley Page Hampden aircraft sent to Russia. As commander of the RAAF 455 Squadron he was mentioned in dispatches. After the war he commanded the Air Training Corps in Western Australia.*

Darwin: February 1942
By Tom Griffith, ex-sgt, RAAF

We knew that the defences were inadequate. 'Tokyo Rose' [the name given to all female Japanese propaganda radio broadcasters] had been telling us all about ourselves and how Australians would be able to have races every day and plenty of beer when the Japs took over. One night shortly before the raid she announced that the RAAF had been camouflaging the hangars for several days — just to hide a few ineffective Wirraways.

Singapore had fallen — then Ambon and other islands.

We didn't have long to wait ...

Bernie Slattery (of Perth) [Corporal Bernard James Slattery] and I are having early lunch prior to going on duty. The sirens sound as they attack, and we race for the trenches with machine-gun bullets zipping all around us. Looking up I can see the eyes of the pilots through their goggles some 20 or 30 feet overhead.

Bernie says, 'Just hang on a minute, Tom, while I duck in and get me tin hat.' But I don't consider, even for a split second, waiting outside the mess in an open area while Bernie gets his helmet.

Fortunately there is a happy ending — or beginning — as Bernie joins me shortly afterwards in the trench, to reach which I have broken all records. The Zeros zip up and down, machine-guns blazing while the dive-bombers do just that, and we see the bombs that the Zeros tumble out.

Making sure my tin hat is on tight, I peer out and see one just outside the 'drome — the bomb flops out, falling over end for end, heading for what appears to be the place we were drinking last night. There is a tremendous *whoosh* as lots of things go up (and my head goes down because the Zeros are still coming).

Gleaming in the sun, the silvery bombers present a magnificent spectacle (in other circumstances) in perfect 'V' formation.

They're the worst. I can see the bullets cutting the daisies, and then the bloke's gone past. The dive-bombers I can see as well as the bomb, but those high-level bombers at 15,000 feet and the scream all the way down — wow! It's a relief to hear the explosion even though there are great shuddering earth movements with dirt, and who knows what, falling everywhere. It is from one of these that some of our airmen are buried alive with a direct hit on the trench. Our army boys on the perimeter are doing their best but the shells are puffing harmlessly 3000 feet below.

And Bernie had said, 'Hang on a minute while I duck in and get me tin hat!'

History has recorded much about that raid and, after all, history is people's opinions — the truth can be the lie. It is a fact that the life of every single human being is a history that can never be repeated and for this reason I want to record some of my own thoughts and impressions.

It is a fact that RAAF personnel were ordered to leave the aerodrome. I do not, for one moment, consider this was meant that they should run away but merely to disperse to points adjacent. It was commonly said that invasion was imminent, so the order to disperse may have come from officers not authorised or qualified to give it.

It might be borne in mind that many of those officers were actually civilians in uniform — doctors, dentists and other professional men. Most had probably never undergone combat training in any shape or form. But lack of proper training applied not only to the officers; men of the NCOs and other ranks were tradesmen. Oh yes, they had handled firearms and faced discipline — perhaps two weeks' training as 'rookies' under a bellowing sergeant major (much of it forming 'fours' and marching on a parade ground) and then shot out to a squadron to do their normal work as fitters and turners, wireless operators and so on.

Even so, there were very few of the airmen at the base who had been issued with firearms. In our quarters there were perhaps 20 per cent. Rifles were on hand to be issued to all, but they had been sitting in cases outside the orderly room for some 10 days before the raid, waiting for someone to do something about them.

They went up in a bomb explosion in that first raid.

We of the met. section were fairly well-off for staff. Due to the evacuees coming from Kupang, Ambon and other islands, we had something like 19; from memory I believe our establishment was five. So we were not overworked and shifts were shortened.

On being told to leave the 'drome we went to a swimming-hole in a nearby creek for a few hours.

The Listening Post, Winter 1992

Thomas Allan Griffith *was born at Dalby, Queensland, on 18 April 1922, and enlisted in Brisbane in April 1941. He was discharged in February 1946 with the rank of sergeant. His last posting was with 30 Operational Base Unit. He died 24 April 2003.*

Darwin, 1942: A Pilot's Close Call
By Harold Stuart McDouall

I commenced my air force career in December 1940, after about 12 months in the Bingara Troop of the 24th Light Horse Regiment. I had two months' initial training at Bradfield Park, Sydney, including drill and theory pertaining to flying, and was lucky enough to be chosen for pilot training. I was posted to Tamworth for elementary training on Tiger Moths, on No. 8 Course of the Empire Air Training Scheme.

On completion I was posted to Amberley for advanced training on twin engine Avro Ansons, and finished with 'above average' and 'recommended for commission' stamped in my logbook. This was a four-month course but owing to an injury to my hand I finished on 10 Course with a commission and a promotion to pilot officer. I was posted to 6 Squadron at Richmond for six weeks as second pilot on Lockheed Hudsons, then to Laverton, Victoria, for a special three-month navigation course. Near the end of that course, 2nd Squadron (which was based there and also flying Lockheed Hudsons) was posted to the Darwin area and islands north. Volunteers were called for from pilots on the navigation course and I was accepted.

We took off for Darwin very early on 8 December 1941. When we stopped at Oodnadatta to refuel we heard that Pearl Harbor had just been bombed and that the Japs were in the war.

We continued to Darwin and then were based at Kupang in Timor for a short while before moving on to Ambon, a small island to the west of New Guinea. We were there up to February 1942, when the Japs were making their big push southwards with far superior numbers of aircraft, ships and personnel. Their fighter aircraft, the Zero, was very superior to anything that we had. We only had a few Wirraways as fighters and really they were only a training aircraft and completely outclassed.

We didn't have much chance of stopping the Japs, so it was decided that Ambon be evacuated and the RAAF and army personnel return to Darwin. A large fleet of Jap warships and transports were heading for Ambon and not very far north. Two Hudsons and crews were given the job of keeping an eye on the Jap fleet, and I was second pilot/navigator in one of them. Our job was to keep reporting the position of the fleet but keep our distance. The Hudsons, which were only a light bomber/reconnaissance aircraft, wouldn't have had much chance against the Jap fleet, which had battleships and aircraft carriers bristling with Zeros.

We flew around, all that last day, in and out of cloud, and returned to Ambon at dusk to refuel and load as many personnel as possible for the flight back to Darwin. The other Hudson was intercepted by Zeros and shot up but managed to get back to Ambon. They had a bullet hole in one of their fuel tanks and were trying to seal it. We took off thinking that they'd soon be able to follow us but the Japs got there before they were able to. We heard later that they were taken prisoner and that they all had their heads chopped off.

We took off into the darkness, grossly overloaded with bods, and straight into a tropical storm. I was navigating in the nose of the aircraft with my maps. The rain was so heavy it came in all over my maps, and then my light went out. After that it was navigation by intuition. God was with us, because after more than four hours we came out of the cloud and there was Darwin straight ahead.

On 19 February 1942 we had just returned to Darwin from a reconnaissance flight and had parked our aircraft in line with others on the airfield perimeter. We were walking across to the hangar and just as we got to the middle of the field we heard the drone of aircraft. We looked up to see what appeared to be hundreds of planes, high up, approaching from the east. Our first thought was that it was nice to see reinforcements arriving. Then bombs started falling and the air-raid alarm sounded. All we had time to do was make a dash to the nearest slit trench, which was right beside our hangar.

We had five P-40 American fighter planes there, which were supposed to be en route to Java, and they attempted to take off but were shot down before they were properly airborne. The Japs had it all their own way. We had nil defence: no anti-aircraft guns, no anything. So after the high-level bombers dropped their bombs, the dive-bombers and the Zeros came down to ground level and finished off our hangars and our aircraft — all nicely lined up for the Zeros to strafe. Out of the 100 or so of our aircraft on the field there was only one Hudson left serviceable.

We got out of the slit trench and everything was on fire, with ammunition and anything explosive going off with a bang. A few of us grabbed a firehose and hung on to it tightly while someone else turned on the tap. However, nothing came out as the water mains had been bombed.

That first wave of bombers and fighters not only did the aerodrome over, but also the ships in Darwin Harbour. About 50 ships were hit, most of them sunk, and the bombs also wreaked havoc on Darwin township.

When we realised there was nothing much that we could do at the field, we made our way to the quarters which, up until that stage, hadn't been touched. We hadn't been there long before the second wave came over, and this time they concentrated on the quarters. Once again, we all jumped into the slit trenches. They made a real mess of the quarters and we were right in the thick of it. With bombs exploding all around the noise was rather damaging to the eardrums, so it's no wonder my hearing hasn't been too good ever since.

After the second raid, it was decided that our lone remaining Hudson should be taken up to look for the Jap fleet that they

Darwin, 1942: A Pilot's Close Call

thought all of the bombers had come from. We drew straws to choose a crew and I drew a short straw. We took off, dodging bomb craters on the runway, and got out to sea just past Bathurst Island. We saw smoke on the horizon and thought, *Oh, shit, that must be the Jap fleet.*

When we got closer we found the smoke was coming from one of our own ships that had been bombed by the Japs. It was sinking and survivors were out in the lifeboats. We went on further and found another of our ships in the same condition. Luckily for us, we didn't find the Jap fleet, but found out much later that the bombers had come from Kupang, which had been taken a day or so before. The fighters had taken off from aircraft carriers closer to Timor than we had got.

Things were a mess back at the quarters. There was no water to drink but there was beer untouched in the mess so we quenched our thirst and eventually got to bed. I hadn't been asleep very long when I was woken about 1 a.m. Our ground crews had managed to get another two Hudsons serviceable and crews were needed to fly the three planes down to Daly Waters. We needed to get them away from Darwin as the Japs were expected to have another go later that morning.

Once again, I drew a short straw, and we took off into a pitch-dark night to try to find Daly Waters. In those days Daly Waters was only a post office which had a paddock for an aerodrome. It was hard enough to find in the daytime, let alone at night, and with no navigation aids. Daly Waters is about 520 kilometres down the track towards Alice Springs and Katherine is about halfway along. It was about 2 a.m. when we took off. I was navigating and by dead reckoning thought that a few lights I saw must have been Katherine. Not long after that a tropical storm front appeared ahead of us, and the skipper flew here, there and everywhere trying to get around it while I was trying to keep track of where we were. By the grace of God the track that I gave him brought us back over Katherine about 3 or 4 a.m.

At Katherine there was only a paddock and no flare path. Everyone on the ground was asleep so we flew around in circles trying to wake them up, and I went back to a window and started flashing the Aldis lamp down in their direction. Eventually we saw a few lights moving about as vehicles made their way to the paddock and made a sort of flare path. After six attempts we finally landed and just as well because we were almost out of fuel.

In the next day or so they got another Hudson serviceable. We then started flying all our aircraft in bombing raids against the Japs in Timor and other islands, day and night, to give the impression that we had more aircraft than we actually had. After a few weeks, a squadron of Yanks flying P-40s arrived. The Japs had been over every day, bombing Darwin and the vicinity, and having it all their own way, so they got a shock when they were attacked by the P-40s and some of their aircraft were shot down. Then some of our ack-ack gunners arrived, after having experience in the Middle East, and they also accounted for some of the Jap aircraft. Our morale went up quite a bit and the Japs weren't so cheeky.

Reveille, 2017; edited by Sandra Lambkin

Harold Stuart McDouall, *known to all as Jim, was born on 3 March 1920. He was discharged from the RAAF on 28 February 1946, with the rank of flight lieutenant. He died on 26 June 2016 aged 96.*

The Fourth Mine
By Flight Lieutenant Leo M. Kenny

To me, as an RAAF member of an 11-man Liberator crew of No. 159 Heavy Bomber Squadron, 4 July 1944 stands out vividly from a jumble of memories, because of the grimly amusing culmination to a mining operation.

My logbook records that Liberator 'B Baker' took off at 0540 hours from Digri Airfield, Bengal, India. The target — to mine the entrance to the Mae Klong River, west of Bangkok.

In case you don't remember, the river is at the top left-hand corner of the Gulf of Siam [Gulf of Thailand]. On arrival at the river entrance, we opened the bomb doors and proceeded to lay four 1000-pound parachute mines — two acoustic and two magnetic, just to be awkward.

By fateful coincidence, a naval launch, flying the Siamese flag astern, was crossing the channel along which, under British Navy orders, the mines were to be accurately laid. By a still more fateful coincidence, that Siamese launch happened to be almost directly beneath the fourth mine as it parachuted gracefully into the blue waters of the gulf. Salt water from the splash splattered the bows of the trim little craft.

Maybe the launch expected the mine to detonate. Maybe it would have been better for them had it done so. That unfortunate launch had to be sunk — and quickly — before the skipper could report the positions of the mines to the Japanese minesweepers.

We baulked sharply and swung right around, the nose gunner raking the launch, followed by the belly gunner as we passed overhead. The tail gunner picked up the target as it dropped astern. For good measure, we baulked to give the mid-upper turret some air-to-sea practice.

We made five runs over the launch, turning it into a Siamese sieve. After the third run, it hove to, and we saw the crew members dive overboard. Understandably, they'd had enough. But to prove the point beyond all question — to our cruel amusement — a crew member managed to climb back on board and haul down the Siamese flag, till then fluttering, tattered, in the breeze.

Then we headed full throttle for home, with two Jap fighters for 'escort', just out of range. The launch was settling as we left. The fighters did not close in on us and we reached home safely enough, but those Siamese sailors would have had a long swim.

Mufti, May 1954

Leo Martin Kenny *was born on 20 December 1914, enlisted in the RAAF in Sydney in May 1942, was discharged in February 1946 with the rank of flight lieutenant, and died 20 December 1984.*

An Amazing Rescue After Air and Sea Attack
By Pilot Officer Keith Shilling

At about 0505 hours on 6 April 1945, Flight Lieutenant S.L. McDonald in Liberator A72-81 took off from Fenton Strip [near Adelaide River, NT] to attack a Japanese cruiser and escort vessel reported in the vicinity of Sumba Island [to the west of Timor]. I was first wireless operator in this aircraft.

The convoy was sighted at 0930 hours, 20 miles east of Sumba Island. Squadron Leader J.G. White, 21 Squadron, was formation leader, with Flight Lieutenant Court as number two and Flight Lieutenant McDonald as number three. We went into attack formation with our flight as the third element.

On the first bombing run, at approximately 13,000 feet, two enemy fighters attacked from 10 o'clock level in line astern, closing to within 50 feet and breaking away underneath. Cannon shells burst under the flight deck in the vicinity of the nose wheel and the auxiliary power unit. Fire broke out immediately and spread very rapidly. It was the first enemy fighter that got us. No hits were seen on the enemy.

The engineer, Sergeant W.J. Wignall, used the fire extinguisher, which proved to be absolutely useless. The fire drove him into the bomb bays and I didn't see him again.

The captain ordered the crew to bail out. The second pilot, Flying Officer K.R. Brown, escaped through the bomb bays. I followed about 30 seconds later. Two minutes later another member jumped. He did not appear to have a parachute.

I went out the bomb bays head first, counted six, and pulled the release cord. The parachute opened immediately and I was pulled up with a terrific jerk. It took me about 12 minutes to come down, during which time I counted six members parachuting from Flight Lieutenant E.V. Ford's A72-77. An additional member appeared to drop without a parachute.

A72-81 disintegrated about 3000 feet above the sea. It did not explode. A72-77 exploded on impact with the water. Enemy fighters did not attack parachutists.

I was using an American-type observer parachute with no quick release on the harness. I started to release the harness at 3000 feet. Of five clips, two were still to be released when I hit the water.

On hitting the water the American life jacket (Mae West) kept me afloat while the remaining two clips were undone. My legs were entangled in the shroud lines and I had to cut them away with a bowie knife. I jettisoned my revolver and equipment on account of weight.

Although I had seen someone land about 50 yards away, heavy seas prevented me from seeing him. The seas were running at about 4.5 feet. I then endeavoured to swim towards where I estimated the other members to be. I never saw any member of my crew again.

About 30 minutes later the enemy cruiser came within 100 yards of me. She was heavily laden with troops, and equipment under tarpaulins was clearly visible. A machine-gun opened fire at the position I had been making for. I deflated my Mae West and sank. At this time the bullets hit the water within six feet of me. The cruiser then passed on.

Some 15 minutes later an escort vessel of 1000 to 2000 tons passed within 100 yards of me. This vessel was also heavily laden with troops and equipment. The only armament I noticed was either four or six twin Bofors and numerous machine-guns.

This vessel continued on for five minutes, turned, and came directly towards me, passing close enough for the bow wave to throw me sideways. I could hear voices from the deck. No attempt was made to pick me up or shoot me.

An Amazing Rescue After Air and Sea Attack

Some minutes later a Zero passed overhead low and appeared to be looking for survivors. I deflated my Mae West again and sank to avoid detection.

Ten minutes later seven Liberators circled low and after some five minutes dropped me a K-type dinghy which landed 50 yards away. Later I reached the dinghy and found the CO2 bottle had broken off and half the air had escaped. I plugged up the hole with one hand and hung on to the dinghy with the other. While I was doing this, a Catalina arrived.

Twenty minutes later the Catalina taxied close enough to pick me up. Sergeant W.W. Sayer from Flight Lieutenant Ford's crew was aboard, having been picked up earlier. I was exhausted and cold. I had swallowed a lot of salt water. We taxied around and picked up Warrant Officer C.G. Vickers, also from Flight Lieutenant Ford's crew.

The Catalina took off, landing again to pick up another survivor, whom I believe to have been Flight Sergeant Ian Faichnie. He was completely exhausted and was being pulled in over the gun blisters when the Catalina was attacked by a Zero from 12 o'clock. The aircraft caught fire immediately and sank three minutes later. No member of the crew or survivors was hit.

I had undressed, as ordered, and was going to be in a bunk in the waist, then had been called forward for the landing and was in the navigator's position when the attack was made. The order was given to bail out and I made my way aft. On the way a fuel line burst above me, pouring blazing petrol onto my back. This was extinguished by Sergeant Sayer, who smothered the flames with a sleeping bag. I escaped out the port blister, naked, and with no Mae West.

A few minutes after the Catalina was hit, the air-sea rescue Liberator dropped two large dinghies and one supply canister. They landed 600 yards away. After an hour's struggle, nine of us reached the dinghy. One crew member and Flight Sergeant Faichnie were floating some distance away, still alive. We secured the second dinghy and supply canister and set off towards the other two, whom we never saw again.

Another Catalina was directed to us by the Liberator. It landed after half an hour's battle with heavy seas and wind. We were eventually picked up. One dinghy was cut in half by the port wing float. As the last survivor clambered aboard, an Irving [Allied codename for a Japanese J1N1 Nakajima fighter escort] was sighted, making for us. The enemy made his first attack as we were taking off and scored no hits. Our return fire did no visible damage to him. A running fight ensued for 20 minutes. The attacks ceased and we headed for Darwin, reaching there about 2230 hours.

The Listening Post, Winter 1989

Keith Roy Shilling *was born on 18 July 1922 at Preston, Melbourne, and enlisted in Perth in April 1941. He held the rank of warrant officer at the time of this incident, and was discharged in February 1946 with the rank of pilot officer. The target for the Liberators had been the Japanese light cruiser* Isuzu, *part of a convoy evacuating troops from Timor.*

The crew on board Liberator A72-77, which was the first aircraft shot down, were Flight Lieutenant (Flt Lt) Eric V. Ford; Warrant Officer (WO) J.O.R. Vickers; Flt Lt L.D. Crowther; Flt Lt W. Laing; Flying Officer (FO) B.T. Jordan; WO A.N.J. Collins; Flight Sergeant (F Sgt) L. Raine; F Sgt J.M. Waddell; F Sgt I. Faichnie; F Sgt K.J. White; Sgt W.W. Sayer.

The crew of the second Liberator A72-81 were Flt Lt Sidney Leonard McDonald; FO K.A.R. Brown; FO P.A. Mouatt; FO A.G. Worley; WO K.R. Shilling; F Sgt L.K. Walmsley; F Sgt J.S. Thomson; F Sgt R.J. Banks; F Sgt T.E. Bowen; F Sgt A. Davis; Sgt W.J. Wignall.

Keith Shilling was the only survivor of these attacks. He died on 29 December 2010.

On Stage and Back Stage

'It was a very silent service ... We're still finding people who've suddenly realised that's what it was they belonged to.'

— Flight Sergeant Joy Granger

Among the First Army Servicewomen to See Operational Service Overseas
By Ailsa Jean Livingstone

I'm going to tell you a smuggling story — one surrounded by secrecy. On 10 January 1945, I was one of three AWAS [Australian Women's Army Service] sergeants, strangers until that day, and two AWAS officers, who travelled from Brisbane to Amberley by bus to board an American Douglas C-47 aircraft bound for New Guinea. The trip did not begin well as the bus broke down at Oxley and our party spent an anxious time in the dark, seated by the roadside, waiting for another bus. When we finally arrived at the airport we were hustled into a room to change into tropical kit — strange khaki trousers and safari jackets, heavy boots with gaiters, a large felt hat and other necessary equipment — then rushed out to the airfield and onto the plane. There was no one to wave us goodbye; no one to wish us a safe trip; not even any air force personnel around to wonder at the hushed activity. Within minutes we were smuggled out of the country.

The plane offered no comforts, such as padded seats, refreshments or ladies' rooms, and we slept on the floor until the plane arrived at Townsville at 1.50 a.m. We all tumbled out onto the airfield where we were served coffee and doughnuts, provided by the Americans. Within half an hour we were away again and our next stop was at Finschhafen in New Guinea. The blast of heat as we stepped onto the tarmac was almost unbearable but within a very short time we continued on to Hollandia [now Jayapura], a forward post in what was then Dutch New Guinea.

On arrival, it was with pleasure that we found ourselves in the mountains and that we were to be quartered with approximately

300 American Army women (WACs). The camp was actually situated on a levelled mountain top. We three sergeants shared a large square tent with three WAC girls and we were very warmly welcomed. We made special friends with the WACs and one of our favourite enjoyments was to hold tea parties in the tent. We soon settled into the routine of camp life and even did our share of KP [kitchen patrol] duty, which started at 5.30 a.m.

Jeep transport was provided to take us to work — our offices were about 15 minutes' drive away. We worked from 8 to 11.30 a.m. and from 2 to 4.30 p.m. with evening work from 7 to 9.30 or 10 p.m., five nights a week. Our workplaces were large wooden sheds, some four steps up from the ground. The top half of most of the walls opened for ventilation and all had iron roofs. The 'conveniences' were a five-minute walk down the side of the mountain and consisted of a long plank with holes and no partitions. It was friendly, to say the least. We also suffered frequent earth tremors, air-raid alarms, insect attacks and constant, draining heat — and we loved it!

The other sergeants and I soon located the Australian HQ and were invited to visit at any time for tea and army biscuits, or just a chat. I was delighted to meet up with the personnel I had worked with at 'Z' Special Unit Advanced HQ in St Lucia. The Australian personnel were wonderful to us, taking us on frequent sightseeing tours and trips to the picture shows. We also had to visit to draw our pay or for medical and dental appointments. While we enjoyed living with the Americans, visiting Australian HQ during our time at Hollandia was like going home.

When we had been in New Guinea for about two months, an American war correspondent visited us and wrote a story about our group. He also took lots of photos. His story eventually appeared in the newspapers — but not until after we were safely back on the mainland.

Unfortunately, that time came all too soon as on 13 April 1945 we were advised that we had to return to Australia. Our units were moving on to Morotai and although our superiors requested that we be included in the movement (and the American girls had already moved on) the Australian prime minister, John Curtin, was adamant that we return to Australia immediately. In mid-1945 the War Cabinet eventually allowed a large contingent of AWAS to go to Lae in PNG but it seems that permission was never actually granted for our deployment. On 23 April 1945 we left Hollandia for the long flight home, and I went back to 'Z' Special Unit HQ.

Reveille 2016; edited by Sandra Lambkin

Ailsa Jean Jarman (Livingstone) *was born at Gympie, Queensland, on 27 December 1922. In August 1943 she joined the Australian Army Medical Women's Service before transferring to the AWAS and in October 1944 being posted to 'Z' Special Unit to work in the Special Reconnaissance Department. She was discharged on 31 January 1946, two months after her marriage to Ralph Livingstone, an RAAF medical orderly.*

On Stage with Peter Finch
By Pat McKenzie

Under her maiden name of Rhodes, Pat McKenzie played one of the more enjoyable roles of the war — entertaining the troops — while sharing the limelight with one of the great stars of Australian theatre, Peter Finch.

When war was declared I was working for the Cunard White Star shipping line. I had been working for a Japanese importer, but I think the manager there knew — he'd sit there and brood, and smoke, and the smoke would come up around, and then he said to me, 'Look, I think you've got plenty of time but look around for another job.' So then I went to Cunard White Star, and they were dealing with the four troopships — the *Queen Mary*, the *Queen Elizabeth*, the *Mauretania* and *Aquitania*, and I think at one time there was another one.

I stayed in contact with the Japanese company and somebody reported me. I was called to the manager's office and here was this huge man, a detective sergeant. I nearly died — to think that I was passing secrets over about the troopships! I couldn't believe it! He accepted my story but he said I must not have anything more to do with them.

Eventually I managed to get released and joined the army and did my 'rookies'. I wanted to be posted to transport, but they said no, you're a stenographer so you've got to go back into office work. So they sent me to movement control, which happened to be in the same building, on the same floor, as Cunard White Star. We were dealing with the movement orders for the troops who were going on the troopships. I quite liked it. It was a good place to work — they were very nice. But I got a bit restless and I wanted a change.

I was a member of the play-reading group that Dennis Glennie was running, and he introduced me to Peter Finch. He said, 'Okay, come out to Pagewood and have an audition.' And I did that and he said, 'Okay, you'll be right,' so I transferred over to Pagewood, to 1st Australian Entertainment Unit. Peter was forming this army theatre. It was going to be the first concert party using real, live girls instead of female impersonators! And of course we weren't popular with the female impersonators. They thought we were taking their jobs.

Colonel Jim Davidson was in charge — he was a major at first — and he used to be bandleader. Peter Finch had been in the army and had been at Tobruk and other places, and he was in charge. We did two plays, both by Terence Rattigan, *While the Sun Shines* and *French Without Tears.*

So there I was on stage kissing Peter Finch — being kissed by Peter Finch — but while he was kissing me his eyes were darting all over the stage, making sure everybody was in the right place, so it wasn't all that thrilling. And he'd yell — he'd have me in tears sometimes — and then another time he'd say, 'You're the best of the lot tonight.' He didn't want me to marry the chap that I was engaged to — he was the officer in charge of our group. Peter Finch said, 'No, you should stay on in the theatre life.' But no, I had to get married.

Our numbers kept increasing. When we first started in Victoria and NSW camps we were in halls. But when we went over to New Guinea, the boys first had to erect a stage and so they needed some extra hands. There were just under 20 of us in the end, I think. The ship we were to have gone on was in dry dock and wasn't ready to sail, so we didn't embark until September 1945. Because there were still so many troops over there they decided they'd still send us, to keep the troops happy.

We went to Lae — that's where we were based — and then we travelled all round that area. We went up as far as Nadzab and we had to cross swollen rivers. I was in a jeep with another girl and the driver, and we had to be towed across by a big bulldozer because there were other jeeps floating down the river and overturned. And on the way back, at night, there was this huge tree across the road. This bloke, the lieutenant I finished up marrying, put a couple of trunks up onto the thing and drove the jeep up, and we flew through the air, so we girls got back to barracks but the boys had to wait till the next day because they were in the trucks.

That was the time we were told we had to cut out the kissing scene in *French Without Tears*. I was the French girl, daughter of the professor, so I was introduced as 'number one piccaninny'. We had to cut out a lot because some of the natives were going to be in the audience.

We flew to Rabaul. We had a lovely theatre there, which they'd built. We gained a hairdresser girl — we pinched her from the musical comedy. One night we were on stage in Rabaul, in full flight, and there was an ammunition dump close by. We didn't know. All of a sudden there were these terrible noises — *Bang! Bang!* We thought we were under attack, but it was the ammunition dump going. And there was shrapnel and stuff falling onto the stage. I think somebody just lit it, to send it off. Peter Finch couldn't come with us because he was unfit for a hot humid climate so we had to get used to somebody else playing the part.

Others in the group were John Store, from 3XY in Melbourne and very well-known there from *One Man's Family*, a radio play; the other girl was Gloria Robbins — she used to sing in clubs before the war, and she lives up in Taree now; Ron Patton; and there was Colin Croft, who became a big name in the early days of television.

We came back from Rabaul on the *Westralia*, right down in the bowels of the ship. It was rerouted to Brisbane so I was stuck up there. My wedding had been set down for 18 May because my husband had been recalled — he was in Sydney waiting and I didn't get back to Sydney by troop train till the day before. So I didn't have a medical or dental, and I was discharged on the 17th and married on the 18th.

Reveille, January–February 2004, interview with author

Patricia McPherson Rhodes (McKenzie) *was born at Hornsby, Sydney, on 17 August 1919 and enlisted at Moore Park in November 1942. She was discharged from the Australian Women's Army Service in May 1946 with the rank of private.*

Service Totally in the Dark
By Joy Granger

Joy Granger says she 'served in Intelligence, but didn't know until after the war!' Her experience sheds light on a largely unknown aspect of Australia's wartime effort — the role played by thousands of analysts, cryptographers, typists and translators who received, processed and distributed intelligence material.

It's something that I didn't even know I belonged to — that's what it was like. It wasn't until about 12 years ago when I was watching the Anzac Day march on television and this little group came along and the announcer said, 'Now here's a little group we haven't seen before. Central Bureau Intelligence.' And they had only started to find who the people were who had worked with them.

There were about 4000 altogether — a most extraordinary group of people. They were the interceptors and cryptographers and translators, that sort of thing. I was communications. Mind you I didn't start with them — I started with the Air Board in St Kilda Road, where I was one of the operators working the London watch. Then we were moved to Frogmore, which was the big communications station in Victoria, and they did everything there — transmissions, reception, cryptography and so forth. Unfortunately they found out that I could type and it was always disastrous for anyone to learn that, so I was then asked to teach the teleprinter to new intakes of young airmen coming through, because they were running out of men. So I did take several courses and taught them. Then the CO announced that a new machine had arrived and I was to go and have a look at it, and I was posted to Brisbane. That's when I went to this place at Henley Street, Ascot Vale, and I was in a little room with a Morse key and a telex device, which was the machine I'd had a look at. And that's where I spent the next year or so.

I didn't ever see anyone. I seemed to be on night shift most of the time. I didn't even know anyone there. Whatever I had to send was pushed through a hole in the wall, so I was totally in the dark as to what I belonged to. And that applied to practically all of them, even the ones out in the field.

It was all code of course, and I had no idea what I was sending, or even where the people were that I was sending it to. It was a very silent service — it really was. That was from 1944 to 1945. We're still finding people who've suddenly realised that's what it was they belonged to. I graduated to flight sergeant — that was a big deal — and I wore uniform all the time. There were a lot of academics among them — the cryptographers, and those who'd learned Japanese.

When we were doing Morse code and transmitting to London, it was such heavy traffic that a machine was used, very old fashioned now when you think of it — it was called a Kleinschmidt, obviously German, and it looked like a big teleprinter. You typed as you normally would — letters or figures — and it punched holes in a tape and that was the Morse code. And that was fed onto a machine and transmitted at very high speed on to London. We got it back the same way and slowed it down, and typed it up.

Then I was sent to Melbourne and was working at Royal Park where they were demobbing those coming back from overseas. Eventually my demobbing came through and I went home to Sydney and went back to the ABC where I had been immediately prior to the war. I had been in the newsroom and fortunately they opened up a station in Port Moresby, and I asked if I could go and so I went and spent the next six years there.

It was started by two army blokes, obviously by arrangement with the ABC, and we were out in a gully near Jackson's airstrip, and we had two studios, nothing air conditioned, and we had three announcers, a log typist and a music director, and I was a programmer, secretary to the manager and dogsbody.

I loved it! I think I was in the first lot of Europeans going back there post-war. That was an interesting landing because Jackson's airstrip had been very heavily bombed and they'd put down heavy metal strips all along, so when you landed you bounced up and down the airstrip. And the manager greeted me with a glass of rum — I'd never tasted rum in my life!

It was an extraordinary experience. It was great because I did a lot of flying while I was there, over to the other side, to Rabaul, and was there during the war trials. And I went up into the highlands.

Reveille, January–February 2004, interview with author

Joyce Eileen Granger was born in NSW on 1 September 1921, enlisted at Rose Bay, Sydney, in September 1941, and was discharged with the rank of flight sergeant in December 1945, her last posting listed as RAAF Command. She died in March 2016, aged 94.

A Story of Mateship
By Connie Noble

WWII was having a bad effect on Australia, and seeing placards everywhere saying 'Join the WAAF and serve with the men who fly' encouraged me to enlist in the Women's Auxiliary Australian Air Force in March 1942 as a clerk typist. As I did so, I stood alongside a girl named Rhoda Matheson who, 72 years later, is still my best friend. My number was 94294 and hers was 94295.

We went to Sydney and did our rookie training at Bradfield Park. By the end of the training we were very surprised to learn we were going to Townsville. Although we enlisted as clerk typists, after successfully completing our rookie training we were posted together to No. 3 Fighter Sector in Townville and worked as plotters, which entailed plotting all sea and air movements in Townsville and northwards.

Rhoda and I were billeted at what had been St Anne's School, slept on the veranda on straw paillasses, were transported to work in a closed-in truck and were told never to tell anyone what we were doing.

We had to line up to start the eight-hour shift, and the door would open as one shift took over from another. We often plotted Japanese planes over Townsville, but they were reconnaissance planes, always flying high. We were told that Townsville could be bombed, but probably never would be.

We were told that Townsville could be invaded and, if it was, we were on our own, so we should keep to bushland and find our way south.

Fortunately that never happened, but there were three bombing raids on Townsville, the main one being on 21 July 1942. Rhoda and I had been plotting unidentified planes for some time and were due to go off-duty at midnight. A few minutes before then, the planes were identified as Japanese, and because of the seriousness of the situation, we had to remain on duty, and the shift ready to take over from us was sent out to the safety of the slit trenches. We had to don our tin helmets and gas masks. Townsville was blacked out on the sounding of the air-raid warning, but the building we worked in had to remain lit as we needed the lights to continue our work plotting the Japanese planes. Not knowing where their bombs would be dropped and hearing our fighter planes and ack-ack guns in action was a scary time.

Fortunately the bombs were dropped in the water, and as we plotted the Japanese planes out of the area, the sound of 'all clear' was music to our ears. We were finally signed off-duty at 2 a.m. and transported back to our barracks, shaken but with a feeling of some excitement at what we had experienced.

The basis of this story is mateship. Rhoda and I have remained lifelong friends. So far as we know we are the only two survivors of this experience, and we are both in our nineties. My late husband served in the 2/4th and also had lifelong friendships until Alzheimer's cruelly took his memories and then his life.

RSL Queensland, May 2014

Constance Caldwell Lawrie (Noble) *was born on 2 November 1922 at Brisbane and enlisted on 9 March 1942. She was discharged in November 1945 with the rank of corporal and died 29 October 2015.*

Rhoda Farnsworth (Matheson) *was born on 27 June 1923 at Seymour, Victoria, and enlisted in Brisbane on 9 March 1942. She was discharged in August 1945 with the rank of corporal.*

I Was Sixth Divvy's Telephonist
By Marien Dreyer

Sixth Division HQ in St Kilda Road, Melbourne, was, when I got there in September 1939, a gaunt, empty building where office furniture and typewriters were being unloaded, and where I was given a typewriter and table and told to show the incoming staff how to handle things.

Subsequently the camp commandant (Captain I.G. Webster) discovered I could handle a telephone switchboard, and from then on I was the voice of Sixth Division.

I wasn't only the telephonist. I organised morning and afternoon tea, arranged for lunches to be telephoned through and delivered to the building, taught potential batmen how to make tea that was hot, strong and drinkable, and how to darn socks.

I sewed on stripes as they were earned (and unpicked them as corporals fell back to the ranks), gave advice on girlfriends, wedding presents, etc. etc. Consequently I was 'in' on all kinds of things.

There was the concert up in the Exhibition Building on the night before the march through Melbourne on 26 January 1940. Connie, who worked with me at Sixth Divvy, came along too — we had special passes to get us (and our escorts — civilians, continually mistaken for radio technicians) into the building.

Connie and I were half the feminine audience — Lady Blamey and a woman companion comprised the other half. It was a sight I shall never forget, and which I would have liked to have preserved with a colour camera.

Thousands of khaki-uniformed men, all of a pattern with sun-reddened faces, backing up against the poison yellow-and-brown walls of the building. A brown-and-yellow, red-and-khaki colour scheme broken only by the big blue velvet drapes left over, I think, from the performance of *Hiawatha* by the Melbourne Philharmonic Society a year or so previously.

The boys were in fine form, enjoying themselves uninhibitedly, and I met people I hadn't seen for years — including 'Abdul', who had been a gripman on the Bourke Street cable trams when I was going to school. He was prowling around keeping a fatherly eye on the youngsters who might have been tempted to scoot out for the night.

The concert got underway, and every act was a howling success. As the theatres closed, comedians and acts came along to do their share, and it was getting on to midnight, with no sign of the show ending, when we decided to give it away and go home.

'How do we get out?' asked my escort.

'Way we came in,' I said, airily, and headed for the Nicholson Street entrance — not realising that some of the boys — quite a lot of them — were undressing to go to bed.

My appearance had a frightful effect — like a greyhound coming into a paddock full of rabbits. The spectacle of numerous males in shirt tails and underpants diving under blankets was not unlike rabbits diving into burrows — white tails everywhere.

Petrified youths stood clutching towels and blankets around them. Panic set in. Such a state of dither as ever there was, and me unmoved by it, accustomed as I was to art schools and backstage in any theatre. Eventually, I hung my head, closed my eyes, and had my escort lead me out.

The boys at HQ next day greeted me with roars of joy. I never lived that episode down, nor the day that ...

It was the first Saturday night of the ballet season in 1940. I hadn't been able to get to the opening night, so compromised on the Saturday night, and since we were going all formal, decided to have my hair set and made an appointment with my hairdresser for 12.05.

Now, to get to this salon, I had to take three trams, and I didn't finish work until noon. Couldn't possibly make it in five minutes at peak hour, so I spoke sweetly to the transport sergeant. He approached the CO, and permission was granted for Miss D. to be taken round in an army car.

General Blamey wasn't in Melbourne at that time — I've forgotten where he was — but the big maroon Rolls-Royce, loaned him by the lord mayor, was in the transport lines.

I closed the switch, grabbed my purse, my laundry (delivered that morning) and bolted — all in the one movement — and found I was to have the Rolls. Not only did I have a chauffeur, I had an orderly and two motorcycle outriders. They pushed me in and off we went — a most imposing cavalcade, except that it was only the telephonist with the laundry!

In case any irate taxpayer or brass hat wants to know why — at this late date — they had to go out to Caulfield Racecourse to pick up some visiting officer, I was just ballast for the outward trip.

Off went the escort, traffic opening up respectfully, and so to the beauty salon where the outriders swung round with great verve, the Rolls followed — causing a mild traffic jam — and stopped with military precision right outside the beauty salon door. The orderly leaped out, opened the door and gave a truly wonderful salute. A small crowd gathered, expecting someone Very Important.

I stepped out with what I prefer to remember was superb poise, inclined my head to the orderly — and the string holding my laundry broke, dealing various bits and pieces over the footpath!

The boys collapsed limply on the running board of the Rolls and laughed. Laughed? They roared and bellowed and writhed, while I tried to pick up the laundry and cram it back into the paper, which was torn. After a minute of this futile business, I joined them, and we sat there laughing until the tears ran down our faces. Then they picked it up, piled it in my arms and whizzed off, still laughing.

They were still laughing on the Monday morning — so was I.

I like to think that perhaps when the going was tough and there wasn't much for them to laugh about in the later years of the war, that they could remember those two things and have a reminiscent chuckle at the Girl Who Went Out the Wrong Way and who dropped the laundry by the Rolls!

Reveille, 1 June 1951

Marien Oulton Dreyer *(1911–1980), writer and journalist, left her convent school in Melbourne at the age of 14, then worked as a stenographer and was a telephonist at 6th Division headquarters in 1940. In the early 1940s Dreyer settled in Sydney with her husband and maintained a prodigious output of stories, serials and plays for magazines and radio. After the birth of her second son, Dreyer began writing a popular column for* New Idea *magazine. In 1959 she shared the Walkley Award for a non-fiction magazine article.*

Abbreviations

AA	anti-aircraft
AAMWS	Australian Army Medical Women's Service
AFC	Air Force Cross
AGH	Australian General Hospital
AIF	Australian Imperial Force
AOC	Air Officer Commanding
AWAS	Australian Women's Army Service
CB	Companion of the Bath
CBE	Commander of (the Order of) the British Empire
CO	Commanding Officer
CSM	Company Sergeant-Major
DCM	Distinguished Conduct Medal
DFC	Distinguished Flying Cross
DFM	Distinguished Flying Medal
DSC	Distinguished Service Cross
DSO	Distinguished Service Order
GC	George Cross
GOC	General Officer Commanding
IO	Intelligence Officer
KBE	Knight Commander (of the Order) of the British Empire
MBE	Member (of the Order) of the British Empire
MC	Military Cross
MM	Military Medal
NCO	non-commissioned officer
OBE	Officer of the (Order of the) British Empire
OC	Officer Commanding

OP	observation post
OTU	Operational Training Unit
POW	prisoner of war
RAA	Royal Australian Army
RAF	Royal Air Force
RAAF	Royal Australian Air Force
RAANS	Royal Australian Army Nursing Service
RAN	Royal Australian Navy
RAR	Royal Australian Regiment
VAD	Voluntary Aid Detachment
VC	Victoria Cross
WO	Warrant Officer
WX	weather
WX	Service number prefix indicating a Western Australian enlistment

Acknowledgements

The various State Branches of the Returned and Services League of Australia made this volume of World War II experiences possible by providing me with access to their libraries, and in particular to their collections of magazines. These are a national treasure, reflecting as they do Australia's military history and the roles played by so many individual men and women in times of war.

A number of the stories in this book resulted from my own interviews with veterans, conducted 15 years ago with residents at RSL LifeCare, Narrabeen. It is sobering to realise that they belonged to a generation which is fast disappearing, and I am grateful to them for sharing their experiences with me.

Wherever possible I have given brief biographical details for each of the veterans, and for others who are mentioned by name in the text. The Commonwealth Government's WWII Nominal Roll has been an invaluable resource in this regard, along with the Australian War Memorial's collection of unit histories and biographies. The *Australian Dictionary of Biography* has also been a useful reference work.

Special thanks are due to Hadyn White of the Department of Veterans' Affairs who checked my biographical notes against department records and was able to confirm the dates of death for many of those whose names appear in this book.

My wife Sonya put in many hours of typing, transcribing pages of photocopied magazine articles into a coherent manuscript. Kate Goldsworthy then cast a very analytical editor's eye over that manuscript and made many useful suggestions. At HarperCollins/ABC Books, Katie Stackhouse and Lachlan

McLaine have provided invaluable support in bringing this book to fruition.

More than 993,000 Australians served in the armed forces during WWII. There could have been almost a million stories so this collection represents only a small snapshot of their wartime experience. I hope it does justice to their service and in some small way preserves the nation's gratitude.

John Gatfield

About the Editor

John Gatfield has spent most of his career as a journalist in commercial television news, current affairs and documentaries, including thirteen years as the foundation anchor of Australia's first 24-hour news channel.

From 1995 to 2017 he was an advisor to the NSW State Branch of the RSL, and has contributed throughout that time to the RSL magazine *Reveille* including from 2015 as its editor. Since 1997 he has played an active role in promoting the Kokoda Track Memorial Walkway at Concord, Sydney, and been active in fundraising for Concord Repatriation General Hospital and the ANZAC Research Institute. He has also served the RSL and the NSW Premier's Department as MC for commemorative services and events.

As a volunteer, John has been the media director for the Australian team at three Commonwealth Games and a media consultant with the Australian Olympic Committee at four Olympic Games. A keen thoroughbred horse breeder and owner, he is currently seen as a host on Sky Racing.

Index of military units

Battalions
2/1st Battalion 135, 164, 263–7
2/3rd Battalion 102–7
2/3rd Machine Gun Battalion 52, 182
2/5th Battalion 88
2/6th Battalion 94, 262
2/9th Battalion 26–31
2/11th Battalion 108–13, 243, 257, 259
2/13th Battalion 185–6
2/16th Battalion 116
2/19th Battalion 66
28th Battalion 116
2/28th Battalion 81–7
2/32nd Battalion 116
2/33rd Battalion 100–1
2/43rd Battalion 85
2/48th Battalion 116, 131–3, 135, 137, 138
58/59th Battalion 89
11/66th Battalion 90

Brigades
13th Brigade 86
15th Brigade 94, 95
16th Brigade 102–107, 159
17th Brigade 95
20th Brigade 188
24th Brigade 81–87, 188
26th Brigade 81–87, 132, 188

Divisions
3rd Division 91
6th Division 102, 135, 176, 177, 180, 243, 333–336
7th Division 77, 80, 81, 145, 178–184
8th Division 8, 26, 31, 36, 142, 146
9th Division 68, 81, 86, 131, 182, 185–186

Squadrons
2 Squadron 308

343

3 Squadron 285
4 Squadron 16
6 Squadron 308
24 Squadron 284, 285
41 Squadron 284–285, 286
49 Squadron 300, 301
159 Squadron 313–314
183 Squadron 290
198 Squadron 289, 290
405 Squadron 284
455 Squadron 302, 304
460 Squadron 277–279
467 Squadron 280, 283–284, 284
486 Squadron 285
617 Squadron 284

Other military units
1st Australian Entertainment Unit 325
2/3rd Reserve Motor Transport Company 49
23rd Field Company, Royal Australian Engineers Militia 153
90th Australian Transport Company 121

General index

For names of most ships, see entries beginning with HMAS, HMS and SS.

A
Ajax (racehorse) 174–5
Akashi, Taijiro 68
Allen, Arthur Samuel ('Tubby') 75, 77
Ambon 308–9
Anderson, George Charles 268–71
Auschwitz 269
Australian Army Medical Women's Service 69–70, 125–7, 172
Australian Comforts Fund 161, 165
Australian Women's Army Service 321–3

B
Baber, Dick 167
Banks, R.J. 318
Bannear, Albert Edward ('Alby') 187–9
Bardia, Battle of 159–65
Barnden, Leo Edward 253–58
Bathurst Island 153–7
Benness, Edwin Charles 87
Bennett, Gordon 27
Berlin 277–9, 281–2
Binstead, Francis John ('Banjo') 52
Blamey, Thomas Albert 118
Borneo 50–1, 67–8, 131–3, 134–8, 139–41, 142–7
Bowen, T.E. 318
Brooks, John Wigram 87
Brown, K.A.R. 315–18
Burma Railway, see Thai–Burma Railway
Button, J.C. 290
Byoki Maru 50–2

C
Carroll, Stanley Lawrence 237–43
Chancellor, June Douglas 69–70
Changi (Singapore) 8, 29, 45, 57, 65,
Clarke, Hugh Vincent 53–7

Clarkson, Reginald Thomas 253–8
Clulow, John Cecil George 298–301
Cobb, Henry William Albert 78–80
Coleman, Dudley Mark 244–8
Collins, A.N.J. 318
Cologne 281
Cooper, Arthur William Frederick 227–32
Cowra breakout 156, 235
Cressey, Dallas Lowther 44–9
Crete 177, 180–1, 207, 210, 228–32, 234, 237–43, 244–8, 251
Croft, Colin 326
Crouchley, John 85, 87
Crowe, Vincent John 97, 99
Crowther, L.D. 318
Cyprus 180–4, 206

D
Dalton, Hazel 125–7
Darby, Alvin Drummond 114–15
Darwin 153, 305–7, 308–12
Davidson, Jim 325
Davis, A. 318
Death Railway, see Thai–Burma Railway
Derrick, T.C. 131–3
Donohoe, George Frederick 116–18
Dowson, Dorothy Joan 148–52
Dreyer, Marien Oulton 333–6

E
Ebner, Edward Robert 78–80
Egan, Hubert Leo ('Hughie') 91, 94
Egypt 166–7, 171–3, 173–5, 178, 179–84, 187–9, 234, 241–2
El Alamein 166, 167, 187–9
Empress of Asia 204
Essen 293–7

F
Faichnie, Ian 317, 318
Farnsworth, Rhoda 331–2
Finch, Frederick ('Frank') 216–19
Finch, Peter 325
Finschhafen 120, 321
Ford, Eric V. 318
Foster, Norton Henry 251–8
Funk, Paddy 142–7

G

Garland, Ronald Selwyn ('Commando') 88–96
Gibson, Guy Penrose 284
Gill, Frederick Arthur 210–15
Glennie, Dennis 325
Glover, Frank 203–5
Granger, Joyce Eileen ('Joy') 328–30
Gray, John Robert 23
Greece 206–7, 227, 233, 237, 251–8, 180
Green, Bob 28–9
Griffith, Thomas Allan 305–7
Grinyer, Norman Robert 178–84

H

Hakata (Japan) 53
Hammer, Heathcote Howard 93–4
Hannah, James Felix ('Pat') 84, 87
Harrington, W.H. 204, 205
Harrison, Frank Bernard ('Brian') 90
Harris, Sir Arthur 284
Haydon, Frederick Bernard 79–80
Heath, Sir Lewis 8
Hertzberg, Albert Abraham 168–70
HMAS Australia 199, 201
HMAS Ballarat 204
HMAS Bendigo 204
HMAS Canberra 205
HMAS Colac 222
HMAS Deloraine 139
HMAS Kanimbla 137
HMAS Kuttabul 205
HMAS Latrobe 139
HMAS Leeuwin 197, 231
HMAS Manoora 123–4
HMAS Parramatta 203–5
HMAS Penguin 209
HMAS Perth 206–9
HMAS Rushcutter 202
HMAS Shoalhaven 214, 215
HMAS Shropshire 232
HMAS Stuart 212, 227, 228
HMAS Swan 203
HMAS Vendetta 212
HMAS Voyager 227–32, 231, 234
HMAS Warrego 203
HMAS Waterhen 210
HMAS Westralia 326

HMAS Yarra 193–7, 203–5
HMS Argonaut 304
HMS Defender 210–15
HMS Formidable 148–52
HMS Grebe 215
HMS Havock 181
HMS Jervis 166
HMS Jupiter 44
HMS Resource 215
HMS York 228
Holmes, Robert 302–4
Hooper, Keith Horton 260–2
hospital experiences 148–52, see also Australian Army Medical Women's Service
Huon Peninsula 81–7

I
Ikin, Leonard Leslie 58–61
Isaacson, Peter 279
Isles, Donald William 62–6

J
Jackson, Harry W.S. 145
James, Enoch ('Jimmy') 5–8
Japan 50–1, 53–7
Jarman, Ailsa Jean 321–3
Johnson, Slim 275–6
Johnston, George Henry 73–7
Jordan, B.T. 318

K
Keast, Una Clara 233–6
Kenny, Leo Martin 313–14
Kerr, June Douglas 69–70
Kimber, Hazel 127
Kirk, Edward Gladstone Gilchrist ('Ted') 288–92
Klagenfurt–Vienna railway 263–4
Kokoda 75, 76, 77, 126
'Krani' (author) 67–8

L
Lae 81, 120, 123, 135, 323, 326
Laing, W. 318
Lawrie, Constance Caldwell 331–2
Libya 159–65, 168–70, 190, 227
Livingstone, Ailsa Jean 321–3
Lumby, Noel Percival 253–8
Lynch, Maxwell William Edward 119–21

M

MacArthur, Douglas 74, 75, 77, 81–7, 200
Mackrell, Harold Gordon ('Snow') 220–3
Macris, George 97–9
Malaya 26–31, 44
Maletti, Florence C. 171–3
Mant, Graeme Smyth 283–4
Manunda 75
Marburg 263
Matheson, Rhoda 331–2
Matthews, Lionel Colin 142, 144
McDonald, Sidney Leonard 315–18
McDouall, Harold Stuart ('Jim') 308–12
McDougall, Iain Donald Hay 159–65
McGregor, John 29
McKenzie, Patricia McPherson 324–7
McWilliam, John Mathew 190
Meares, Wallace Archibald 88–96
Mills, Una Clara 233–6
Milne Bay 116–18, 120, 123, 126, 199
Montgomery, Bernard 167
Montgomery, John 122–4
Moore, H.J. 166–7
Morris, Basil Moorhouse 74, 77
Mouatt, P.A. 318
Muar 26–31

N

Nadzab 81, 100, 114–15, 326
Nagatomo, Yoshitada 46, 49
Nakhon Nayok POW camp 62–6
Neilson, Christian Henry Ernst 26–31
New Guinea 19–25, 73–7, 78–80, 81–7, 88–96, 97–9, 100–1, 102–7, 108–13, 114–15, 116–18, 119–21, 122–4, 125–7, 132, 135, 183–4, 236, 321–3, 325–7
Newbery, John Collin 85, 87
Nielsen, Robert Stanley McFarlane 277–9
Noble, Constance Caldwell 331–2
Norman, Colin Hugh Boyd 81–7

O

O'Dowd, Bernard Shelley 108–13
O'Keefe, Emmett Walter James 131–3
Orton, Alfred George 193–7
Osborne, Henry John ('Aussie') 253–8

P

Palestine 178–80

Papua New Guinea, see New Guinea
Patton, Ron 326
Percival, Arthur 8
Plant, Joseph Vernon 253–8
Port Moresby 73, 77, 100–1, 126, 135, 329–30
Powell, Leslie 153–6
Price, Ernest William Alfred 94

Q
Queen Mary 233

R
Rabaul 19–25, 73, 119, 326–7, 330
Raine, L. 318
Rankin, Robert William 193, 205
Revigny-sur-Ornain 298–301
Rhodes, Patricia McPherson 324–7
Rhodes, Rodney 214
Robbins, Gloria 326
Robinson, Max 26
Rowell, Sydney 77
Ryan, Urban Gerard 259

S
Salamaua 88, 97
Sandys, Duncan 260–2
Sattelberg 132
Savige, Sir Stanley 91
Sayer, W.W. 317, 318
Shilling, Keith Roy 315–18
Singapore 5–8, 9–16, 26–31, 32, 44, 45–6
Slattery, Bernard James 305, 306
Smith, Roy Kenneth 32–6
Spencer, Terence 286–7
SS John Trumbull 218
SS Limerick 220–3
SS Strix 216–19
Store, John 326

T
Taylor, Frederick James 206–9
Testro, Rex Clifford 173–5
Thai–Burma Railway 33–6, 42–3, 46–9, 58–61, 65, 208–9
Thailand 62–6, 313–14, see also Thai–Burma Railway
Thiele, Keith Frederick ('Jimmy') 280–7
Thomson, J.S. 318
Tobruk 163, 164, 168–70, 185, 203, 210–15

General index

Townsville 331–2
Toyoshima, Hajime 156
Turner, Florence C. 171–3
Turner, Tom 139–41
Twohill, Berenice 19–25

U
Ulungura, Matthias 156

V
Vickers, J.O.R. 318

W
Waddell, J.M. 318
Waller, Hector MacDonald Laws 207, 209
Walmsley, L.K. 318
Warfe, George Radford 89, 90, 93
Warren, Roy 87
Watt, Alf 78–9
Wau 88, 97–9
Wells, Frank Morris 134–8
Wells, Mark Ernest 134–8
Wewak 108–13
White, J.G. 315–18
White, K.J. 318
Whyte, Lorna 25
Wignell, W.J. 315–18
Wilson, Alexander Vincent ('Alec') 85, 87
Winterflood, John Stuart 88–96
Woods, Gilburd William Edward 198–202
Worley, A.G. 318
Wright, John William 9–16

Y
Yamashita, Tomoyuki 27, 31
Yates, E.C. 42–3

You may also enjoy these other military history titles from HarperCollinsPublishers and ABC Books.

THE RSL BOOK OF WORLD WAR I

True stories of Aussie courage and mateship from the annals of the RSL

Edited by John Gatfield with Richard Landels

VOICES from the AIR

The ABC war correspondents who told the stories of Australians in the Second World War

TONY HILL

'Kieza has made the life of Australia's greatest general open to a broad audience ... well-crafted and extensively documented'
Weekend Australian

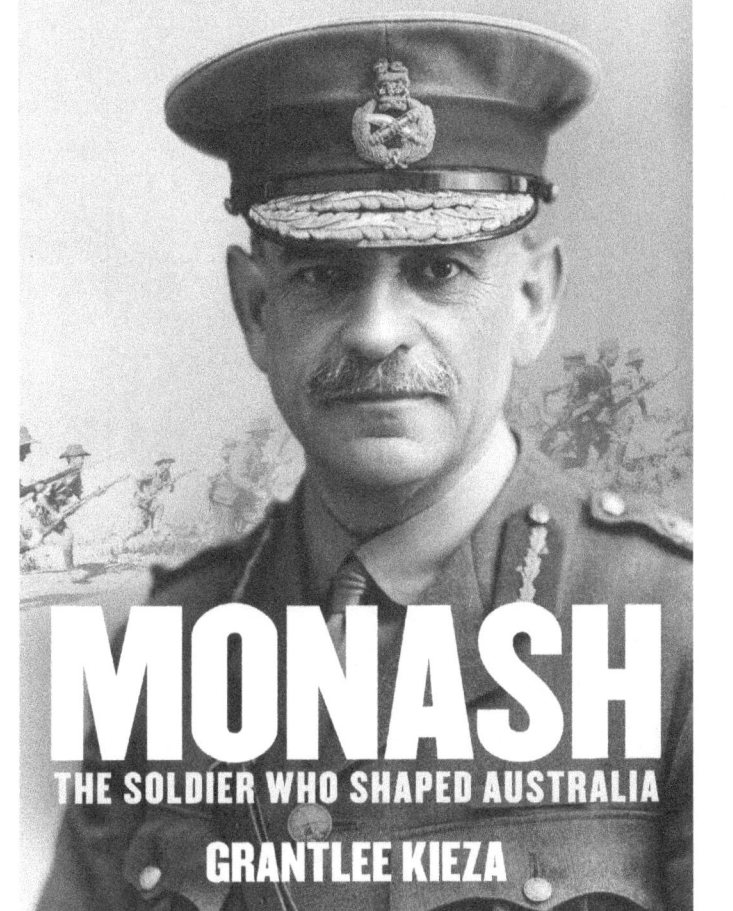

MONASH
THE SOLDIER WHO SHAPED AUSTRALIA
GRANTLEE KIEZA